AF269660

THE CITY AS A SYSTEM

METABOLIC DESIGN FOR NEW URBAN FORMS & FUNCTIONS

DAVID DOOGHE,
ERIC FRIJTERS,
CATJA EDENS,
MATTHIJS PONTE,
THIJS VAN SPAANDONK,
CHRISTOPHER DE VRIES,
JET VAN ZWIETEN (EDS.)

TRANCITY✕VALIZ

Contents

Introduction
A Different
Look at the City

> "'Perhaps the mystery is a little too plain",
> said Dupin. '... "A little too self-evident."'
>
> — *The Purloined Letter*,
> Edgar Allan Poe, 1845

In one of his most extensively analyzed stories, *The Purloined Letter*, Edgar Allan Poe, the literary godfather of the horror and detective story, assembles three men smoking pipes. The company, consisting of the Paris prefect of police, the protagonist, and his friends and master sleuth C. Auguste Dupin, are sitting in comfortable chairs in the twilight to ponder a seemingly unsolvable enigma. At stake this time is not a murder or large-scale fraud, but a stolen letter. A trifle, one would say, were it not for the fact that the sensitive content of this letter, which was taken from the Queen's writing desk, composes a threat to the balance of political power. The question is not who took the letter — the Queen witnessed herself how it was exchanged for another one in her presence. It is therefore also perfectly clear who now is in possession of the letter and for what purpose. The perpetrator, a cabinet minister who is also a mathematician and a poet, uses the letter to blackmail the Queen for the sake of his own political position of power. Now, the minister must have hidden the letter somewhere, but no one has been able to find it and so the extortion continues. The prefect has had the minister's house searched several times, looking in every nook and cranny, even checking chair legs to see if the letter was hidden in there, but to no avail. It simply cannot be found and now the desperate prefect has called upon the two renowned detectives sitting by the fireside. Perhaps, Dupin boldly suggests, the police are unable to locate the letter because the solution might be too plain, too self-evident. And indeed, it is. Shortly afterwards, Dupin triumphantly hands the letter to the police, earning the finder's fee that had meanwhile been put up. He realized the letter had never been hidden at all, but was in plain sight. The police simply forgot to look for it at its most obvious location: the thieve's card-rack.

The clue to the solution was taking a different approach. Solving the riddle, says Dupin, did not so much require a better search, but rather a completely different way of thinking than the police are inclined to apply when handling a crime. Poe's story subtly demonstrates that solutions for a specific type of dilemma and challenge require a different approach, so that new possibilities and relevant locations may be considered. The difficulty often does not lie so much, or at least not exclusively, in the execution but primarily in obtaining the required knowledge, discovering new opportunities and a fresh approach that suits the task at hand. Dupin's example shows that it pays to question one's own intuition, tried-and-tested methods and practices. Difficult problems do not always require far-fetched solutions, but in order to arrive at the solution a change of perspective may be in order. In other words: solutions for tricky problems may be there for the taking for those who know where to look but remain invisible for those who choose the wrong approach and stick to set methods and practices.

This book advocates such a change of perspective in the study of the urban environment. It posits that designers who wish to truly improve the functioning of the city and solve tricky urban problems cannot afford to focus only on the spatial manifestation of the city, but should also conduct thorough research into the underlying system, into the operation, use, and performance of the urban fabric.

Solutions for tricky problems may be there for the taking, like the purloined letter that is hiding in plain sight.

Research by design is, in our view, the pre-eminent method for meeting this challenge. Therefore, this book looks at what effect research by design has and can have on the current design practice. We explore what the result of the increasing availability of data is for our understanding of the system of the city: what new methods come up at designers' desks in order to apply improvements with an eye for that system, what fields of activity may thus be opened up, what new type of neighbourhoods, cities, and buildings may emerge and how their aesthetics relates to the familiar shapes of the city.

In our research we view the metabolism of the city as that of a living organism. After all, the system of the city shows all sorts of striking resemblances with the bodies of humans or animals. Both can be understood as a system of flows and materials that interconnect and collaborate in all kinds of ways. Both are also exposed to all kinds of external influences, just as they in turn constantly influence the situation around them. Not least because the city, in order to keep functioning, demands the input of many raw materials (food, energy, materials) and produces a lot of waste. This use of resources is one of the biggest problems of urban life in the Anthropocene, the age in which the influence of human activity on the climatological and geographical condition of planet Earth is decisive. In order to change the impact of our actions in a positive way, we consider it a given that our use of resources should change drastically. The urban body — as the place where much of our use culminates — plays a crucial role in that transition.

The role of designers in this process is potentially decisive — that is, if they meet the challenge. It is up to them to design this transition. It requires a spatial transformation, but also a systemic one in which the functioning of the city changes radically. The urban body must become healthier and more efficient in its use of resources, if we are to stop pillaging the planet. At the same time, the city must continue to house its residents in a comfortable and inclusive manner, bolster their social, economic, and cultural position, and improve their health. In order to have the city perform these various functions on a permanent basis it is necessary to work towards multiple spatial solutions. Towards designs that will fulfil not one but a multitude of functions. The office building of the future must be capable of much more than providing its users with conference tables, workspaces, and canteens. It must also contribute, for instance, to storing CO_2, preventing urban heat islands, and promoting the health of its users. The same goes for the future design of urban streets and neighbourhoods, but also for the surroundings of the city and the infrastructure that connects the city internally and externally. To make such layered designs possible we need a much more extensive research practice that utilizes the increasingly more available and easier accessible datasets. The transition of the city, in brief, starts with solid processes of research by design.

The role of designers in this process is potentially decisive — that is, if they meet the challenge. It is up to them to design this transition.

Research by design was also the main subject of the 2017 publication *Urban Challenges, Resilient Solutions*. It was the conclusion of the first four years of research by Future Urban Regions (FUR), the research group for research by design of the six Dutch Academies for Architecture. The current book is its sequel and coincides with the conclusion of the research group. In *Urban Challenges, Resilient Solutions* we surveyed the possibilities and the importance of research by design as a tool to obtain more grip on the urban metabolism, laying the foundation for a methodology for shaping the research into healthy urbanization. We identified six themes that are decisive for the metabolism of the urban environment and the study of it. Three of these are of a physical nature, i.e., energy, materials, and infrastructure. The other three are of a societal nature, i.e., health, economics, and social conditions (or, in a modern phrase: inclusion and liveability). In *Urban Challenges, Resilient Solutions* these flows were also interpreted as ambitions: a healthy city needs a resilient infrastructure, sustainable energy, and a materials cycle that is as circular as possible. Such a city also promotes social cohesion, a vital economic climate, and the health of its residents. These six themes manifest themselves at all scales; that of the city as a whole, of the street, and of the building. The pursuit of a healthy metabolism at all of these scales also requires unique interventions. FUR's focus is not primarily on concrete design intervention but is mainly aimed at the preparatory stage, the research phase that precedes the spatial intervention and enables it.

Research by design into the metabolism of the city is a method for working on 'wicked problems'. The wickedness of urban problems is a direct result of the interconnectedness and mutual dependency of the various flows within the city. Each problem is therefore also a symptom of another problem. Any flow is always affected by and its course co-defined by all kinds of other flows. For example, a bad waste situation in a city or neighbourhood may be related to an economic problem while at the same time leading to a bunch of side issues, for instance in the areas of health, liveability, or impoverishment, which in turn may all be causes of the problem. This complex intertwining means that a solution found for one place has an effect on all kinds of other places and themes that are at play in the city. The consequences of an intervention are therefore hardly foreseeable, if at all. Even more so: with a 'wicked problem', according to the definition of the German design theorist Horst Rittel and his American colleague Melvin M. Webber, you know beforehand that an intervention may provide a solution for one thing, but that it will often also create a new problem. Solutions are therefore not so much right or wrong, but can be an improvement all the same. Because wicked problems are so characteristic of the city, the commissions given to designers for improvements are becoming less and less clearly defined. Research by design is the pre-eminent method for bringing clarity and concreteness, thereby arriving at a stricter definition of the commission.

A process of research by design does not follow an established path. Still, we managed to outline what a general course of a research process is by using three models. The Design Thinking Process diagram traces how the research develops from abstract and broad to concrete and concentrated. The diagram also places the research within the longer trajectory from idea to design and realization. The DTP diagram comes in the form of a series of diamond shapes that keep shrinking. Each diamond shape represents a phase of research that first diverges and broadens before it converges again and eventually consolidates, taking a step forward in the research. In the diverging phase data are collected and combined with existing insights. This leads to knowledge that can be identified and concentrated in the converging phase into a new question leading to a slightly smaller diamond shape. In this way the project becomes more concentrated and more clearly delineated. The research steps within the diamond shapes are explained in more detail

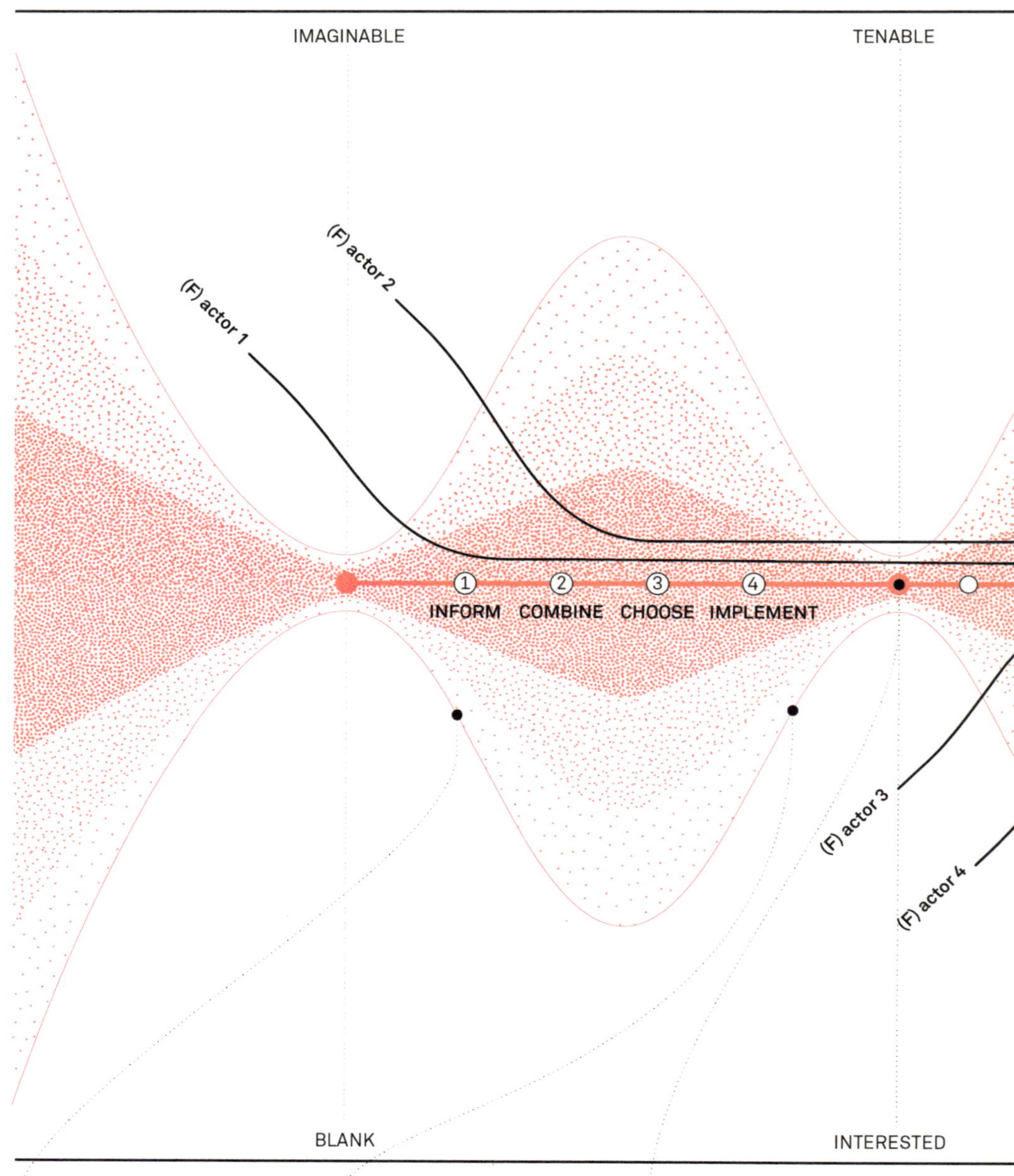

diverge:
INFORM + COMBINE

- add facts, take position, formulating arguments

- brainstorm, philosophize, take position, formulate arguments

- the idea is subject to deformation and development

converge:
CHOOSE + IMPLEMENT

- focus on new reality

- summarize, narrow down, negotiate concessions, choose, come to agreement

- The idea becomes shaper and more mature

consolidate:
C3 CUBE

- determine and capture a new representation of the idea

- new facts, opinions, relations and relevant stakeholders

- the idea becomes tangible through a new comprehensible representation

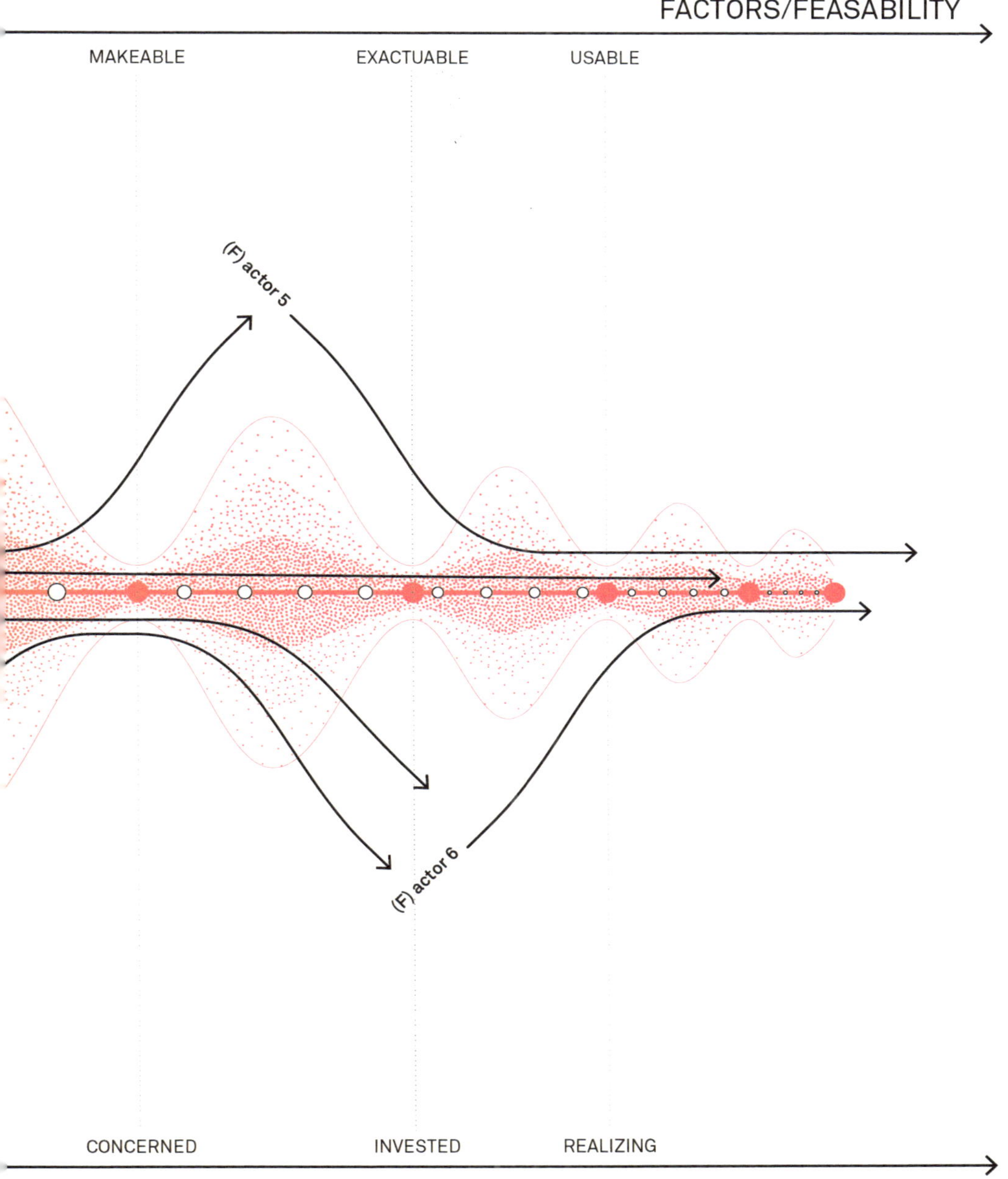

Diagram describing the Design Thinking Process (DTP)

in the ICCI Model, which identifies various common processes within a research phase. The fact that working on the wicked problems of the city is always layered and that problems manifest at various levels and themes with effects on different stakeholders is expressed in the C3 Cube. At the beginning of the process, it is often unclear where in the Cube the problem at hand is primarily concentrated. It is only when the diamond shapes in the DTP diagram become smaller and the research focuses on a more and more clearly formulated question that it also becomes clear where in the Cube the researcher now is.

In the interview included in this publication, the young Spanish urbanist Daniel Ibañez adds useful terminology to this method. He identifies three ways, or moments, to approach the city as a metabolic system. The first one is 'urban metabolism' and focuses on the analysis of the metabolism of the city. A second approach, 'metabolic urbanization', is a critical reflection on that metabolism and thus also a first step towards a design intervention. In this book we are interested in both, and also focus on yet a third perspective on the metabolism of the city, an approach that Ibañez calls 'metabolic urbanism'. This metabolic urbanism is future-oriented; it projects. It explores the future of the city from the realization that it is organized as a body that needs to become healthy to prevent it from destroying its own residents and the planet itself. In that light metabolic urbanism explores new value models, new neighbourhoods and building typologies, as well as methods that enable a different relation with the urban fabric.

That we really need a different relation to the urban fabric is, in our opinion, beyond any doubt. The impact of humankind on the Earth is big, can be felt globally, and is inextricably linked to our concept of the city. We regard the city therefore not only as the place where individual buildings are gathered in high density, but we also look at the city in its systemic interwovenness with the environs. This means that we also look at the places without which the city as we traditionally define it could not exist. For example, the city is then also the places where the food is grown that is eaten in the city and where the energy is generated that is used in the city. This blurs the distinction between urban and rural areas. Looking at it this way requires some flexibility in how we relate to the various scale levels in the analysis of the city. We have to look through the scales, as it were. During the process of research by design we look at the system 'city' as landscape architects, as urban planners, and as architects, all at the same time.

Reading Guide

This book explores, in five chapters, an inspiring array of new possibilities for understanding the city as a system, based on a metabolic approach to the wicked problems we find there. In doing so, we alternate theory with practice and reflection with conversation. The various chapters consist of theoretical reflections that are developed by using concrete examples. Between the chapters, four conversations have been included with distinguished researchers and designers who reflect, each from their own working practices, on their methods for approaching the city and the results that these different methods yield. The five chapters each deal with an important aspect of the search for a metabolic approach to the city, i.e., the gathering of knowledge, the handling of a task, the discovery of new places, the reconciliation of competing spatial tasks, and the designing of a different spatial future.

The impact of humankind on the Earth is big, can be felt globally, and is inextricably linked to our concept of the city.

The first chapter deals with the importance of thorough knowledge of the present performance of the urban fabric. This requires a detailed analysis of the underlying physiology, processes, flows, and use of the city. It also means more data and other ways of measuring, looking, and searching, and experimenting with the city. The ambition to fully understand the urban metabolism goes hand-in-hand with the trend of emergent digital measuring and processing techniques for gathering and opening up new data. These techniques greatly expand the view on the functioning of the system 'city', leading to more chances for design to improve the performance of that city. We therefore further discuss in this chapter how applying different data sources also leads to new designs and we highlight three specific data sources: first of all, there is a huge amount of already available data that are being gathered and stored by all kinds of larger administrative, public, and private parties. A second continually growing set of data is actively being gathered by all kinds of sensors that are by now part of the city. A third source comes from more sociologically oriented research in which the data may be limited in a quantitative sense but do have a high qualitative value.

In the second chapter we take a look at what forms of analogue research enhance our understanding of the city and what shape such research currently takes in the everyday practice of various design firms. We look at scenario thinking as a method for exploring the bandwidth of a task. Scenario thinking is a good way of involving cultural and social aspects in the research. They play an important part in a method such as crowd building, which is aimed at bringing together a large group of end users in the very first stage and give them an explicit role in the design of their future living and/or working space. In the process of crowd building spatial designers must assume a new role. This opens up new fields of activity.

In the third chapter we look at how new analyses lead to new tasks and come to the conclusion that these new tasks are not always found in obvious places. We look at a number of these new places and tasks, which manifest at national, regional, and local scales. The various cases also show that it may be possible to define a task at a specific scale level, and that the spatial translation into concrete places demonstrates at the same time that a metabolic approach cannot be accommodated within that single scale level.

In the fourth chapter we look at how a different use of the city leads to new design questions and to a need for new spatial typologies at different scale levels. One important observation is that a metabolic approach of the city generates a need for mixed functions, in order to have buildings, neighbourhoods, and cities function better with regard to various issues at the same time. The city can only be organized smarter and more sustainable by bringing together various functions within a single design, promoting the exchange of residual flows. The concept of the mixed city may seem obvious, but the spatial elaboration is still far from evident. To meet the demands of this task and unite the sometimes seemingly conflicting interests, designers must navigate a field in which the value models, shapes, and functions are not yet known.

In the final chapter we ask ourselves how a metabolic approach of the city will influence its spatial expression. What will the healthy city of the future look like? What shapes will result from the solutions for the current complex tasks? The requirement of circularity and use of local materials with a small ecological footprint forces designers to expand and test their aesthetic abilities. By thinking about these enforced limitations in the use of materials and space we reflect on the opportunities that present themselves as a result. This is not a matter of secondary importance. In addition to sustainability and optimized performance, values such as beauty and cultural expression are crucial for the success of the city of the future. It is inevitable that this city will look radically different. It is in the hands of the designers whether this conclusion will be a pleasant one or not.

Gathering Knowledge

'Beauty is not the goal of competitive sports,
but high-level sports are a prime venue
for the expression of human beauty. This
relation is roughly that of courage to war.
The human beauty we're talking about here
is beauty of a particular type; it might be
called kinetic beauty. Its power and appeal
are universal. It has nothing to do with
sex or cultural norms. What it seems to
have to do with, really, is human beings'
reconciliation with the fact of having a
body.'

— David Foster Wallace, *Federer Both Flesh
and Not*, 2006

The documentary *De machinekamer van Tom Dumoulin* follows one of the world's best-known racing cyclists of recent years in the spring of 2019 during his preparation for the Giro d'Italia, the race he managed to win two years earlier becoming the first Dutchman in history to do so. Dumoulin's erstwhile team is known for subjecting its cyclists to an extreme regime of protocols and rules with the goal of maximizing control and minimizing uncertainties. Exerting maximized control over the body in this way aims to create the ultimate, resilient sporting physique. One which can resist any potential attack, overcome it, and eventually use it to its advantage. To achieve that goal, Dumoulin's body is constantly subjected to processes of detailed analysis and extensive test strategies in order to draw a very accurate and intricate physiological map on the basis of the generated data. This map can then be used to navigate his body and alter minute details to maximize the production of power and therefore the potential for competitive results. This may sound extreme, and it is, but at the same time this approach to the physique of top cyclists has now become the norm in the world of professional cycling. Cycling, the sport that is drenched in epic stories and romanticism about the heroic use of our most analogue means of transport has also become *the* sport in which technological developments and ingenuity can make the difference between winning or losing. In that sense the Giro victory of Tom Dumoulin is both a unique personal sports achievement, and also a victory by an interdisciplinary team consisting of all sorts of scientists, doctors, dietitians, trainers, and technicians who triumph thanks to their minute analysis of that one vehicle: the body of the cyclist concerned.

Such a top performance therefore presupposes a profound, specific, and focused knowledge of the initial situation of that body, its maximum long-range endurance and peak performance, its capacity for recuperation, its need for nutrients and rest, but also well-founded knowledge of the anomalies and exceptions that both threaten the body in question and allow it to excel. It is a way of thinking that has not only become quite normal in sports, but also in medical science. Measuring, analyzing, and if necessary, adjusting the flows, processes, and substances in our bodies provide the basis for making our species healthy and keeping it healthy.

Detailed monitoring and analysis of the cyclist's body position and performance

This book understands the city as a body that should be treated likewise. We expect and demand more and more from our cities. It is the place where we ourselves wish to be and remain happy and healthy, but it is also the place where many of the problems facing the planet can and must be addressed. This means that the urban body has to deliver a top performance not unlike that of a top athlete. And not just in one area but in a whole range of themes the buildings, streets, neighbourhoods, and environs of cities must contribute to improving the conditions of the Earth and the humans, animals, and plants living there. In order to reach that goal, the city should not be approached only in its physical appearance; rather, the system underlying that appearance must also be scrutinized. We understand that system as a body that is comparable with that of a living organism, with its own metabolism. The system city goes beyond what is traditionally considered the city. We view the surrounding countryside as part of this body, as space that has a great impact on its performance.

This book details a metabolic approach for designing the city. This makes it necessary to first make a thorough analysis of the current performance of the urban fabric. Analogous to the example of Tom Dumoulin, making such an analysis first requires the gathering of large amounts of data about the underlying physiology, processes, flows, and resource use of the city. We conclude that much more data is needed than is currently available to adequately make that analysis. If we are to understand the functioning of the city better, we will have to measure, look, and search at the city and experiment with it in a different way.

Systemic Knowledge of the City

The tendency to approach the city not only as a space but also as a system with a complex concentration of infrastructure is an insight that already caught on in the second half of the twentieth century.

This interest has since then gone hand-in-hand with the advent of new research methods. In order to get a grip on the complexity of the city, spatial professionals and scientists have been experimenting with new technologies and innovative work forms since the sixties. They wanted to gain more insight into the underlying structures that help shape the city and they wanted to make the accompanying planning and design processes more efficient. This development runs parallel to the rapid rize of computer technology and it therefore comes as no surprise that there is often synergy between these two domains. In both the systemic and the spatial aspect of urban planning all kinds of processes have been subjected to automated experiments through computer technology ever since. Many of the technologies and methods that are still crucial for the work of the contemporary researcher by design have their origin in the sixties. New ways to apply them are still found today and their development continues. We outline this history below to see whether the contemporary research by design can continue to inspire, nourish, and deepen. And also, to place the revolutionary aura of the contemporary synergy between computer technology and design somewhat in perspective.

An early exponent of the digital experimental zeal with a relevance for spatial research was the British former fighter jet pilot Roger Tomlinson, who held degrees in both geography and geology. After completing his studies in the sixties, he worked as manager of the department for computer mapping at Spartan Air Services, where he was given the task of determining the best location for a large timber plantation in Kenya. Tomlinson experimented with various analogue methods for overlaying all kinds of ecological, cultural, and economic variables. These methods turned out to be very useful, but also quite costly and time-consuming. He decided to develop a method that could be applied with the aid of computers. This led to a breakthrough. Shortly afterwards he sold his inventions to the Canada Land Inventory, a government agency that is responsible for collecting and applying data for its spatial planning activities and land-use planning. As elsewhere in the world, following the report by the Club of Rome, there was a growing awareness in Canada that the natural resources on Earth were finite. The organization was tasked with developing a resource map of one million square miles of the inhabited and productive land of Canada. Together with a team of designers and programmers, Tomlinson coded and scanned aerial images and thus created the Canada Geographic Information System, the world's first automated geographical information system.

And so, Roger Tomlinson became the brain behind the development of GIS, a system designed to record, store, manipulate, analyze, manage, combine, and present all sorts of spatial and geographical data. This new technology generated much knowledge while at the same time saving a lot of money and time. Without GIS the task of mapping

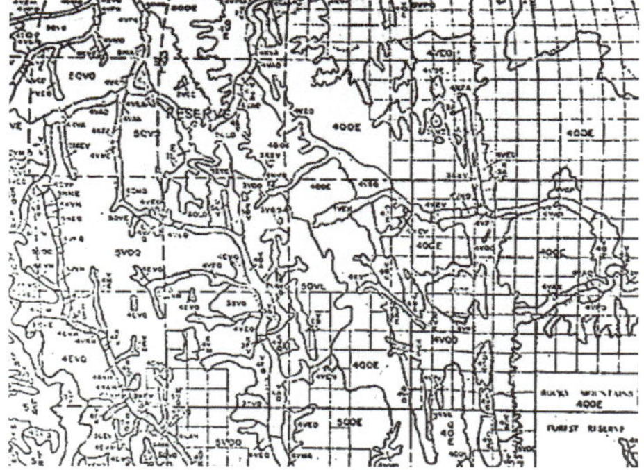

The world's first automated Geographical Information System (GIS)

all the available natural resources of Canada would have taken more than three years, while the entire process now took only several weeks. The cost was reduced to a quarter of the original eight million dollar budget. Even more important though, was the scientific gain. Tomlinson was the first geographer to demonstrate that data technology enabled us to better understand space. For the first time, it was now possible to maintain dynamic maps of those places on Earth that contained deposits of raw materials, where flows of materials took place, and to translate this complex information, in an intelligible way, into knowledge about the spatial system of the city.

In the following years, developments quickly succeeded each other. The computational power of computers and the possibilities to program them increased, as did their ability to fathom complex spatial situations. Via the Harvard Laboratory for Computer Graphics and Spatial Analysis (LCGSA) data technology became available to spatial designers for the first time. In the sixties the lab started to experiment with the possibilities provided by GIS but also with automatically generated designs and three-dimensional visualizations. In those days, LCGSA was the epicentre of innovation when it came to data-driven design tools. Among other things it led to Computer Aided Design (CAD).

Researchers at LCGSA further developed the first version of GIS because it enabled them, for the first time, to easily superimpose layers of information on maps and thereby analyze them. Also, much of the work at LCGSA focused on visualization and computer graphics. In addition, the institute also developed its own software systems to further operationalize the technique and make spatial design and data technology enhance each other. Another breakthrough was developed by architect Eric Teicholz. In 1969 he was the first to write

Peter Rogers and Carl Steinitz at the Laboratory for Computer Graphics and Spatial Analysis (LCGSA)

a computer program that could automatically generate a design plan based on a set of rules. Bruce Donald took this one step further and created the BUILDER software, a CAD program by which a computer could actually start drawing independently.

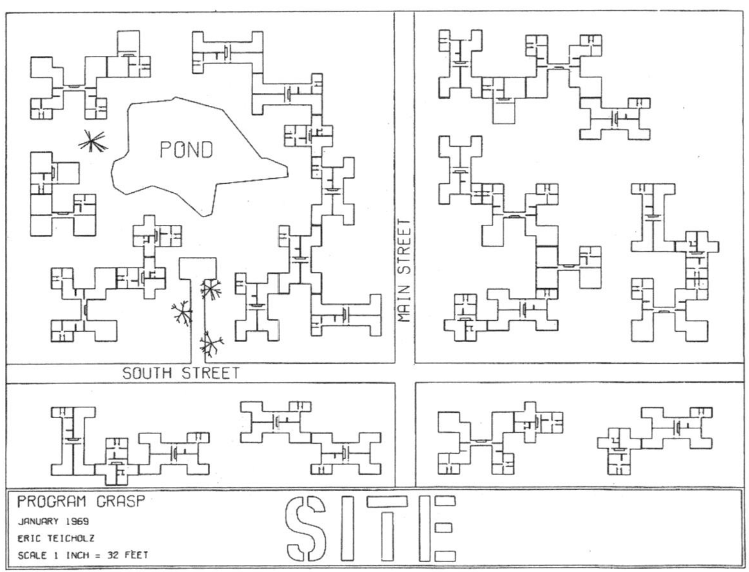

The first experimental, computer-generated, rule-based design plan

In the eighties the Odyssey team at LCGSA developed a holographic 3D representation of the demography of the US, literally producing a new look at the map of the United States. Landscape architect Jack Dangermond — who developed ArcGIS — also worked at LCGSA, before he founded the Environmental Systems Research Institute (Esri) together with his wife Laura Dangermond, in the late sixties. For a long time, ArcGIS was the standard for making spatial analyses; it was an important digital tool for researchers by design who focused on the complexity of the city. Much trailblazing was done by architect and theorist Christopher Alexander. His attempt to split up the design process and rationalize it in logical rules and formulas was an important basis for understanding design processes. In his 1964 book *Notes on the Synthesis of Form* he dissected the design process, identifying a number of conceptual steps that helped to understand the process in a logical and formal sense. His work was an influence on both spatial designers and computer programmers and played an important role in developing programming languages. He also developed a formal analysis of urban problems in his book by positing that these problems were not hierarchically organized but rather worked as overlapping fields of problems with all sorts of complex cross-links and mutual dependencies. By building a bridge between designers and programmers, i.e., between design and technology, between humans and computers, Alexander

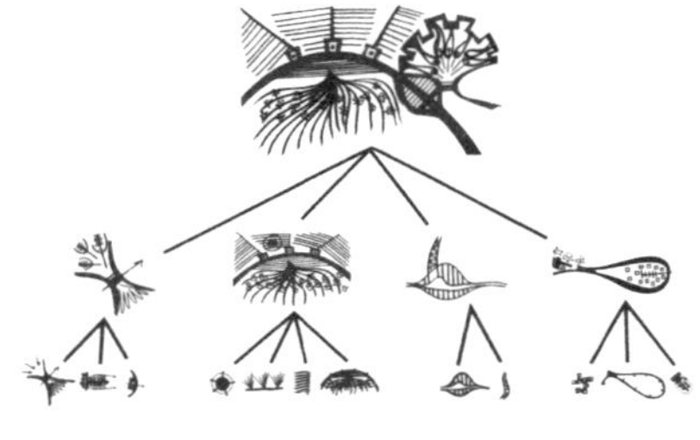

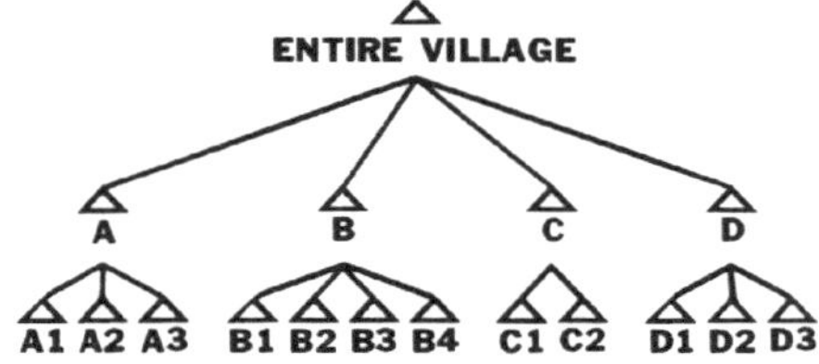

Dissecting the design process in conceptual steps, as shown in *Notes on the synthesis of form* by Christopher Alexander

was an important trailblazer for the metabolic analysis of the city as system.

Innovations in computer technology in research by design also took place outside LCGSA. For instance, in 1967 Nicholas Negroponte founded MIT's Architecture Machine Group. This research group functioned as a laboratory and think tank and focused on new approaches to interaction between humans and computers. One spectacular project was the so-called 'architecture machine': a computer controlled a number of robotic arms to stack blocks in a bin where mice lived. The mice went to work with the blocks by moving them and using them as climbing objects. The idea was to thus gain insight into the interaction between living creatures (in this case mice, but by extension also humans) and computers, as well as into what takes place when the two start building a city together. The experiment came to an unforeseen end when the mice decided to no longer cooperate but to escape instead.

Not just research processes, but also design projects are supported by computer technology since the second half of the twentieth century, both at LCGSA and elsewhere. An early example of generative design in which the computer takes over the design process was conceived of by the British architect Cedric Price in the 1976 Generator project. He would generate floor plans on a grid. The algorithm he used could adapt itself to specific input, in the case of the Generator formed by the needs and wishes of the user. The user therefore had a decisive role in the resulting design, which was fully organized on the basis of the desired effect in terms of future use and financial means. In the course of the

Simulating the spatial interaction of artificial and real life intelligence in the 'architecture machine'

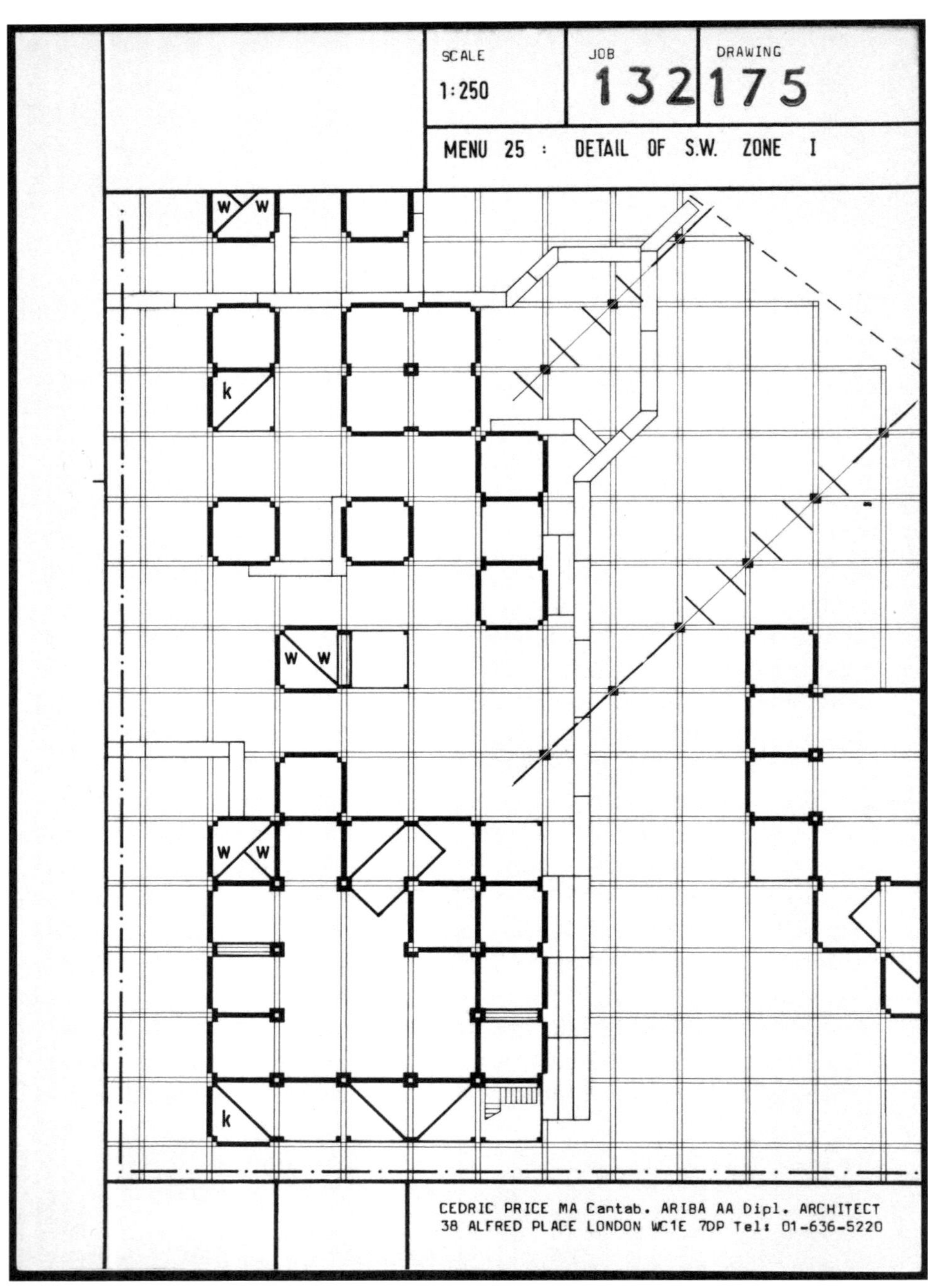

Cedric Price's The Generator Project

design process, it was possible to immediately adapt conditions when the expected performance, such as the cost of the design, turned out more or less favourably.

Traditionally, the design process is an artistic, intuitive activity and, as such, seems to be the opposite of and irreconcilable with the rational, factual connotations of information technology. However, the previous examples show that the two can also be quite complementary. Ever since the advent of the computer, various architects and designers have integrated information technology into their work. Cedric Price described himself as an anti-architect, as 'someone who withdraws from his authority in exchange of becoming a member of a multi-disciplinary team of experts and cybernetic automation'.[1] It is an expressly multi-interpretable and plural definition, the core of which is that automation allows for adding a whole new register of potential knowledge to the design process; that this brings an increase in complexity of such a magnitude that it is no longer thinkable for this process to be managed by a single discipline, let alone an individual, or a simple logic. In the multiple identity of the Anti-Architect, the Architect, the authentic artist, the genius, transforms into a multidisciplinary network of knowledge carriers and knowledge generators, both human and robotic. The Anti-Architect obviously may not have the romantic aura of his opposite, but this is compensated by a huge gain in depth and knowledge about the complexity of his object.

The complexity of generated designs can result in aesthetically quite pleasing buildings that would otherwise have been unimaginable.

Also, the complexity of generated designs can result in aesthetically quite pleasing buildings that would otherwise have been unimaginable. The recent interest in parametric design, in which a design can be generated on the basis of data or relations between parts, is interesting in this respect. In part thanks to the continuously growing computational power of computers, more and more complex and exciting design possibilities present themselves. In parametric design the use of the computer is not so much — exclusively — about enhancing efficiency, but about being able to expand the complexity of the design and thereby being able to draw shapes that cannot be drawn by hand. This complexity stems mainly from the irregularity of the various elements of which buildings designed in this way consist. These elements are never identical. Realizing such buildings is therefore only possible by also manufacturing the various parts in a computer-guided process. A famous example of such a design is the Guggenheim Museum in

Bilbao, by Frank O. Gehry. The titanium skin of the museum — which gives it its characteristic glow that changes its colour under different weather conditions — and the limestone and inner layer of glass are supported by a complicated skeleton of steel slats and cross-laths around which the visible material has been folded. In order to keep that skeleton and its complex curves and lines upright, Gehry developed his own CATIA software (Computer Aided Three-Dimensional Interactive Application). This software has become a product in its own right and later would find application in, for instance, the aeronautics industry.

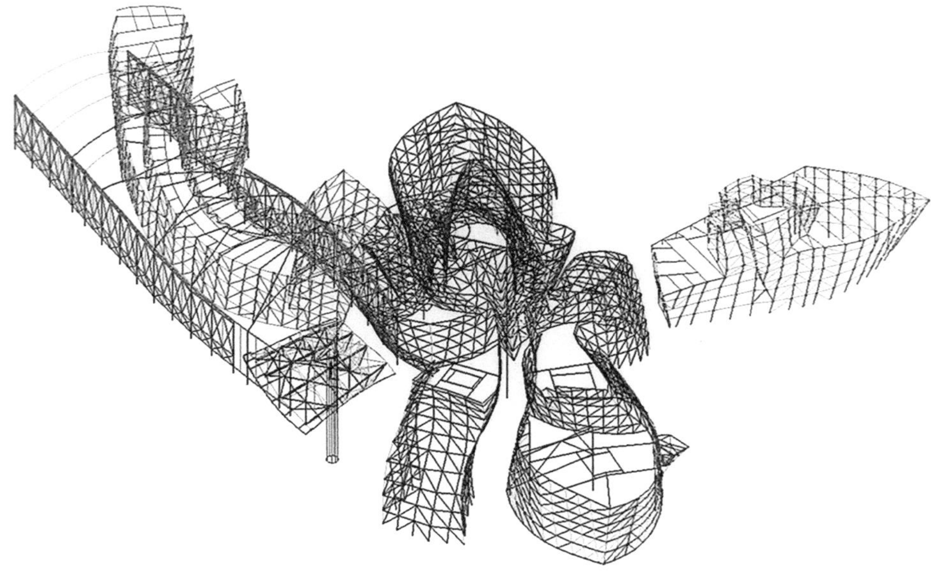

Computer analysis model of the Guggenheim Museum in Bilbao, Spain
made with CATIA software which was developed by Ghery

Experiments with computer-guided design are still being done at a different scale as well. The fascination with a city that designs itself is still very much alive. The most recent linking of public datasets in the area of urban tasks is the development of the Toronto Waterfront by Sidewalk Labs. Until recently, this subsidiary of Google was working on what was probably the most advanced plan in which urban development and data technology met in practice. Where smart city initiatives often tended to focus on measurable physical flows of resources, materials, and energy, Google widened the scope by adding human interaction with the city as a system to this palette. This, in essence, makes it a complex, digitized continuation of Negroponte's experiment with mice. The plan for developing the Toronto Waterfront was cancelled in 2020, but if it had materialized it might have been the first project in which the main role in the design process would not be fulfilled by designers but by a tech company. This obviously says something about the often frightening and limitless ambition of powerful companies such as Google to be involved in the monitoring and nudging of all aspects of our daily lives and social interaction. At the same time, it says something about the potential of applying technology in the spatial organization of our cities. Designers would be wise to fathom and apply this potential — consciously and in an ethically responsible manner, but nevertheless fully — in their daily practices. Because before you know it, these companies will relieve them of their task.

The latter is at once one of the more important arguments for designers to start experimenting with the possibilities of information technology in their own practices: to not be put out of action. And there's a number of other good arguments as well. For one, computer technology opens up the possibility of addressing more complex research and making it scalable by visualizing processes that are not easily derived from direct observation. So, it is not just about the quantitative processes that are expanded or made more efficient by data analysis, it is also about qualitative improvements of the research. In tandem, this may generate important new knowledge. In order to test what the current technological possibilities have to offer to do research into the system of the city, we scanned the city of Amsterdam on six themes that in our definition together define the condition of the metabolism of the city: economy, socio-cultural cohesion, use of materials, use of energy, infrastructure, and the health of residents.

New Technology for the Contemporary Designer: The Metabolic City Scan

The ability to apply new technology effectively requires learning some new skills, but this does not present a large obstacle per se. For example, a relatively simple script allowed us to scrape data from Google Places. With these data we were able to visualize how busy shopping areas were at any given time of the day over the course of a week. In an animation of space — mainly shops in Amsterdam — and of use in time and number of visitors per hour, the flows of people through the shopping streets of the city can be reconstructed and visualized.

In a similar manner, Google Street View can be scraped for data. Analyses of Street View images expands our view of the spatial organization of a particular street or area into knowledge of how the city is being used. With the aid of an Image AI and through machine learning protocols, the computer can take a sample survey of this use by analyzing images and, for example, counting how many shops there are in a given street, but also by studying the number of parked vehicles and determining how many bicycles and scooters we find, how many pedestrians walk by and how many of them are probably tourists — identifiable by their wheeled suitcases and the cameras around their necks. Using this information, urban planners can enrich their street profiles with actual information about how the street is used. One thing that stands out is that the Image AI shows that the use of a street is actually much more chaotic than what we usually think we observe. Thanks to this knowledge there are now also possibilities to not only visualize static data, but dynamic data as well. More detailed visualizations give designers more fact-based authority. Also, visualizations support interdisciplinary collaborations if researchers from different disciplines can develop a common visual language.

It is not always necessary to use Google for this. Open sources and techniques can also reveal many characteristics of the city. For example, we have used Principal Component Analysis for measuring gentrification phenomena in urban environments. To this end we made an aggregate of average developments in income, the price of houses, the size of households, and the age structure of the residents of a neighbourhood. Yet another method, the Space Syntax Analysis, provides information on the quality of street connections within a city. Weighted Raster Overlays, in turn, are very interesting for analyzing rural areas and recognizing soil suitability for specific forms of agriculture. For example, with this technique, a researcher can overlay data on elevation, soil hydrology, and specific types of soil in various maps. It is a technique that can also be applied to the city, for example to overlay all sorts of health variables such as air quality, noise, green structure, and the presence of shops selling healthy products onto the map of Amsterdam. It results in a map in which various layers reveal which areas in the cities are best able to support healthy living.

In addition to human flows, less 'physical' ones such as air quality, incidence of light, or noise can also be captured, analyzed, and described better than before. Before, these are often simulated but it is now increasingly possible to use concrete data from sensors that measure traffic, monitor noise, or keep an eye on air quality. We marshalled such data to calculate the potential for sustainable power generation in various districts of Amsterdam and compare them with the energy consumption of the buildings there. To do so, one can, for example, combine sunlight simulations with generic datasets on energy use from the grid operator. This provides information that helps in preventing peak loads of the power grid of the city while at the same time providing insight into the CO_2 footprint of various city districts. Such information lays the foundation for future interventions

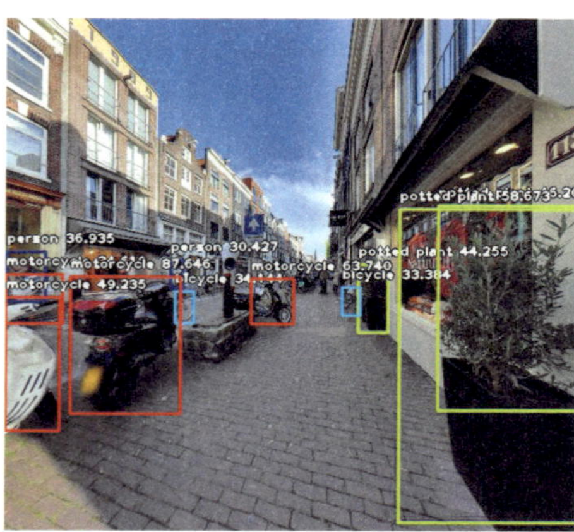

Image AI scrapes data from Google Street view to analyze the use of urban spaces

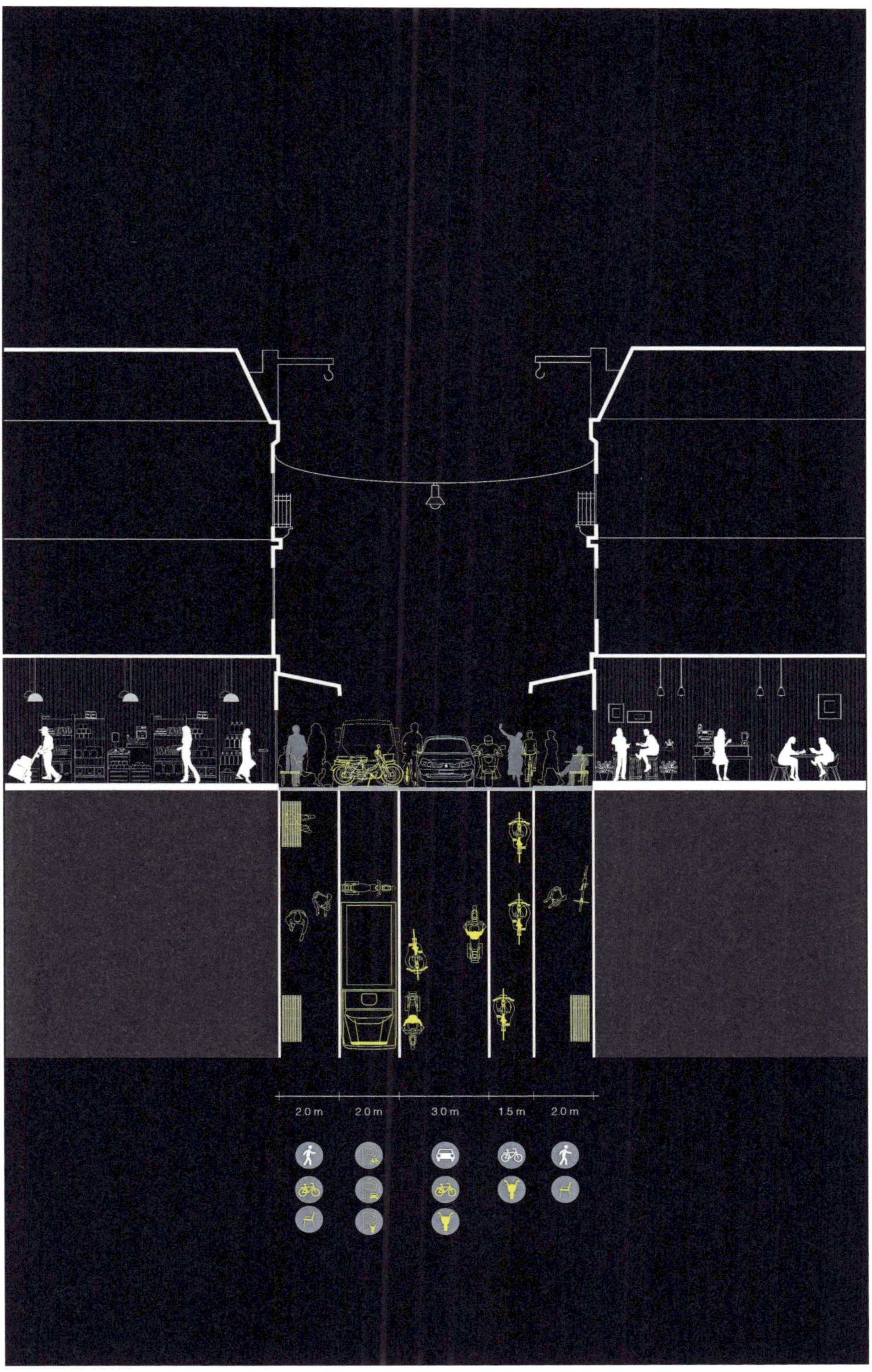

City street profile showing predicted use in contrast to actual spatial use
of the street, based on expectation and data collection

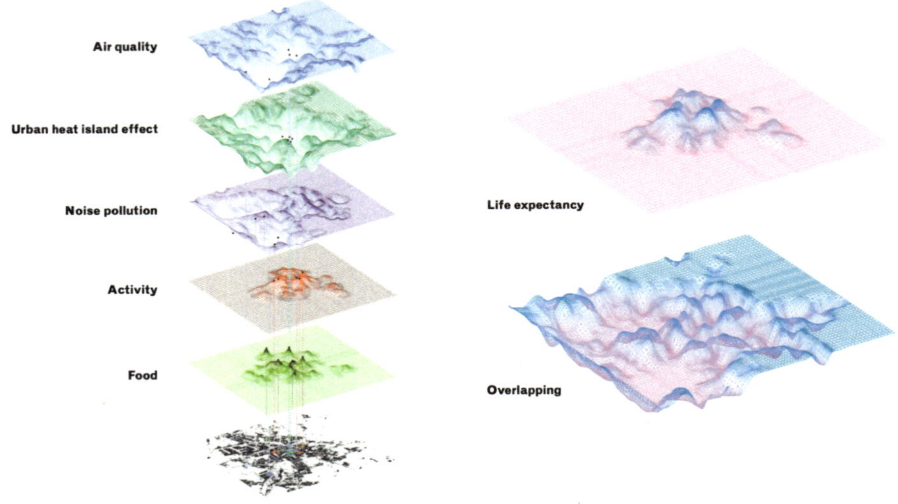

An analysis of which areas in the city of Amsterdam provide inhabitants the best conditions for leading a healthy life through weighted raster overlay

at neighbourhood level for making the city more sustainable and more efficient in energy use.

To study the economic viability of the city we tried to use data analyses to predict where, in the urban fabric of Amsterdam, 'city streets' are needed or will spontaneously emerge. City streets are strictly defined main arteries of the city. Based on this definition spatial indicators can be seen as the starting point of a process of spatial machine learning. In this process a large number of datasets about the facilities in the city, density, length of the street, are combined with data about, for example, the time spent by visitors in a street. We managed to build a machine learning model that can distinguish between city streets and non-city streets. City streets tend to have more shops, less offices, and a higher density. Also, on average, users tend to spend more time here than in other streets, if only because in city streets there are more public transport stops. By using this model, we can not only analyze existing city streets in cities, but also predict where such streets are likely to develop in the future. It is then possible to make a projection of how the city will develop, where economic activities can emerge, and what other effects this will have on the city's metabolism.

In a study of materials cycles and circularity in Amsterdam we devised a calculating model to evaluate for the entire city what the effect would be of a decentralized form of processing vegetable waste, compared to central processing. Economic and environmental impact is relevant but so are the amount of energy and number of movements required for transporting the waste. The model enabled us to sit at the computer and write a fairly accurate plan for the chances of an efficient and healthy approach to the problem of organic waste in Amsterdam.

A politically somewhat sensitive analysis, as it had a potentially big financial impact, was the one we made of the load bearing capacity of the quays and bridges of Amsterdam, a seventeenth-century city that was not built with the current traffic load in mind. We were able to map many bridges and quays that need renovation or have already been renovated (**the white squares, triangles, and circles on the map on the next page**) By looking at the density of shops and catering facilities, which both generate many logistical movements, on the one hand, and assessing the pressure of traffic among other things on the other hand, we looked at which quays and bridges were mostly in need of renovation because they were overburdened.

These forms of metabolic analysis thus support the visualization of the spatial aspects of the city, such as learning to identify city streets, and also help in generating knowledge about less visible but influential aspects of the underlying system of the city. What is striking about this brief survey of the search for the applicability of data technology, is that it provides access to complex problems in an efficient manner. This does not mean that the solution for these problems is within immediate reach, but that there is a perspective on having a fertile starting point for a spatial analysis that can lead to intervention.

Data: Opportunities and Risks

The metabolic approach we advocate fits within a wider trend, in which all kinds of new measuring techniques are applied for collecting data about what the city is and how it is being used. This development runs parallel to the emergence of new datasets that are being collected with modern measuring instruments, sensors, and computer technology — and through the widespread use of mobile phones. These datasets provide lots of opportunities to gain a much deeper insight into the individual performances of the city. Later in this chapter, we will address how other data sources provide opportunities to arrive at original design perspectives and we will highlight three data sources that according to us are especially relevant for designers. First, we will discuss in more detail the question of what are data, what benefits they bring to the design process, and what the possible pitfalls are in using them.

Before diving deeper into the use of data in spatial research, let's briefly clarify the terminology used. When we speak of data here, we literally mean the 'givens': the un-ordered collection of facts and things given to us. These givens in themselves do not mean anything yet. They only acquire meaning when converted into information. We regard 'information' — just as literally — as an ordered collection of data that has been analyzed and as such has been shaped 'in formation'. So, information is data that have been processed into, for example, a text, an image, a diagram, or a map. It is only from information that we can arrive at 'knowledge': the interpretation and understanding of

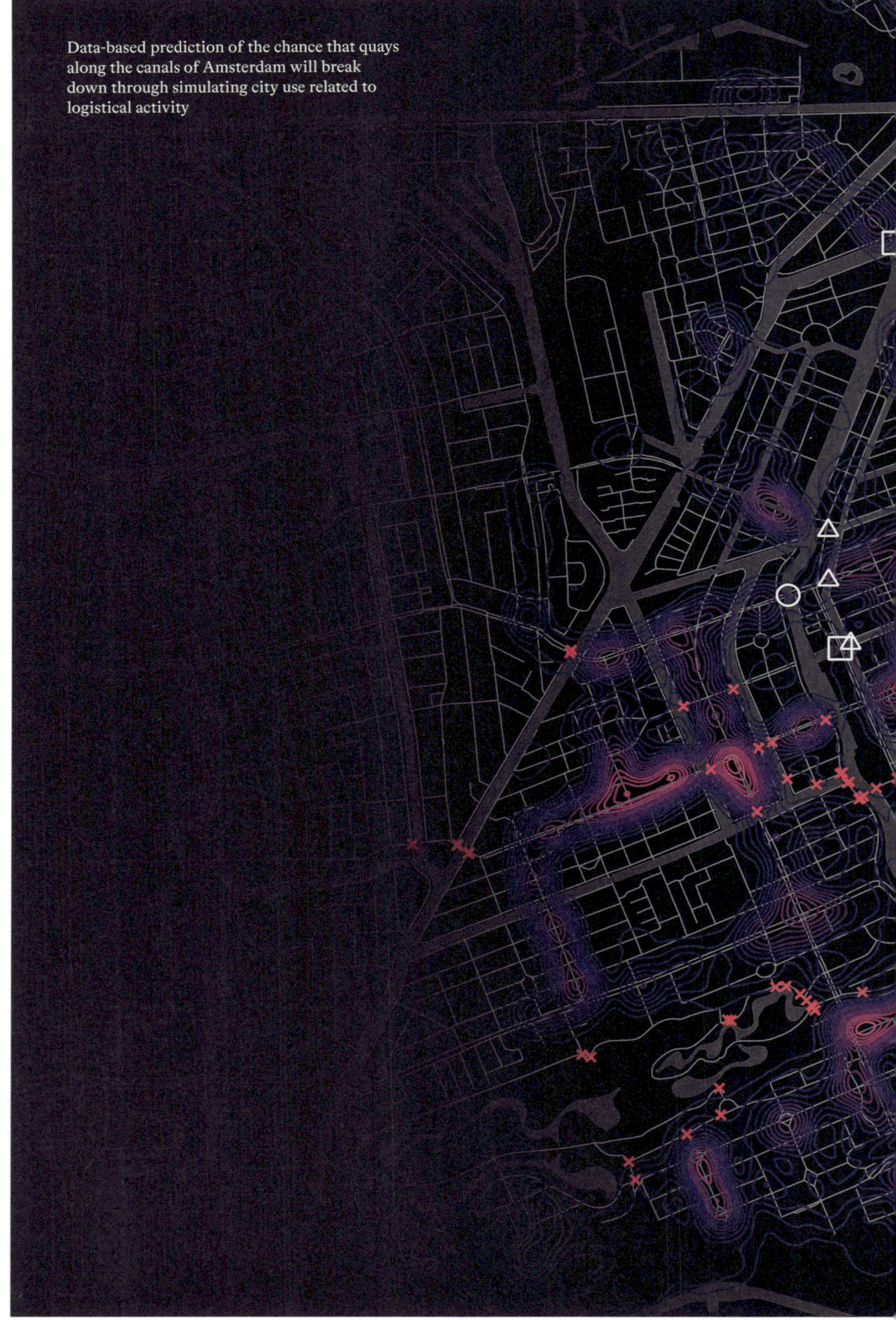

Data-based prediction of the chance that quays along the canals of Amsterdam will break down through simulating city use related to logistical activity

Charles Booth's poverty map

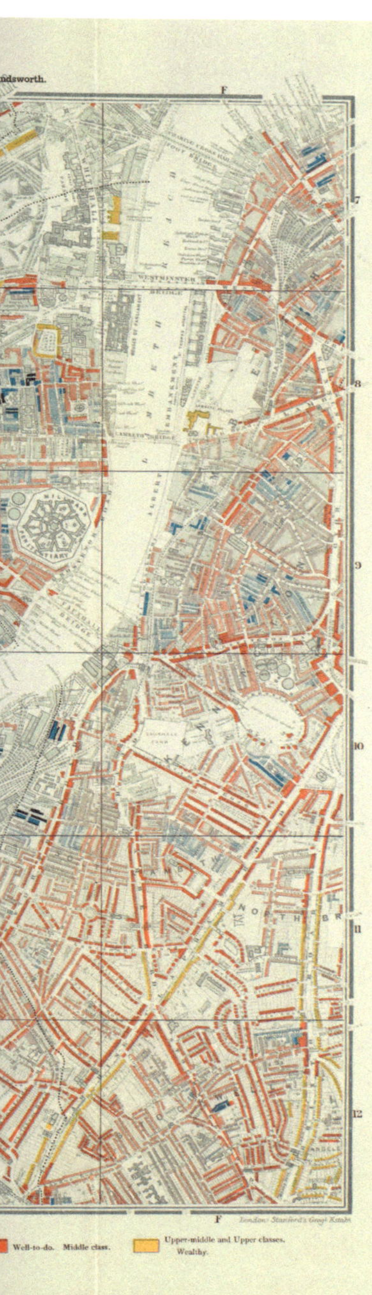

the meaning of the acquired information. So, if we speak of 'knowledge of the system of the city', we are referring to the process by which we construct, analyze, and process datasets in order to then — on the basis of the gathered information — gain an understanding of the workings, use, and performance of the city. The availability of large amounts of data about the city therefore in no way replaces the importance of human observation and interpretation. It is precisely through the observation, interpretation, and visualization of newly available data that knowledge emerges. Only after this last step we discover the design opportunities for improving the performance of that city.

The wish to be better informed about the situation of the city and to be able to make informed decisions based on factual information obviously did not arise with the advent of the computer. Between 1889 and 1903, social researcher Charles Booth collected, by hand, data on the income level of families in London. Together with some twenty young students Booth went from door to door to interview people and gather data on their financial situation. Armed with these data he not only managed to verify the assumption that a quarter of London's residents were living below the poverty line, but was even able to adjust this figure upwards. In reality one third of Londoners turned out to be living in deplorable conditions. Booth classified the outcome of this research by identifying eight separate income groups, which he then also mapped visually with different colours. With this spatial translation of the poverty problem, he managed to place the issue on the agenda of local politicians, thus delivering the foundation for his plea for an old-age pension.

Mapping the performances of the urban system by hand can still be a very good tool to get an idea of the state of the city. It is just no longer necessary in all cases. The availability of large datasets and the ability to analyze them often make handwork redundant. In the design phase, datasets provide greater possibilities for making applications and visualizations, which makes it easier to share and discuss the results of the design process.

In design proposals various parts of the system can be easily translated and combined. As with Booth's map, images can convey insights to a wider audience and lead to new action and interaction. They open up the road to interdisciplinary collaboration in design processes. After the conclusion of a design intervention, the availability of data from the research provides an explanation for the choices made in the design and also clarifies how the design influences underlying processes. This latter aspect has yet another advantage: it makes interventions repeatable, also at different scales.

The most striking advantage of data analysis for the design process is that it has the potential to provide us with a clearer view of defining systemic processes and correlations. From this clearer view on the urban fabric opportunities arise for designers to intervene in essential processes. This immediately accelerates and enriches the understanding of the performance of the city, the action perspective of the designer, and, as later examples will show, also their work fields and clout. Data analysis also makes it possible to quantitatively test and falsify anecdotal knowledge and instinctive hypotheses. This allows designers to underpin their research and design more clearly.

An important realization for anyone who uses them is, therefore, that algorithms are never neutral but always biased.

So, data research comes with many advantages. However, using large datasets also entails serious risks. One always looming problem is an unwarranted pretence of objectivity. There is always the great danger that the datasets themselves are biased, and their processing by algorithms as well. An important realization for anyone who uses them is, therefore, that algorithms are never neutral but always biased. This was illustrated once again when the Russian computer scientist with a passion for computer art, Denis Malimonov, demonstrated with a few simple examples that high-resolution portrait photos generated from pixelated images by the StyleGAN algorithm have little in common with the heads of the originally photographed persons.[2] The idea behind the algorithm is that photographs that are made hazy on purpose can be converted back into an image that should resemble the original photograph. And the algorithm appears to be quite successful in this. Until you apply it to photographs of people with a skin tone other than white.

To illustrate this, he applied the algorithm to a pixelated photo of Barack Obama. The result: a photograph of a white man. In itself the photo is convincing and at first sight could very well be a portrait of

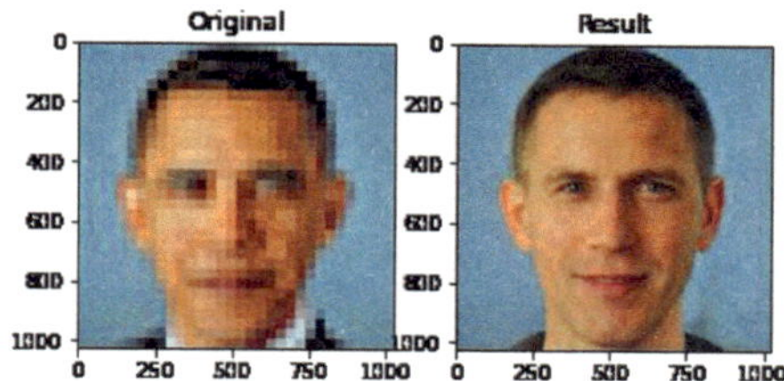

A demonstration of bias in machine learning models using the StyleGAN algorithm

an existing person, but it isn't.[3] Malimonov's result was no accident but the outcome of the structural preference for white people ingrained in the algorithm: it repeats the same error time and again. Whatever photograph you feed it, the result is always a white person. By pointing this out, Malimonov not only unleashed an almost endless stream of memes in which Mohammed Ali and Martin Luther King are being morphed into white men and Super Mario into The Joker, but also provided the insight that the outcome of the computation of an algorithm is to a large degree determined by the blind spots in the thinking of developers and the selective composition of the dataset that is used. In this case those limitations appear to be the result of the personal background of the developers and the overwhelming representation of white people in the dataset that serves as a reference. As a result, the specific algorithm literally does not see the possibility that an individual can have any other skin colour but white, making the outcome of the calculation by definition far removed from the actual situation. That is not a healthy basis for sound research, nor, it seems, for our trust in the objectivity of the computing power of algorithms. After all, what this example so clearly shows is that the results of algorithmic computations may look impressive and convincing, but that they are at the same time full of hard to discover assumptions, which compels us to be careful and modest in judging the results.

This example does however also show us something quite different and much more hopeful, namely that the community of online active data researchers has a very good checking and regulating capability. The bias of this algorithm is after all not only disturbing, but was also neatly discovered and interpreted by an attentive member of that community. This is a special quality of working with computer-generated data. Because these technologies either originate or are tested in open-access online environments, they are constantly subjected to rigorous checks by the active online community of researchers, who also have publication channels to share their findings and objections directly with the world, as on Twitter, in this case. The power of this community works especially well when it comes to algorithms, technologies, and data that are publicly available and the source code of which is published and freely accessible and thereby testable. That is, open-source technologies that are approved by a critical community of researchers. This is no guarantee that there will be no bias, but it is an important step in reducing the risk of bias and also a method to uncover it where and when it occurs.

This risk of bias can also affect the work of designers. Earlier, we mentioned as an advantage that data visualizations help in sharing and discussing design results and that the resulting images can assist in interacting with a wider public. At the same time, designers often work from an inflated enthusiasm for making use of opportunities. The graphic representation of data by designers therefore often leads to visualizations that are coloured by a profound optimism (new opportunities!) or even opportunism (new tasks!) and are far from neutral in that sense. It is not uncommon that data are treated rather carelessly in the presented images, for example to achieve a desired visual effect. Consciously or not, this is a form of manipulation. So, with the designing look and the power of visualization also come responsibilities.

In relation to this, designer and mapmaker Joost Grootens speaks of 'the inevitable rhetoric of maps'.[4] Unlike maps that are made in academic cartography, the maps made by designers, artists, spatial planners, and other mapmakers link geographical knowledge to political power structures. A map is then not a neutral representation of the situation but should be understood and read as a rhetorical argument. Any map that presents itself as neutral, says Grootens, after 'critical cartographer' John B. Harley, uses 'the rhetoric of neutrality' — and is therefore especially coloured. A map always attempts to not only give us insight: it also aims to convince. That fact is not the result of bad intent, but of the nature of maps, which are by definition the result of a process of subjective interpretation. This conclusion makes Grootens, always want to let the maps testify to that process. He advocates 'ambiguous maps', maps that make their users actively aware of the rhetoric that they contain. He gives the example of a map he made for the Belgian Pavilion at the thirteenth Architecture Biennale of Venice. This map, entitled *A Land Never* (an anagram of Vlaanderen — Dutch for Flanders), shows an area of 30 × 8 kilometres south of Antwerp, between the municipalities of Temse and Lier. The size of the map is 15 × 4 metres and so has a scale of 1:2000. The size of the map makes it possible to present details that would normally be lost in the representation of a between-area as depicted here. It enabled Grootens to show the real use of the area, which is characterized by all sorts of variations in living, producing, growing, nature, and infrastructure. The messiness so typical of this landscape would not be visible at all on a different scale. Usually, such an area is reduced to a piece of emptiness between cities with some infrastructural connections overlaid. By focusing specifically on every nuance in the landscape that is often overlooked, this apparent emptiness is now filled and assumes an identity all of its own. In Grootens' map the emptiness is filled with what the maker experienced while navigating the area, with all the subjectivity this entails. By doing so, Grootens wishes to pay attention to the undefined, unstable, and ambiguous nature of spaces and environments that are otherwise written off as desert-like no man's lands. Such a working method asks a lot of the creative process and at the same time it demonstrates how much a map is an expression of a subjective process. By explicitly expressing his subjectivity in the map, Grootens reveals a truth about maps in general: that also when this ambiguity is not made explicit, as in most maps, but remains hidden under a veil of neutrality, one is still essentially always looking at a subjective projection of a space.

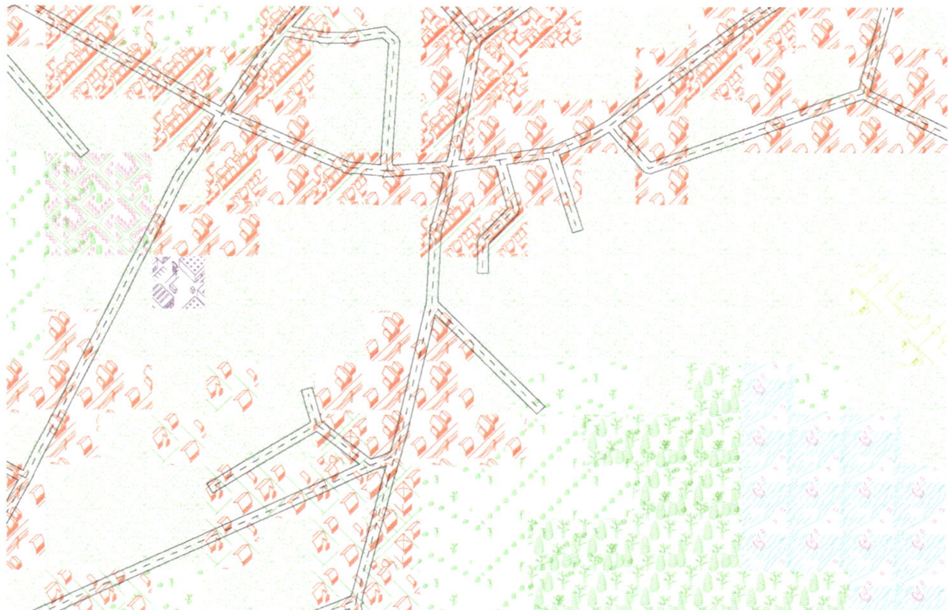

Installation view and detail, Joost Grootens, *A Land Never*, Venice Architecture Biennale, 2012.

Knowledge Through Representation

The insights of critical cartographers such as Grootens make maps more complicated and ethically and politically charged, but they also make the process of creating them, and the results, more interesting. It is only in the interpretation and representation of the gathered information that meaning is assigned to found data and knowledge about the city is produced. A traditional drawing is usually no longer the most obvious instrument to record the designer's imagination. A drawing is by nature static and therefore less suited to represent the dynamics of the use of cities. New information also requires other forms and other representations.

One company that applies itself fully to the effective visualization of use data of the city is Habidatum. Habidatum often collaborates with governments and companies to make analyses of urban use over the course of a day. The result are dynamic maps, which they call 'chronotopes': maps that visualize the urban environment by linking the factor time to the factor place. Chronotopes analyze the urban system and in the process highlight as yet unused opportunities for the city. To make them, Habidatum combines, among other things, mobility data, field research, and experiences of the space as expressed on social media, consumer behaviour, and energy use. This may result in maps of, for example, the behaviour over time of various communities in Dubai and their movements through the city, but also in maps of how tourists appreciate the various sites in Barcelona at different times of the day. This appreciation is interpreted on the basis of statements in public posts on social media such as Twitter. Any conflicts between tourists and the local population can also be visualized in time and space, based on such statements.

Habidatum combines experiences of space, with
behaviour in space by city users in this Chronotope

Habidatum shows that it pays to explore new forms in which the use of the city is included in the visualization of research data. Another example of a more dynamic visualization of a city is a cross-section of the busy Haarlemmerdijk, a street in Amsterdam. It not only represents the shops, houses, and infrastructure, but how they are used is added as a layer. Based on data from field research and the analysis of images on Google Street View the static drawing is thus enriched with how the street is being used daily. Likewise, the representation of the health climate of Amsterdam as a layered landscape map — the result of the study described earlier — is an example in which a dynamic layer is added to a static map. Data about air quality, heat island effects, noise, sports facilities, and food supply are superimposed on Amsterdam in order to provide more insight into the health situation on the neighbourhood level. In the representation of cities, 'use' is a new theme. The analysis of the use of space has hardly been part of design processes, if at all. Now, the technology providing access to that is available.

Relevant Data Sources
Where do designers find the necessary data to base their own research on? We list three types of data sources that are relevant to a metabolic approach to the city. First of all, there is a huge amount of already existing data that is being gathered and stored by all kinds of larger administrative, public, and private parties. These datasets are often not readily accessible, but they hold the promise of a treasure of usable information once these archives are opened up. Here, the innovation is not so much the utilization of data from these sources, but rather that a metabolic approach brings designers to use these data for spatial applications. A second continually growing set of data is actively being gathered from the use of all kinds of sensors that are by now part of the city. Like the data from the first source, these data still need analysis, visualization, and interpretation in order to become information that can be shared. A third source comes from more sociologically oriented research in which the data may be limited in a quantitative sense but do have a high qualitative value. These data often have been gathered from a specific outlook and have therefore already been subjected to interpretation. That latter aspect is a risk. If the underlying documents of these data (for example interviews that have been written out) are not available, extra caution is required when using such data. We will briefly go into the first two data sources to illustrate how they can be relevant for the design profession and to our search for a better understanding of the functioning of the urban body. The more analogue third source will be discussed further in the next chapter.

Finding and acquiring dependable datasets is often not an easy task. By far not all relevant datasets are publicly accessible. More and more data are collected on a large scale by private parties who store them behind locked doors. This makes it increasingly difficult, if not impossible, to make use of those data. Professor of Geographic Information Science from Liverpool, Alex Singleton, sees the not-being-public of data as a growing problem. He notices a decrease in publicly available relevant data not only with private parties, but also observes how governments are more and more inclined to block access to previously open data, even for scientists and researchers. He therefore advocates better standards to ensure that more data can be made available for research in a safe and privacy-friendly way.[5] As long as such standards have not been set, getting hold of reliable datasets or even finding out where to look for them remains a laborious process. Illustrative of this is a map of the distributed storage of relevant data of and about the municipality of Amsterdam. It is a network of various departments and on- and offline datasets that they store in different places under different licenses. The map makes it immediately clear how complicated it is to locate, collect, unravel, and decipher the right data in the right manner, even before one can even hope of being able to apply them. Also, experience tells us that even if one succeeds in obtaining the data, designers have to make high demands upon them in order to apply them in a meaningful way. Designers tend to have extensive and specific wishes. Being able to assess local interventions in the fabric of the city, for example, does require a certain level of detail in the data. The naked fact that more and more information about the city is being gathered, does not as such make life of the student of metabolism of the city much easier.

The Observing City: Sensors as Data Source
A second, continually growing source of data is to be sourced from the sensors that can be found in increasing frequency and numbers in our cities. After all, data flow freely through the city and are more and more often picked up by all kinds of robotic noses, eyes, and ears that share their observations with us as freely. Contemporary researchers no longer need to hit the streets themselves to gather data; more and more the city is equipped with gadgets to continuously monitor itself and these gadgets report on their findings in an automated manner. As a result, not only governments and businesses have access to a mountain of data on how the city is used nowadays, but everyone who takes an interest can now have increasingly easy access to datasets about the state of the city. This is also good news for concerned citizens who are suspicious of the data that are being gathered and interpreted by their municipality or the big companies in their neighbourhoods. For example, the people living in the vicinity of the Tata Steel factory in The Netherlands decided to gather their own data about the emissions of toxic substances, such as high concentrations of lead and PACs. They feared a connection between these emissions and the in their region acknowledged high risk of serious health problems such as cardiac complaints, diabetes, and lung cancer; a connection that governments and

research agencies are always hesitant to make as a result of too strictly formulated research questions and, as a result, scientifically inadequate research data. So the residents decided to crowdfund their own measuring equipment and start collecting data with the aid of drones and underwater robots. The residents of Flint, Michigan — who in 2014 were confronted with large quantities of lead in their drinking water after the city decided to change the source of their drinking water for budgetary reasons — also decided, out of anxiety, to start testing for poison in their water themselves. They managed to prove that some hundred thousand residents were structurally exposed to a high level of lead in their water. A heavy legal and political battle followed, resulting in officials being sued, high damages being paid, and repair work being done.

The naked fact that more and more information about the city is being gathered, does not as such make life of the student of metabolism of the city much easier.

A fine example of applying sensors in a design process in Amsterdam is Amsterdecks, a project by design firm Rademacher de Vries Architects, in collaboration with Waag Society and the water company Waternet. Amsterdecks are smart swimming decks in open water. The decks allow swimmers in open water to safely go into the water while at the same time providing all kinds of information about the current water quality. In addition, they are equipped with aerators that use screens of air bubbles to convey any poisonous blue-green algae to the deeper and darker parts of the water, where they die. The decks not only monitor the water quality, they also actively contribute to it. The results of the measurements (temperature, oxygen content, conductivity, PH value, and turbidity) are not only made available to the swimmers on location but can also be followed remotely on a companion website. This means that other parties can use the data as well. Besides providing a nice starting point for swimmers, this also makes Amsterdecks an example of a private series of sensors that measure flows in the city and collect data from them. Worldwide there are numerous of such initiatives — both advanced and less advanced — emerging in hacker spaces and companies where often relatively simple sensors are assembled by hand and then collect data. For example, with Sniffer Bike, SODAQ developed a sensor that can be easily attached to the handlebar of a bicycle to measure air quality. The data are shared on a platform that displays the fine-particles values measured by the sensors as the participating volunteers ride their bicycles.

On a different scale, Sensor.Community combines the data from globally distributed open-source sensors and displays them on maps. The goal is to generate open data about global environmental conditions. They also show where and how you can put together a sensor yourself for little money and hook it up to the network. By now they collect valuable data with more than 14,000 sensors in seventy-seven countries.

Sniffer Bike

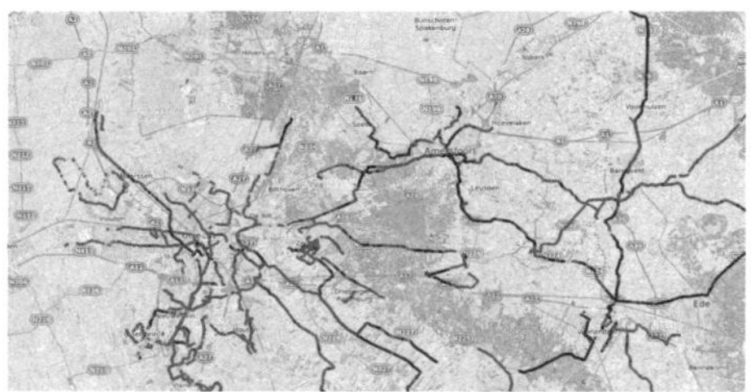

Air quality measured by cyclists on Sniffer Bikes

Citizen science: self-assembled sensor collecting data in Stuttgart, Germany

The work of Sensor.Community is an example of 'citizen science', making use of eminent scientists and enthusiasts to help gather relevant data. The data compiled by such initiatives are open-source and can thus be relatively easily applied in one's own research. It is important that the value of the resulting datasets is properly evaluated time and again and to realize what limitations the dataset contains, what conclusions can be drawn from it, and to consider what data should be added to arrive at high-quality knowledge. To enhance the reliability of the data it may be necessary to find an extra dataset, for example by engaging the services of a commercial partner. This latter option, for example, was required in the Waste Streams project of the MIT Senseable City Lab (SCL).

Waste Streams is part of SCL's Roboat project. It studies how a fleet of automated boats may contribute to the existing Amsterdam infrastructure while at the same time working as sensors to monitor the water and air quality and the weather conditions, among other things. In Waste Streams, the Roboats focus on the waste flows in the Amsterdam inner city to investigate whether this waste can be collected and taken away via the water. This could remove the infrastructural and environmental pressure of garbage trucks on the quays. The inner city of Amsterdam also suffers from a great shortage of waste collection points, as there is often not enough space available to place waste containers, and installing underground containers would wreak havoc on the already fragile state of many of the quays. At the same time, the amount of household waste is considerable and the many hotels in the city produce a constant and sizeable stream of waste.

Waste Streams is just one of the applications of the Roboat project, which in general does research into technological innovation on the waters of Amsterdam. The project also looks at possibilities for installing floating bridges, monitoring water quality, and organizing transport of goods on the canals. As a basis for that research, SCL has first made an analysis of the current traffic on the canals. The starting point was a week in 2017, in the summer, when the canals are usually most busy. To obtain data on the water traffic during those days they enlisted the help of a commercial partner: Marine Traffic. This company follows maritime traffic worldwide, tracing it with the help of satellites and so-called 'coastal AIS receiving stations', base stations that process the location data transmitted by ships. Thanks to these data SCL was able to monitor the movements on the water, store the results in a dataset, and then visualize everything in a map. The speed at which ships, ferries, and boats moved was also represented.

To obtain more insight into the current situation additional static data from the city of Amsterdam was processed about the amount of household waste per resident and the accessibility of garbage containers and collection spots in relation to the accessibility of the canal. The standard was chosen as 120 metres between garbage container and canal or front door. Only half of the inner-city residents has access to a garbage container within 120 metres, but eighty percent can reach a canal within that distance. Armed with these data the SCL began to look for mooring places for the roboats to provide residents with collection points within 120 metres. This resulted in a map with 283 locations that were then linked to some six collection points and routes for the automated boats that bring and haul the floating containers. The roboats show how innovative data collection about the use of the city (in this case its water and quays) can enrich existing static knowledge about an old city like Amsterdam — which in many respects was not designed for the current demands placed on it — while at the same time opening up concrete design possibilities for making the infrastructure of the city stronger and more robust.

The MIT Senseable City Lab's Roboat project studies how a fleet of automated boats might contribute to Amsterdam's existing waste collection infrastructure, while also gathering data on the city's water and air quality

Controlling the Controllable

The metabolic approach we advocate is not only aimed at better understanding the city as space, but also to understand the city as a system in order to get a better grip on its performance. It also makes it clear that gathering data to become informed about the functioning of the urban system goes beyond just mapping physical flows. Visualizing human behaviour to obtain insight into how people use urban space is at least as important, if we are to deepen our understanding of the city. Generating data on the functioning of aspects of the urban system has evolved enormously over the past few decades. The door-to-door interviewing and mapping data by hand as, practised by Charles Booth around 1900, can now be supplemented by having computers collecting or processing large datasets. However, the second practice does not replace the first, as ideally both are used together to obtain a richer view of the use and functioning of the city and adapt it where necessary. The impact of technology and its development within the domain of spatial design yields all kinds of new possibilities and perspectives. Technological tools help to simplify and speed up the process of data gathering, but also help expand and enrich it. Embracing complexity in design issues is, therefore, not only advisable in terms of content, but also technologically within reach. Likewise in Amsterdam where, especially since the Covid-19 crisis, there is much focus on crowd management. Amsterdam applied new technology for tracking the flows of people in public space, for example to avoid large concentrations of people in popular meeting places such as the Vondelpark and ensure social distancing. Even when that rule no longer applies, the expertise is still there, ready to play a role in all kinds of other themes in order to get more insight into the patterns of use of the city. Apart from any political and ethical questions this gives rise to, designers should think hard about how it is possible that this technology is further developing day by day but rarely plays a significant role in designing the city.

Of course, this technology certainly does not bring about universal happiness. The system of the city is not fully understandable and controllable either, like, to return to the opening of this chapter, a bicycle race is. In preparing for a major tour, the people in Dumoulin's support team talk a lot about the importance of having as much grip as possible on that which can be controlled in a race: 'controlling the controllable'. But the reason why people love to watch cycling, and professional sport in general, is precisely that most elements cannot be controlled. Of course, the route is known in advance and therefore somewhat controllable and by exploring it you can devise possible scenarios. Of the rivals, it is also known what their specialties are, their strengths and weaknesses, and what results they achieved in which area in the past. However, there are at least as many elements one cannot control at all. The weather may suddenly turn and neutralize the race, as happened during the Tour de France of 2019, when a huge stream of snow and mud blocked the road on a crucial final climb in a decisive leg, thereby prematurely deciding the final results of the race. The wind may suddenly pick up and tear apart the whole pack of contestants, resulting in a loss of minutes. A favourite to win the tour may slip over a pebble in the road and have to give up early. A collision may leave someone without transport, as happened to Chris Froome in the thick of the battle for the Tour de France of 2016. Wearing the yellow jersey, he collided with one of the organization's motor cycles, lost his bicycle, and was forced to continue the mythical climb to the top of Mont Ventoux on foot, running. Also, the body, so meticulously prepared to meet any demand the course may make upon it, can suddenly rebel in extreme situations and display unexpected behaviour. As became clear when Tom Dumoulin almost didn't win the Giro d'Italia in 2017, when sudden tummy trouble made it necessary for him to step off his bike and use the camper of one of the spectators along the route to relieve himself.

Designers should think hard about how it is possible that this technology is further developing day by day but rarely plays a significant role in designing the city.

GC riders in major tours often like the individual time trials: to go as fast as you can over well-reconnoitred terrain. In a time trial the uncertainty has been minimized, the predictability of the run of the match has been maximized, and the energy effort can be optimally controlled. He who manages to put the most force on the pedals for the longest time and has the best aerodynamic posture, is fastest and wins. Most bicycle races are not time trials, however, but chaotic, unpredictable journeys rife with opportunities and risks. The 'controllable' is continuously put under pressure by the uncontrollable logic of the day.

Urban issues have a different time frame in terms of both execution and possible adjustments, but here too there is much uncontrollability and uncertainty in drawing up a strategy. A strategic economic choice to go for tourism as the prominent economic factor in cities such as Amsterdam can lead to a series of problems that are hard to predict in advance. Also because there may be developments in the market that radically change the situation. The popularity of a company such as Airbnb in combination with the popularity of Amsterdam as a holiday destination has for example led to much pressure on an already overheated housing market.

Temporarily renting out apartments to tourists instead of

permanently to the local population had simply become much more attractive from a financial viewpoint. That is, until the Covid-19 pandemic put a halt to tourism and, in another plot twist, turned the lucrative decentralized tourist dwellings into a financial blow for those who had come to rely on this income. Data research cannot prevent such processes from happening, but a thorough knowledge of the situation does make the city more resilient and strengthens the ability to intervene swiftly and effectively when an unexpected development occurs. It makes data research an indispensable element in a thorough process of contemporary research by design.

1   Sevki Türkkan, 'The "Anti-Architect": A Phantasy or a Probability', presented and published at the proceedings of the international conference 'Political Imagination and The City', Santiago de Chile, 7-8 July 2016.

2   See: Vincent James, 'What a Machine Learning Tool That Turns Obama White Can (and Can't) Tell Us About AI Bias', *The Verge*, 23 June 2020, theverge.com/21298762/face-depixelizer-ai-machine-learning-tool-pulse-stylegan-obama-bias, accessed 26 June 2020. And the original Twitter thread: twitter.com/tg_bomze/status/1274098682284163072.

3   The website thispersondoesnotexist.com shows how convincing 'fake photographs' can be. Visitors to the site see only a high-resolution photograph of a non-existing person and when they reload the page they are presented with another one. This website too uses the *generative adversarial network* (GAN) StyleGAN2 algorithm and is often used for generating photographs for fake accounts on social media.

4   Joost Grootens, 'Complexity and Contradiction in Map Design', in *FUR Handbook #01: Information Design*, p. 21 ff.

5   Alex Singleton, 'Challenges and Solutions for the Analysis of New Forms of Data', 2018 CGA Conference, 27 April 2017, Harvard University, Cambridge.

MAPPING THE URBAN METABOLISM

A Conversation with Taneha Bacchin

Taneha K. Bacchin is an architect, urban designer, and researcher. She is assistant Professor Urban Design Theory and Methods at the Faculty of Architecture and the Built Environment, Delft University of Technology, where she also is Coordinator of Research at the Section of Urban Design and Research Leader Delta Urbanism Interdisciplinary Research Programme. Her research and projects focus on the intersection between landscape architecture, infrastructure, and urban form. She has expertise in design and planning of critical territories, being specialized in water-sensitive design in the context of aggravating climatic conditions. Her current work deals with the changing nature of the territorial project, addressing spatial, political, and economic aspects of extreme weather and resource scarcity with projects in the North Sea, the Arctic, Brazil, and India.

In her research Taneha uses water as a lens to obtain an understanding of urban metabolism. She approaches water both as an access-point to start gaining insight into the performance and identity of a city and as an agent and driver of change. As such she identifies four domains of change, spaces where change can come from: societal culture, ecological circumstances, infrastructural & technological conditions, and governance & management. The manifestation of water (its availability, its quality, its safety and security) in an urban context is understood as the effect of the situation within and dynamic relation between these four domains.

The four domains manifest themselves in the design space continuum between air-water-land (interdependencies between atmospheric, water, and land cycles), and the related design elements: layers, processes, challenges, criteria and scales. These design elements are used to organize her research and identify the relevant ingredients that together form a blueprint, or map, of the metabolism of a city and, specifically, of its use of water. That knowledge can be used to explore what potential design interventions can bring systemic changes to the behaviour of that metabolism.

The blueprint Bacchin comes up with is always detailed and layered, in the sense that it identifies all these ingredients at three different scales. These scales can be found on the right side of the attached scheme. From big to small, macro to micro, she named these: territory, object, and ensemble. Those scales, however, are more fluidly interpretable than the scheme might suggest and are very context-dependent, as she explains in the following interview. In it, Bacchin and Frijters discuss the details of her methodology and the results she gained with it. Together they explore a few concrete examples from her work and how her watery lens helped to obtain a deep understanding of the circumstances in different urban areas. In India, for instance, she used this lens to study different secondary cities and the societal role of local water storage facilities in them. Her analyses also lead us to new places for design that before were never identified as such. This is shown in her work on the North Sea, but also in her study on the moving city of Kiruna, where the metabolic analysis brought her to a very concrete design strategy.

Data technology also plays an important role in her work. While initially being somewhat shewed away by the massive availability of data with questionable use for urban researchers and designers, she later realized it also opened up new forms of analysis. She, for instance, values the possibility it opens to represent use as a layer that can be laid on top of the representation of spatial organization, which dramatically increases our knowledge of the urban space as a living organism.

Frijters and Bacchin conclude their meeting with a reflection on the aesthetic effects of design from a metabolic point of view, the importance of maintenance and re-use and how change and transition could drive us towards another, more temporal, aesthetic approach.

ERIC FRIJTERS Taneha, before we start, I would like to give a short introduction on the various topics we want to discuss and maybe test the mutual understanding of some of the notions we will be using. For starters, I would like to share with you my perception of 'city', which I don't conceive as a morphological concept of spaces and voids solely. Rather, we recognize that the city may be even more a system than a morphological expression. In this understanding of cities, we recognize two limits to the discussion on the design of the system. The first are the planetary boundaries: human life on earth is impossible when those boundaries are transgressed. So, we as designers feel the responsibility to prevent that from happening, but only to a certain point. The second, and opposite to the first, are the societal restrictions. There is a limit to what we as human beings can do to relief our collective footprint on the ecosystem of our planet through design, construction, and use of urban territories. The system might demand something more radical than we as people can survive in. Therefore, we have to find a balance in that as well.

In order to find that balance, we should develop new tools to understand its underlying system. As designers, we are of course trained in looking at the city in its morphological appearance. But it's more than just that. Working on the challenges that come with a sustainable transition that is needed in order to make sure that cities start to perform as healthy ecosystems requires a different approach to spatial design. And it demands a different repertoire from designers. It will lead to the invention of new typologies and infrastructures, which will be followed by a new artistic expression. In other words, the search for a more circular city that is based on renewable energy, sustainable resources, and climate-change-ready solutions will appear to us with a completely new design aesthetics. But first things first; do you agree

TANEHA
BACCHIN that cities are a system?

I understand the city as embedded in a larger context. Now, this context can be exemplified by a watershed. I think of our work, the daily quest to understand the urban phenomenon. But to start understanding this phenomenon and the processes behind it, we first have to look elsewhere. The many non-linearities of the urban system show how we should read and understand the city as a living organism that is evolving, that is constantly changing and that has different paces of change. The difference in pace has been accelerated and/or disrupted by crises: climate crisis, societal crises, and economic crises. So, to start unpacking this urban phenomenon, and to understand these non-linearities, I am using the watershed as a logical lens to start my metabolic analysis. From a metabolism point of view, you want to map a specific flow, find the source and sync of it. This can be the use of a specific material, the resource which has been used to make that piece of material, the originating location, or the externalities that have been generated in the place of its extraction. By mapping such a flow, we want to analyze and comprehend the whole chain of production until its final use. To understand the city, we need to fall back on the theory of complexity. And we can only start to understand it if we accept the fact, that it's embedded within other bodies.

EF —You describe how the presence of the city does not coincide one-to-one with the presence of buildings. You are saying that there is a larger system related to what we see, that we always agreed upon as being the city. But under that presence, there's a large number of complex processes that collectively shape this idea of city.

TB You see the manifestation of it. As you said in the beginning, it's not just a question of environmental, but also of societal norms. So, what is actually the specific element that we are looking at, what are the several juxtapositions that made that specific element known? Say, a process, a building, an object, only comes into place in that specific moment in time. So, I also think that when you talk about understanding cities as systems, you should not only talk of the embeddedness within different spatial units, but also of the embeddedness within different temporal scales. Therefore, time is an extremely important factor.

The City as an Agent of Change

EF —Water plays a special role in your analysis of the city. Could you explain this a little more?

TB I am currently coordinating an ongoing transdisciplinary research project on water sensitivity in secondary cities in India funded by NWO-DST Cooperation Programme on Urban Water. It is a bilateral cooperation between India and the Netherlands about the challenge of water in the context of fast-growing secondary cities. In the project we focus on three cities that we use as archetypes of 'the secondary city'.

From a first understanding through careful reading about the history of these cities, we identify what might be things that are not specific and can be extrapolated to other cities. For that we are producing three city atlases for the cities of Bhopal (Madhya Pradesh), Bhuj (Gujarat) and Kozhikode (Kerala), and we do it as a descriptive, analytical, and projective effort. The projective effort already discloses a design position and the orientation that we have as a project. Through this projective lens we try to understand phenomena in the cities in their relation to water.

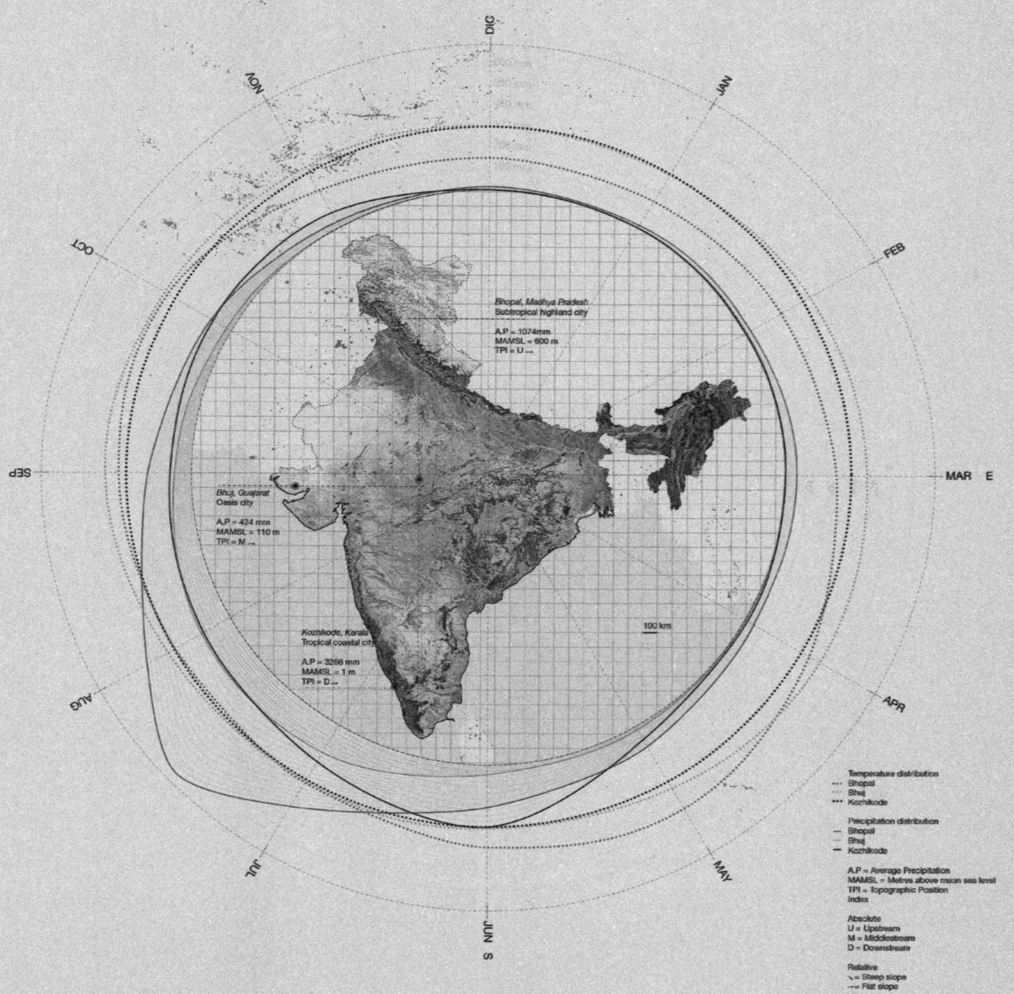

Using water as a lens to look at urban systems in a research project on water sensitivity in the Indian cities of Bhopal, Bhuj, and Koshikode

EF — You have been working on cities all over the world, using water as a lens to look at urban systems. To support this ongoing research, you are developing a metabolic overview.

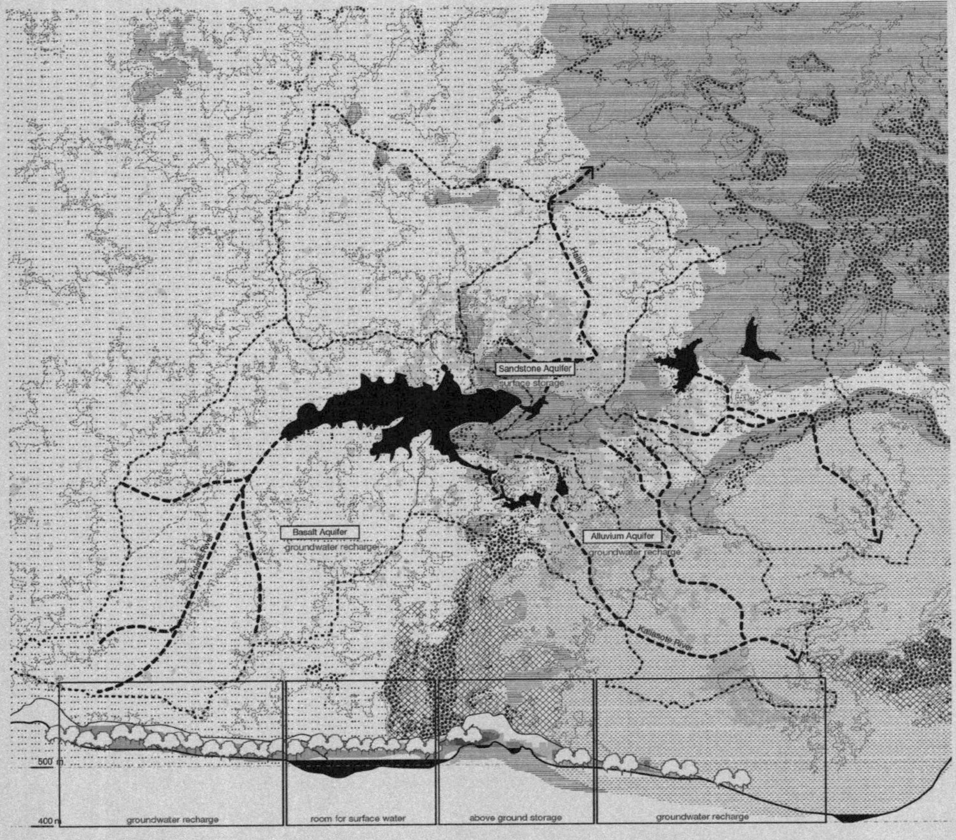

The reading of air patterns and water flows culminates with the understanding and identification of four different strategic zones to manage water

TB   We started from the idea of reading the city as the watershed, but we now use the idea of the continuum. What we mean by that is the fact that urbanization happens not only between the city and its watershed, but also in the continuum of atmosphere, surface, and subsurface — air, land, and water. Therefore, urbanization (as a phenomenon) can be read even in atmospheric patterns. Our mental framework is a complete section, starting with the air above cities and straight into the underground. The amount of moisture that is carried in the atmosphere above cities, is part of our system analysis. With this spatial design approach, we are focusing on change. As you said, we do not perceive the city only from a morphological point of view, but we read it as an agent of change. Let us say that urbanization has the agency of changing surface, subsurface, and atmospheric qualities that are in turn changing each other. When we exhaust the soil, for example, because of a certain form of urbanization (e.g., occupation, extractivism, production and/or infrastructure), we will find out the systemic consequences of it in the atmosphere later on.

EF —In this metabolic overview on page 58—59 I see six design elements or categories represented by six columns: design space, design layers, processes, design challenges, design criteria, and design scale. On the right side, I see scale connected to design challenges and objectives. On the left side, I see what you call continuum, meaning air patterns, water flows, cultural institutions, and land transformations. This complete overview starts to resemble the map of human metabolism.[1] This time I am not looking at the 'chemical processes in the human body', but I see 'water and the city', right?

TB   Yes, exactly. What we have are the basic principles of interdependencies, or the continuum, on the left — as the overarching approach to spatial design encompassing the six design elements or categories — and the three scales that we are using — territory, object and ensemble — on the right. (p.58–59) I would categorize these three as part of the architecture of the territory, or territorial design. The whole scheme could be applied to a specific infrastructural type that we are looking at. So, the scales are more flexible to interpret. The object could be a district, or a part of a district, while the whole city would be referred to by the territory. The ensemble is a unit of design, in which there is a certain process that organizes that unit.

EF —What is the status of this scheme? Is this a complete overview?

TB   Well, this overview is a work in progress, which helps us to coordinate our steps. So, we are looking for what is our design space? What are the design layers? What are the processes embedded in those layers? And what are the challenges of those processes? And then finally: what are our design criteria and main scales of the analysis of the design? The choice of the three scales comes with the idea and the intension of having a synthetic narrative.

EF —Just as an aside: now this scheme is dedicated to 'water', but we could also put in the word 'energy'? You would get the same analysis, the same categories, and the same unfolding regarding any other theme of subject, right?

TB   Absolutely.

Four Domains of Change

EF —On what foundation did you base this overview? Did it come out of the blue or does it refer to something we may already know?

TB   The project is about cross-contamination and it is structured around four domains of change. That means that to change water, you'll have to design with the four domains of change: space of societal culture, space of ecology, space of infrastructure and technology, and space of governance and management. What we understand as the manifestation of water, like the availability of water, its quality, security, and safety, is based on the dynamic balance between these four domains. This means that to address the design challenge we must work for a balanced outcome of governmental action, with the implementation of new and/or retrofitted or repurposed technology, combined with new

air, water, culture, land continuum
four domains of change
how to read

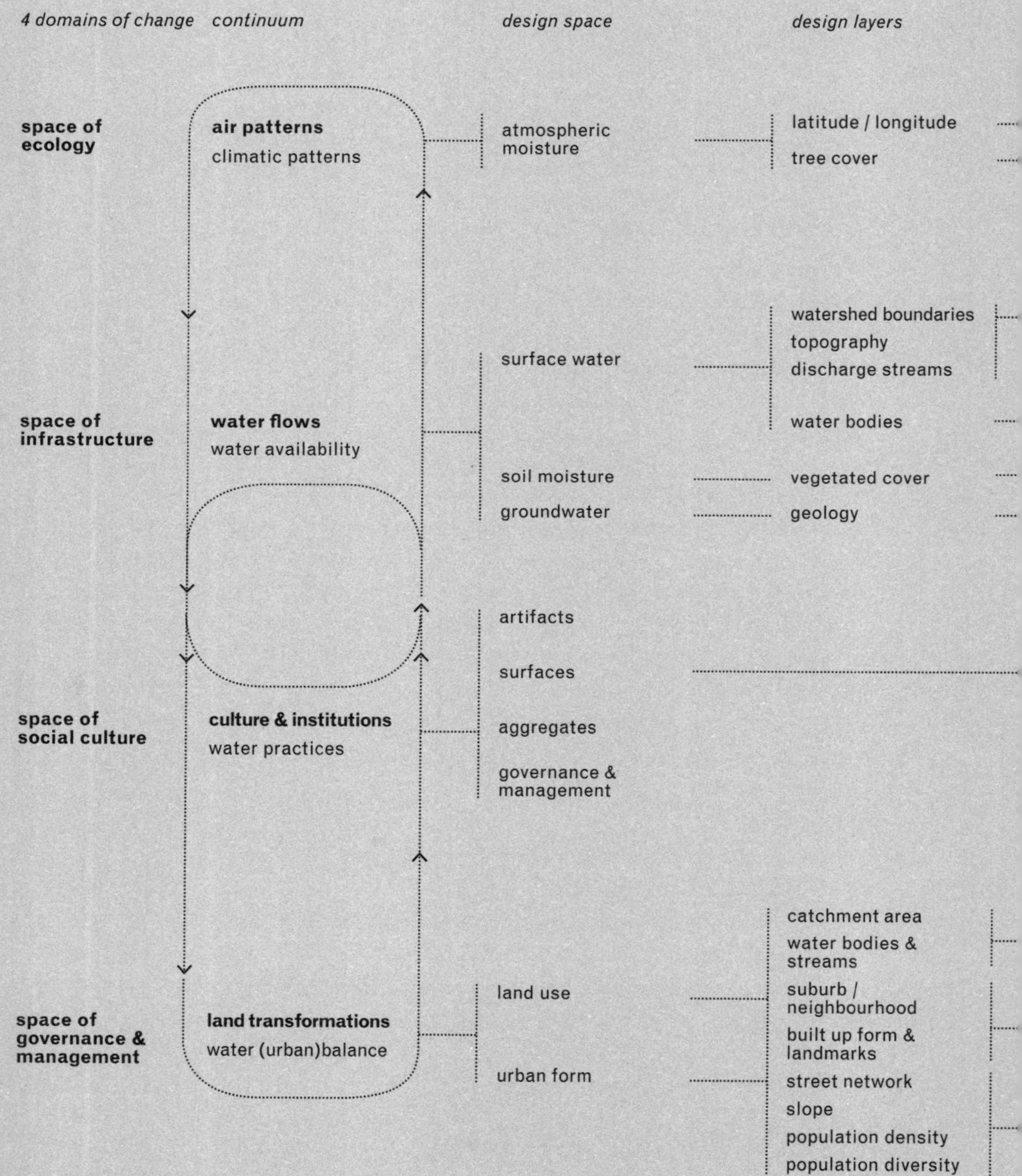

processes	*design challenges*	*design criteria*	*design scale*
precipitation distribution	precipitation exceedance		
precipitation recycling	precipitation scarcity		
	high evaporation (dryness)		
		what, when & where store & harvest in the air, surface, topsoil or and groundwater	**territory**
runoff direction			
recharge			
evaporation			
storage	surface water availability		
infiltration	groundwater availability		
evapotranspiration			
percolation			
responsiveness to uncertainty	dependency on exogenous sources		**object**
responsiveness to urgencies	dereliction of local resources		
sustained water availability	water pollution		
sustained water accessibility	groundwater depletion		
multifunctionality		**who & how** landscape proximity and landscape maanagement	**ensemble**
catchment performance & technology			
cultural landscape & technology	flood prone areas		
space & technology	fluctuant water availability		

societal behaviour and based on environmental interaction. In order to do that, we have to understand what sensitivity to water means in the Indian context, and we need to arrive at an understanding of existing and traditional practices around water that are embedded in institutional and cultural arrangements. After that we wonder what type of systemic changes can be made and whether we should have a focus on changing space, changing infrastructure, or changing governance capacities and behaviour.

When Bill Hillier[2] writes about the social logic of space, he suggests to start from a spatial perspective. What we did to understand the performance of our case study watersheds, was to look into the most representative infrastructural (water-related) practices. We started with the traditional ones, for instance in the case of Bhopal we studied the example of the 'baoli'. (Figure 4) Unfortunately, today most of them are in ruins. It was conceived as a space that collects water — a water storage and supply facility for the city that also has important social functions. That translates even into how the building is made and the shadow that it creates, providing cooling and a place for social gathering with access to water. Therefore, the baoli is a traditional artifact that performs as a multifunctional space. Finally, the question of the project is to see how decentralized systems such as the 'baoli' and centralized systems of water towers appear in a hybrid coexistence for water storage and supply. Therefore, looking into the watershed is important for us to understand the water performance and the different forms of infrastructure that can mutually coexist. And at the same time, we also use it as a base to read urbanity.

Students sitting on the steps of a Baoli

Water as a Lens of Knowing

EF — How important is it to identify the critical scale of intervention in how you approach your projects? Following your work, I noticed that you have been expanding the working areas of spatial design by connecting research-by-design through projects on various scales and topics.

TB From a systemic point of view, the way I was involved in projects was initially based on an assumption of macro, meso, micro, and nano scale. With my PhD research I added the idea of the nano as the process level scale. This trans-scalar way of reading, analyzing, and designing, looking for interdependencies between scales in space and time, is the basis of my way of working.

EF — So, what is the nano scale? Is it nano architecture or even smaller?

TB Smaller.

EF — Is it furniture?

TB It can be. But I would say it is more dynamic than that. When looking at a site, I see the nano scale represented as type of plants or soil. It could be a building as well, but it really depends on the context. In any case the nano would be the singular unit. So, the nano is the building block, or the singular unit of the performance attached to it.

EF — And the micro scale? How would you define, or relate to the micro?

TB From a water management point of view I define the micro as the street segment. It is the street that carries the water within a micro catchment, therefore it is the segment flow that combines the singular performance units attached to it.

EF — It is performance-based. In this case, then, translated into a water system infrastructure. So, whereas the city happens somewhere in that context, its relevance is the expression of that system.

TB That is why I said that I am using water as a lens that allows the city to be read.

EF — The way you apply water as a lens to read the city, is that similar to how Daniel Ibañez uses wood as a lens to observe the urban metabolism?

TB Yes, exactly.

EF — The difference is that your system is always a necessary condition for the city to exist. While I consider wood more as an optional application for cities. You do not necessarily need wood to have a city, but you need water to have it, I would say. But they can both function as a lens, as a translation method of looking at that urban system and understand it from that perspective. I think our readers are very happy with this, at least to get that idea of urban metabolism a little bit more down to earth, formulated or defined, to start understanding it not only as an analogy or metaphor. It can actually be made more tangible by relating it to water or wood or some other flow.

TB Yes, I am constantly making this effort to open the puzzle of the logic in relationships. So, how things relate in space, for instance, by using the boundary of the city and how the city divides itself by catchment areas, and then into sub-catchments and then inside that you have a micro-catchment and then the nano-catchment.

EF — What does this analysis mean for you as a designer? I understand the interaction between these different scales of observation, looking at the same system from different perspectives: on the one hand at eye-level view, and on the other almost at a water universe. But knowing this, understanding this, what does it bring you as a designer? As an urban designer, what can you do now that you could not do before?

TB Again, it is the search for balance. What was eye-opening to me was the possibility of the application of this type of tools, say of design analysis, that lead to the notion that you do not need to solve the whole puzzle in one space. Things are related and dependent on each other. So, you may not be able to change land use and ownership in this specific location in this micro-catchment area for example, but you may be able to mitigate a decisive influence on other portions of the system to reach your goals. What is the type of information that you are taking into the design decision, every step of the way?

EF — I understand, but what still puzzles me is how we will ever be able to really approach the city holistically, which would enable us to justify the idea of urban metabolism. What I mean is, now we have investigated this idea of water, and how that ends up in the city with a certain expression. But that city is of course much more than only water. There is so much else going on: people go to work there, they sleep, play games, and do sports. There is commercial activity. There is of course energy flowing through that same space. All that needs to be climate-adaptive too. Do you see a future in which we would have a similar approach of analysis at all these different levels?

TB   No, maybe not in the same way. We will be constantly asking ourselves: what is the challenge in front of us and that sets the lens of knowing in a specific case. This might then translate into the choice for prioritizing certain scales, or certain subjects and objectives that we are using to read urbanity. I would say that we do need the gaze and the narrative. This is important, because it helps us to select. When I started my PhD at the Bartlett at CASA, which is the Centre for Advanced Spatial Analysis, with Michael Batty,[3] I was very passionate about urban development. And I was interested to use spatial intelligence to understand the growth of cities. But after a while I realized once again the importance of spatial design instead and with Dirk Sijmons[4] I concluded my PhD research designing urban landscapes. I understood that a careful design-driven lens and reading of space is more than just algorithms can tell. You need a design mindset at the same time, to navigate this complexity.

City Analysis and Technology

EF — This method you described reminds me of Bruno Latour[5], who differentiates 'matters of fact' and 'matters of concern' as a tool to prioritize key elements in a complex framework. As a basic formula to start a city we have people living and working there, right? We need some mobility to move around, and at least some resources, such as food, water, and energy, for starters. So that is why I could imagine that at least research into that nexus for these three types of flow infrastructure and how they internally relate to each other, would always be a meaningful analysis. Are you suggesting that we only need a few of those analyses, based on a limited number of themes or lenses? That it would be enough to have the main topics of making city under control?

TB   Well, I believe that we can never control cities since they behave as a living, everchanging organism. I think the main question is how can we close some of their loops. I realize I am not really answering your question. But I think it depends. If you would look into energy, water, or material flows, there are specific ways to map and to analyze their areas of influence and (co-)dependency. I must admit that material flows are harder because they are embedded in geopolitical, logistical, and production processes globally. But doing the suitability analysis in a specific context to understand what type of land use we can have in respect to the carrying capacity of the environment, would still be possible for some flows. But then: what about politics? What about legislation and financial issues? So, to again not answer your question: at this point I do not know if there is a way to have it all.

EF — But when we were trained as architects, or as urbanists, or as landscape architects, we never learned to travel through the different scales of spatial design. This is something you learned yourself. Nobody taught you how to do this, right? So, you taught me two things: one is to start with a flow infrastructure, like water or energy, and secondly start understanding how it responds to space on different scales. Those are the two things you already add to this toolbox of designers of the future. We also touched upon the fact that the complexity of making a thorough analysis of the urban metabolism might be inconceivable in the short term. Do you think that technological developments, such as artificial intelligence, could help you read the data to understand urban systems?

TB   There was a time that I felt overwhelmed by data. The complexity in analyzing urban systems kept on growing, instead of being reduced. You remember how we always defined the difference between data and the action in different steps in between?

EF — Yes, you mean the process of research-by-design, which promotes information into knowledge, knowledge into wisdom, and wisdom into potential action, and finally into plans?

TB   Exactly. So, I felt that design was a way for me to be in control again, to sort of tame the expansion of the amount of irrelevant data into complexity, to not be continuously overwhelmed by it. But I do see that both design and technology are extremely important in understanding urban metabolism. I was using genetic algorithms to model growth, for instance. I think that the work of Christophe Girot[6] at ETH on landscape design and analysis based on pointcloud modelling technology, is an interesting example. He uses a very different form of computational representation to survey and map a site. It is based on computational techniques, but it renders space in a way that we could not see it before. So, for me, that is a good example of how technology and design start shaping an interesting hybrid.

EF — Does this new hybrid also require a new visual language to communicate its message?

TB   Maybe unintentionally? We did a project for Randstad for which we made this kaleidoscopic drawing.

EF — This is actually a method, this type of kaleidoscopic drawing?

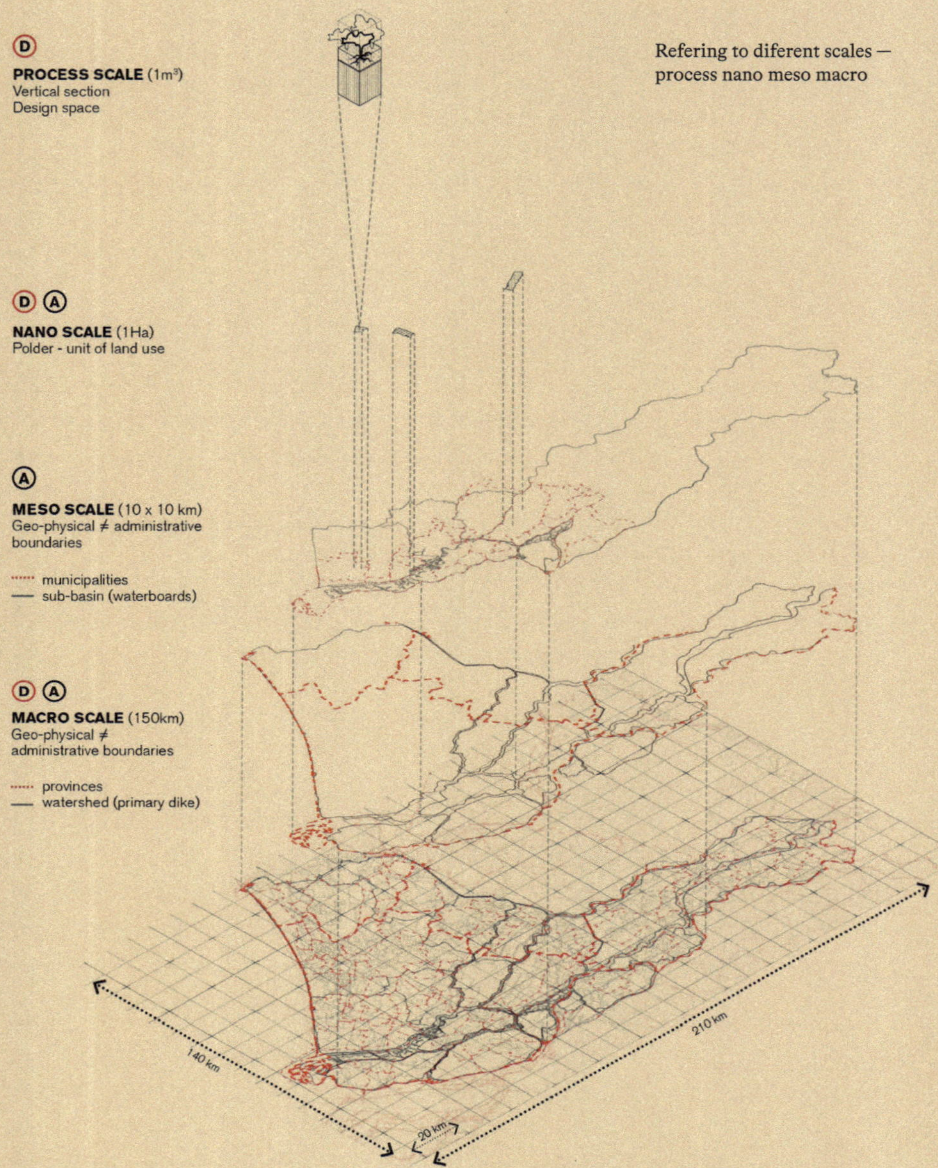

TB   Yes, it is moving between two scales. The main scale is the macro scale, featured here as the urban region as posed by Richard Forman,[7] and the nano, which is the scale of parcels of land use type and their proposed transformations (Figure 5). The project was called NEXT generation infrastructure design under conditions of extremes, a project developed with Filippo La Fleur and supported by TU Delft Deltas, Infrastructure & Mobility Initiative. The main question of this research was what it would take to change or adapt existing land use for carbon sequestration and flood risk management. The basic action of the project proposes a hybrid land use. The aim was to increase the biocapacity of existing land uses when possible, by growing the ecological density, or the amount of vegetation and different forms of vegetation, of the site. So, we took specific types of land use, and we saw how much vegetation, in terms of density and plant species, we could insert. So, yes, this type of representation, although abstract, for us was a synthetic method of drawing, in which we would lay the two scales on top of each other, so the nano on the macro, and we would show the impact of local interventions in changing and/or adapting existing land uses in the larger territorial context. And then the other important point was that we could see land and sea as one system and identify the sea as the largest open space of the Netherlands.

EF — That is quite an observation. So, in this analysis we see that the sea is our solution space.

TB   Yes. It is again also part of the continuum. There is no real distinction. If it comes to climate adaption, that is a matter of what is happening both on the sea and on land. We concluded that the answer to environmental restoration lies in this hybridity. That means working with silviculture and with specific patches of reforestation, but also, in the sea, for example, with seaweed farms. So, it is possible to enhance biocapacity while maintaining existing land use by increasing the presence of designed nature.

The Mobile City of Kiruna

EF — Our suggestion is to read cities as a system in order to host a solution space for a new generation of challenges that roll out over the city, over time, as a phenomenon. What I mean is that the urban area has to start performing and behaving in a new way. To host the production of energy in circular processes that do not exhaust our resources, for instance. Climate adaptation takes space. You showed us more space in places where we never looked; like the North Sea. You showed us that we might find space by increasing the density of uses into new hybrids. But that is not all. There is a third one, in which over time we are allowed to project different uses.

TB   Indeed, and connected to that is the notion of maintenance. Because if performance becomes part of design, maintenance does as well. A few years ago, TU Delft was a partner in a winning research proposal for a three-year research project with the Luleå University of Technology and the University of Innsbruck. The central case of our project was the city of Kiruna and the objective to design a green/blue infrastructure for the new city masterplan called New Kiruna. The research challenge for us was to design and engineer a green/blue infrastructure in a place that normally is covered in ice and snow for nine months a year. What is important to know is that Kiruna is a city in Lapland, Sweden, in the Arctic region, site of the largest and most modern underground iron ore mine in the world. Because of mining activities, the city is sinking and has to be relocated. Therefore, Kiruna is not only a city characterized by its extreme cold climate but also by the fact that it is a moving

The re-location of historically and culturally protected buildings in Kiruna, Sweden.

city. So how do you design a green/blue infrastructure that reflects these two unique aspects? To start — if we only focus on the challenge of extreme cold climate designing and engineering — the question was how to maintain a soft design space based on vegetation and open water. Therefore, maintenance and infrastructure integration became our key concerns. Our objective was to design with nature. That means that the control of the infrastructure is less than a piped infrastructure and it implies that the infrastructure is much more dynamic. You can only control it up to a certain extent. There is an unfolding of things happening and the space will be subject to how it will be used by the people living there. So, an avalanche of new questions entered our domain, which switched from pure technical bases to system analysis. For instance, what is the agency and the contribution given by private and public forms of maintenance? How can you involve the community in maintaining those open spaces that are also subject to snow and ice coverage? Or even more basic, how do you recognize that a bioswale is actually a piece of infrastructure. Maintenance became, in that sense, part of the design.

EF — The way you connect and integrate technical infrastructure, or in this case green/blue infrastructure, as embedded in city and society, sounds very similar to the Indian analysis we discussed in the beginning of our conversation.

TB   You are right. The approach is similar. It was the idea of a way to break down complexity, reading through the different scales, but also the domains that you use in terms of performance objectives. But the difference is the aspect of time that we brought into this project. Since the city of Kiruna is continuously on the move, because of mining activities, we had to place design in a moving context. So, we were forced to design with instability, uncertainty, and the acceptance that the city will continue to be displaced. Therefore, it became important to us to know what would be the backbone. What are the key elements in space that provide the identity of the city? For this we relied on the masterplan that was done by White Arkitekter. They established this identity and what it takes to maintain it, regardless of the future displacements and movements of the city. What we added to that identity structure is this overwhelming change between seasons. It resulted in the inspiring question: what might be the portions of this green/blue infrastructure that actually can provide for the basic performance, and will be capable of vanishing and appearing again, throughout the seasons. So, this is what we tried to model.

EF —So, the metabolic analysis of Kiruna resulted in a design strategy that amplified its specific characteristics, right?

TB   Sure, this seasonality of the infrastructure, with the moving sequence itself, formed the essence of our proposal: the drainage infrastructure that moves from the Old City to the New Kiruna and continues to do so through time. The main axis in the plan is based on an old railway. In the New Kiruna masterplan this axis is used to relocate artefacts of cultural importance and heritage buildings. Another important set of spatial elements were the existing green fingers from the adjacent forestry entering into the new city as well. The design was very much based on working with local climate by carefully designing the new urban fabric in response to the winds that Kiruna is exposed to. In this way, the urban fabric of the New Kiruna became much denser and shaped in a way to improve the micro-climatic comfort.

EF —So, in a sense White Arkitekter already incorporated metabolic knowledge into their design?

TB   Yes, absolutely, and this is also the reason why the Municipality of Kiruna was our key stakeholder partner in the JPI Green Blue Cities research project. It is a very sparse city with very low density. Therefore, the question became: how can we create such a micro-climate that life outside can become more comfortable? The design and engineering question for us was then how green/blue infrastructure could contribute to that.

EF —So, the second version of Kiruna became much more logically embedded into its natural systemic context. Did you reach this by only pointing out core qualities, or did you bring new technology to the solution as well?

TB   Yes, we did. As it was not just a settlement that grew from the mine. It is a designed city, looking into the possibility of having even more outdoor life. For this reason, we envisioned a green/blue infrastructure design framework that is sensitive to the unique climatic, environmental, and cultural conditions of Kiruna. For that, we worked with new technologies in order to integrate different types of infrastructure. For instance, we explored the application of tunnelling and underground space technology integrated with landscape architecture at the ground level. By doing so we aimed to enhance the synergy between surface and subsurface design while maximizing maintenance.

Transitional Aesthetics

EF — What I find interesting, is that new typologies or new infrastructures, as you can see in the previous example, are a result of a new analysis. A new lens, if you will. A metabolic approach of urban design leads to new solutions, looking for synergies between different systems within the urban landscape. The performance of this design was about making microclimates, making a city that is both a winter city and a summer city, and find the synergies in that temporality in such a way that it can become a spatial quality, right? Through its metabolic intentions in its design strategy, the bundle of water and energy infrastructure in Kiruna has unavoidably led to a new typology for infrastructure. What I am curious about is whether this technical repositioning also implies a cultural shift in the way we design and express our spatial solutions.

TB   I think the secret of that aesthetic is the aim for the legibility of the system and specially the performance that you are designing for. Aesthetics play a crucial role in understanding the design through the lens of performance. Its aesthetics make the system comprehensible. An important dimension to that is appropriation. So how do you appropriate space and make it your own? I understand appropriation in relation to care and therefore to maintenance.

We are used to a certain city form, to a certain infrastructure form and the way it is embedded in the urban. It is directly linked to specific lifestyles that we have. Because of the predominant way that we currently inhabit, produce, and built infrastructure we are still far behind from truly transitioning to clean energy, sustainable resources, and healthier environments.

We might increase ecological rehabilitation if we let go of control of certain open and/or abandoned spaces so that nature can return and flourish, most likely in an unpredictable fashion. Here the question is how to encode this indeterminacy as an element and quality of our design and maintenance frameworks.

EF — So, you describe that the inherent distinction of how landscape design differentiates itself from urban design or architecture is by claiming that there is this indirect conditional design in which you create a basis for an ecosystem, but you cannot really control what is coming out, right? So, there is an experimental percentage in the outcome of every design decision. That same outcome will also affect the collateral aesthetics that will characterize architectural and urban designs.

TB   Indeterminacy has a strong aesthetic value and programmatic meaning, as we learned from important projects as the one of OMA for Parc de la Villette. The question is: will these open spaces have a programme assigned to them and might they still have a certain level of control embedded? And the open spaces that do not have any programme assigned, whose function is void, can we perhaps just let nature grow back again? From the perspective of urban safety and security, are we ready to accept this by design?

I do not want to romanticize and I won't, but perhaps we shall seek to increase the adaptation, repurpose and reuse of the existing built and material stock in cities, to work with different temporalities of urban spaces, and allow for more decentralization to take place in time. In my understanding, the aesthetic is an aesthetic of transition. We know that we have to transition to a decarbonized urban form. We live in a carbon-based type of urbanization, which is the legacy of the modern project. We are now realizing that we need to achieve instead a situated urban form, in the entire extent of urbanization, one that is sensitive to climate, ecology, and society. So that is the question of change. We should really start thinking about this aesthetics of transition.

1   See the conversation with Daniel Ibañez.

2   Bill Hillier is Professor of Architectural and Urban Morphology in the University of London, Chairman of the Bartlett School of Graduate Studies and Director of the Space Syntax Laboratory in University College London. He holds a DSc (higher doctorate) in the University of London. He is seen as the original pioneer of the methods for the analysis of spatial patterns known as 'space syntax'. Hillier produced a large number of articles concerned with different aspects of space and how it works and published extensively on other aspects of the theory of architecture. One of his monumental works is *The Social Logic of Space* (1984), which presents a general theory of how people relate to space in built environments.

3   Michael Batty is Bartlett Professor at University College London and chairs the Centre for Advanced Spatial Analysis. It is as an interdisciplinary centre devoted to developing computer technologies with respect to urban applications and city planning and a focus on visualization, modelling and simulation, spatial data, and urban morphology. He is the author of *Cities and Complexity* (2005), *The New Science of Cities* (2013) and recently published *Inventing Future Cities* (2018).

4   Dirk Sijmons is emeritus professor of Landscape Architecture at TU Delft and has a long track record in publishing on developments in landscape planning and design. He asks questions such as: what has happened to the Dutch landscape and what are the future developments? How does the energy transition become visible in the landscape? How do we continue the tradition of making our own land in a good way? And is there still attention for the landscape in politics? Sijmons was one of the three founders of H+N+S Landscape Architects, mainly involved in regional planning. The International Federation of Landscape Architects (IFLA) awarded him the prestigious IFLA Sir Geoffrey Jellicoe Award for his contributions to landscape architecture and more specifically his ability in redefining the profession, its boundaries, its strategy, and its position.

5   Bruno Latour is a French philosopher, anthropologist, and sociologist. He is the author of several influential books and professor at Sciences Po in Paris. From his position as a science anthropologist, he has become a prominent figure in the debate about the Anthropocene and is often seen as one of the most important thinkers of our time. He is mainly concerned with the relationship between science, technology, and society. *Laboratory Life* (1979), *Science in Action* (1987) and *Nous n'avons jamais été modernes* (1991), are some of Latour's most famous publications. In his recent work, Latour focuses on climate change and on our current 'modern' world and explores what life looks like in the Anthropocene, under the title *Facing Gaia*.

6   Christophe Girot is Professor and Chair of Landscape Architecture at the Department of Architecture of the ETH in Zürich. His research covers three domains: methods in landscape architecture and topology, new media in landscape analysis, and perception, history, and theory of Western landscape architecture. Emphasis is given to large-scale landscape design and modelling methods with particular attention to the topology of nature in and around cities. The landscape visualizing and modelling laboratory of the ETH has enabled significant advances in applied landscape design and pointcloud modelling.

7   Richard T.T. Forman, Professor *Emeritus* at Harvard University, is often considered a pioneer of landscape ecology and road ecology. His primary scholarly interest links science with spatial pattern to interweave nature and people on the land. Other research interests include changing land mosaics, conservation, and land-use planning.

In Real Life

Analogue Research into the System

Today, there is a notable tendency to dive into the computer for generating data about the system of the city. And rightly so — so much information is waiting for us there to be included in our analysis. On the other hand, it can be quite rewarding to take an analogue approach. One example of an early study that has resulted in interesting knowledge about the use of the city is *The Social Life of Small Urban Spaces* from 1980, by William H. Whyte. He made a name for himself around the middle of the twentieth century with his now classic sociological study of North End Boston, entitled *Street Corner Society*. Still, it bears mentioning that this study has been often criticized for the bias that supposedly was evident in the predisposed attitude of the highly educated Whyte, who started from an interest in characterizing the 'Italian-American ghetto' where he lived as a student and which was mainly populated by first- and second-generation Italian immigrants. However, for our interest in this study the specific criticism on the outcomes and bias of this research is less relevant, as we are mainly interested in the method Whyte applied to obtain his information. In his book about Boston, he used an early variant of a form of participatory observation, a method from anthropology in which the researcher mingles with his research area, with all the complications this entails, and tries to become part of it. Whether this is realistic or desirable is a matter of debate.[1] However, such forms of embedded research can most definitely yield interesting and useful information. David Gianotten of the firm AMO likes to use embedded methods to obtain knowledge of the environment as part of a research process, as he explains further on in an interview.

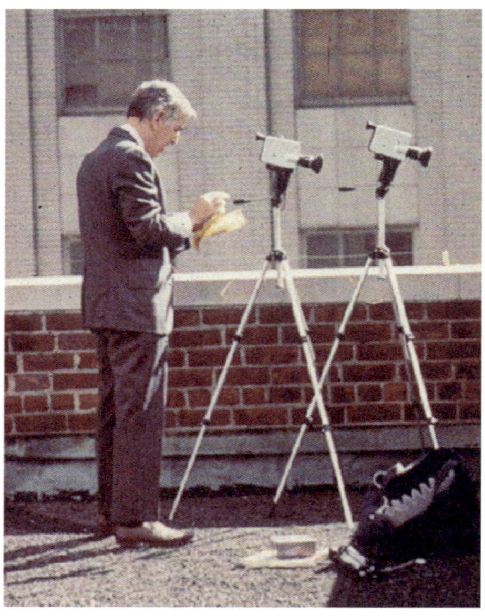

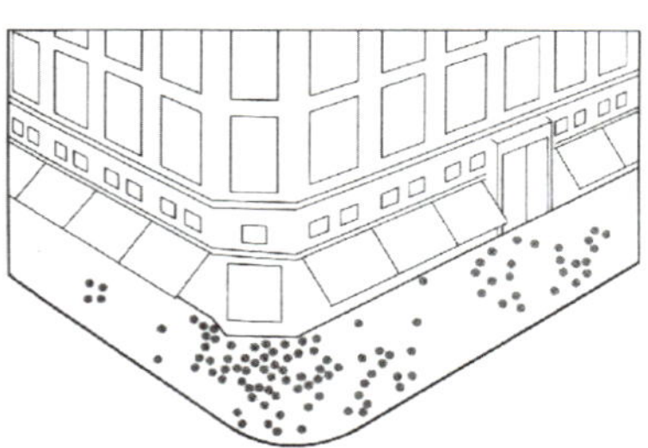

An analogue method of obtaining information through observaing, taking notes mapping and video registration, William H. Whyte (above) *The Social Life of Small Urban Spaces*: location of street conversations lasting two minutes or more (down)

The students attending the Rotterdam FUR studio in the Peperklip building initially also adopted a wait-and-see attitude for their research into making this listed social apartment building in Rotterdam sustainable. They went and lived with the other residents of the building for a time to see how they could involve their temporary neighbours in the sustainability process. In addition to learning how to work on location, the studio also taught the students the importance of interaction and how to work with end users and commissioners; by working with people on location you are not only an observer; you also influence their behaviour.

A similar dynamic is to be found in the work of the young Amsterdam designer Patrick Rogiers. For his project A Sense of Home he studied a group of actors that are hard to reach and about whom there are few data available that a designer can use: homeless people. Not the sort of data anyway that Rogiers needed to get a grip on the question of how a homeless person uses the city as a living environment, as his ambition was. In his research, this designer behaved like an embedded journalist in the world of the homeless in Amsterdam. This enabled him to map the places where they hung out and where they slept. The tools he used as a journalist-designer are part of the design project. A nice example of this was a stall with with a soup made from leftover vegetables from the market. It worked as both a design intervention and as a way of gathering further data. The designer built up

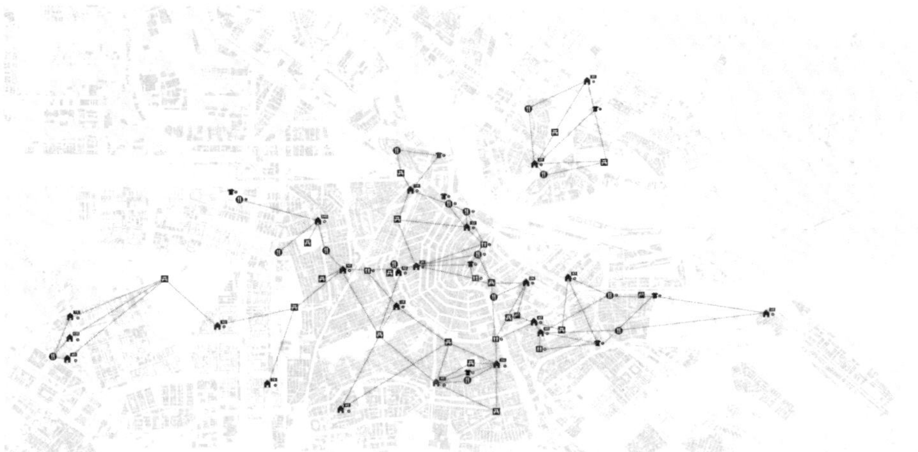

A Sense of Home: fragmented Homeless network Amsterdam by Patrick Roegiers

Observations of a journalist-designer in the Dapperkeuken: A Sense of Home

trust with the actors he wanted to study and in this way managed to gain access to their community. Based on those observations, the designer also made two circular interventions: a soup kitchen, which utilized leftover products from an open-air market, and a sleeping facility, constructed in the 'leftover and in-between' space of the city, made of pressed waste cardboard that can be found in abundance in the streets.

Back to Whyte. In order to obtain information about the use of squares in New York he chose an even simpler approach than the one he had used before in Boston, also thanks to the availability of technological innovations, i.e., cameras. He installed cameras in squares, playgrounds, and parks to simply observe how New York street life organized itself. In addition, he and his team talked to users of the square by using simple polls on how often they came there, where they worked, and what they thought of the square. However, as he emphasizes in *The Social Life of the Small Urban Space*, he mostly sat down with his team to look at what these users were doing.[2] Those data generated a treasure trove of information about the use of public spaces in the city.

In this Parliament of Things researchers immerse themselves in the shape of the objects around them to literally give them a voice.

In the Netherlands too there is a long and extensive urban-sociological tradition, supported by researchers such as Arnold Reijndorp and Ivan Nio. However, simply observing the city with great attention no longer suffices to obtain a thorough insight into its complex contemporary use. These days, such observations can be adequately complemented by experimenting with technological applications for measuring and assessing the operation and performance of the city. Some of the relevant research methods are not so much helpful in gathering raw data about the city but they can put the observations and data in perspective and thus help shape one's own thinking. A somewhat theatrical method is the Parliament of Things, an idea of the French philosopher Bruno Latour. In this Parliament of Things researchers immerse themselves in the shape of the objects around them to literally give them a voice. This can be useful in projects that navigate unexplored territory. For example, the collection of essays *De stem van de Noordzee* explores how animals, plants, and the water — the North Sea itself — would react to human activities that are currently being developed there.[3] The method is quite popular among ecological activists and can be a useful exercise in modesty during the development of innovative design interventions.

Likewise, the Socratic conversation does not generate data, but it does invite ideas and concepts. In a Socratic conversation — loosely fashioned after Plato's dialogues, in which a group of thinkers retreated from everyday life to freely discuss all kinds of subjects — people gather in a safe environment and follow a number of fixed steps in a structured debate about a jointly chosen subject. The interlocutors are supposed not to speak from knowledge based on all kinds of preliminary research, but only from personal experience. That is why the debate subjects are not defined beforehand per se. The ideas presented during the conversation are not judged on their factual correctness, but on whether they are logically sound and suitable to inform the sincere exchange of ideas. This leads to an open and uninhibited atmosphere that can bring unexpected insights. This method too, like the Parliament of Things, lends itself especially as a method for critical reflection on one's own assumptions, either in general, or in a specific design task.

Scenario Thinking

An interesting method, to get design tasks in focus and fully understand them, is thinking in scenarios. Scenario thinking is a way of structurally thinking through the various designs that are part of the task and determine the metabolism of the city in its future development. Scenarios often have an outspoken material aspect, but cultural and social aspects can also be easily incorporated. This method is a form of structured speculation about possible future realities. The process starts from a reflection on .future uncertainties in order to map the complexity of the current situation. It's a method that is often used by government agencies of countries, regions, or cities, and by companies as well. Constructing a scenario starts by identifying the two biggest future uncertainties and putting them on an X and Y axis. The four resulting frames provide room to think about the possible linking of these uncertainties and lead to sketches of four future situations. These imaginings of the future help to develop potential strategies for dealing with one or several of the outlined future scenarios, and with being prepared for the identified uncertainties when they present themselves. Eventually, a strategy is chosen. Should the circumstances in which this strategy is successful change, then the other future imaginings provide insights into possibly new relevant futures and the strategy to follow can be quickly and efficiently adapted to the new conditions. Scenario thinking is therefore the pre-eminent strategy for making your company, region, or city resilient and flexible and for dealing with possible future problems. It's therefore no surprise that scenario thinking was professionalized in the world of corporations, especially in the think tanks of oil company Shell. They used it in the seventies to develop a method for covering financial and business risks. Since then, thinking in scenarios has been a globally applied strategy by companies, governments, and NGOs for finding frameworks of thought in which possible futures can be discussed and reflected upon. In the ICCI method of FUR, discussed in the introduction to this book, scenarios also play an important role. Research by design is after all concerned with imagining and representing future realities. In the ICCI model, scenario thinking is especially used as a tool to, together with a client, bring research one step further towards a concrete design.

To illustrate how scenarios can be actually applied in the field of spatial design, here's an example from the practice of Bureau Bright, who regularly use the method. As in their research into the Dutch 'foodscape', which is on the eve of a number of big changes. The precise development of that food landscape is unpredictable in a variety of ways as it depends on a number of economic choices, consumer preferences, political interests, and technological advances. In such a complex force field it is hard to get a grip, but roughly speaking the designers can define two big uncertainties to form the X and Y axes. One uncertainty is about, on the one hand, the option that the Dutch food production is organized for large-scale production for the world market or on the other hand, the option that there will only be small-scale production for the local market. The other uncertainty is about how much grip technology is allowed to have on our food: on the one extreme maximum grip, and the other hardly at all. The question is whether consumers desire extremely refined innovative food products or rather have an increasing need to eat 'natural' and 'authentic'. From these two uncertainties the designers drew their crosses of X-Y axes, forming four quadrants as the basis for the various scenarios. One axis goes from strong resistance against new technology to wholehearted acceptance of it. The other axis varies between the Netherlands as a large-scale exporting mass producer and a small-scale self-sufficient food nation. In order to translate this into spatial terms they take an average Dutch town with basic amenities such as shops, schools, and transport nodes, surrounded by industrial estates with some greenhouses and silos and around those a rural area with meadows and farms.

The scenario 'Supersize me', in which technological acceptation and increase in scale are decisive, goes wholesale for factory farms and intensive dairy farming with a minimum of animal rights and emission restrictions. A smart infrastructure connects the farms to industry for generating energy. The result is a landscape of a large, anonymous scale with little variation, linked to an effective infrastructure aimed at large-scale transport.

The other extreme, the scenario 'home grown', which focuses on organic, small-scale food production for the local market, results in a completely different landscape with regional farmers markets that sell seasonal, regionally grown food, successfully competing with generic supermarkets. This scenario is characterized by protectionism and keeping out foreign products, with a landscape that leaves room for natural development and agriculture on, around, and between urban structures.

The remaining two scenarios were also translated into a landscape. These are extremes, obviously. In reality, the tendencies they described will mingle and result in hybrids with, perhaps, also a different

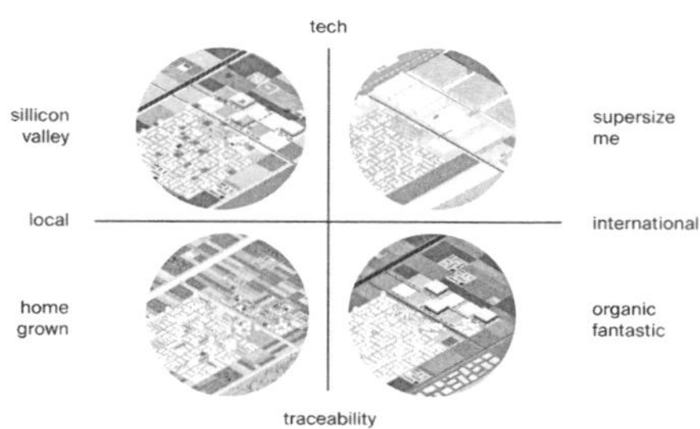

Scenario matrix for the Dutch 'foodscape'

landscape, but the outcomes are interesting for visualizing a possible future and thus influencing strategic choices. The knowledge that is being generated in this project about the future of our food, food production, and the landscape that could go with it is therefore evident. But the question then is how to share this knowledge and convert into a marketable product. The designers chose to convert their findings into a 'serious game'. A game aimed at knowledge transfer for the players and knowledge production (from the input of the players) for the makers of the game. In the serious game 'Ministry of Food' a player assumes the role of Minister of Food and develops a policy for a Dutch food strategy. This fictional policy follows and thinks through the lines of the identified scenarios and results in a variety of Dutch landscapes. The impact of the choices on various actors in the food chain is also highlighted. How they assess the policy is communicated in a live feed of news, documentaries, and reports. In this way the game manages to communicate the complexity, richness, and layers of the food issue, and its spatial implications, while at the same time communicating the fun of thinking about the future of food.

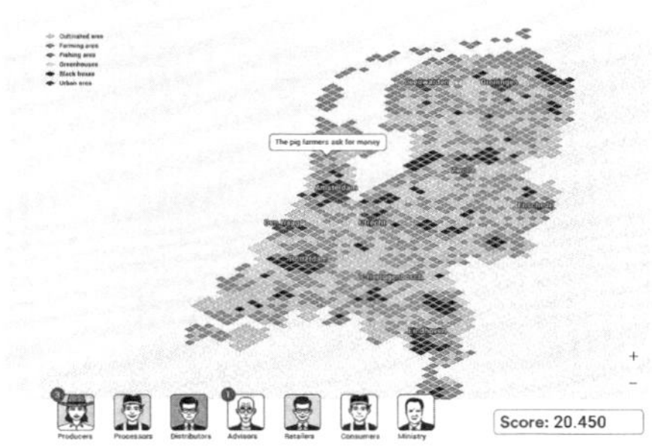

Serious game: 'Ministry of Food'

In this research, the scenario thinking about food is a goal in itself. Developing that research into a game was a much later choice and turned out to be not only a result, but also the consolidation of the research as a permanent method for thinking through the outlined scenarios. A somewhat similar method is the principle of 'forecasting', which is used a lot in design education. This involves speculating about the future by placing the study object in that future. By means of 'backcasting' a reconstruction can be made of the route from the now to the future. What transitions and interventions are needed to arrive in the future scenario? How do we get from now to the new situation and what is the role of the various elements such as the condition of the soil, the water, the infrastructure, the ecology, and the landscape in all this?

The Riotopia project of student Thijs de Boer also uses scenarios, in this case to imagine two different futures for the Rotterdam neighbourhood of Oud-Mathenesse: a utopian one and a dystopian one. The immediate cause is a concrete system task, i.e., the renovation of the

Rotterdam sewer system. The replacement of the sewer system is running well behind and where work is being done, it is without any vision on the relation of the condition of the sewers with other tasks to be done in the city. De Boer developed two scenarios in which the renovation task is linked to new possibilities for future use. By utilizing these scenarios, the initially technical task is opened up to the public domain (whose task is it?), to management (what's going to be done with it?), and to the local economy (what values are being developed?). De Boer looks at the flows of material in the sewer as either a revenue model or as part of the commons and he introduces sewer water as a source for the local economy. At the same time, he makes a spatial translation aboveground of the underground infrastructure.

The serious game developed by Bureau Bright seeks interaction with the public without immediately becoming spatial in the traditional sense of the word. It applies a totally different medium to involve a different and wider public than normally in a spatial task. This is no luxury, as it creates public support and can initiate a societal debate about spatial tasks, but also because providing the right answer to a task may require a different medium. There are many cases in which developing an urban plan or a building turns out not to be the proper reaction to the actual problems of the city. Certainly not in the short term, as architecture is simply too slow and too unwieldy. From initiation to realization a building can easily have a lead time of five years.

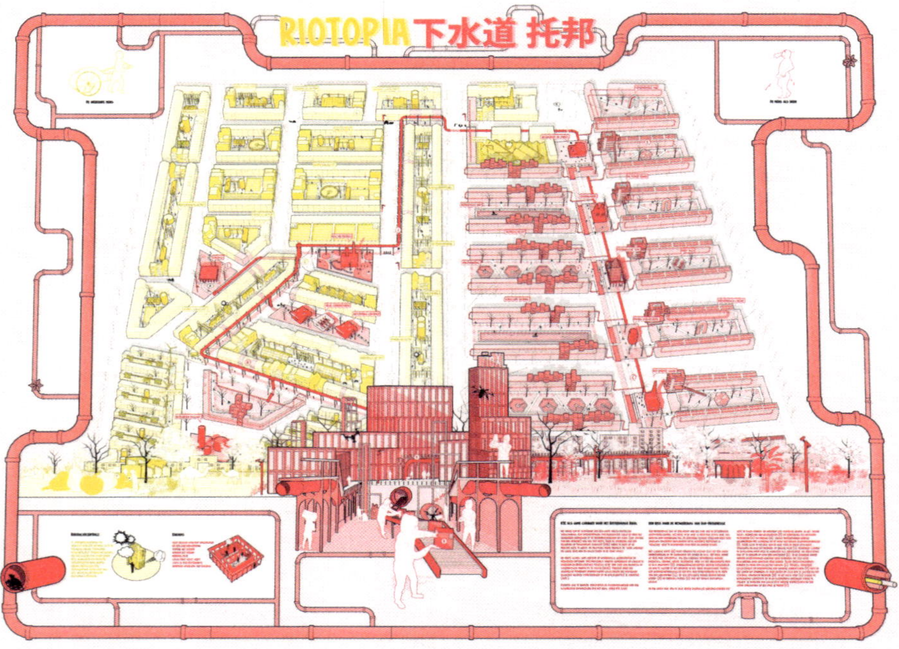

Thijs de Boer's project, Riotopia, addresses and explores the utopian and dystopian potential of the renovation of the Rotterdam sewage system

A fragment from Roadmap 2050 by OMA proposing an integral European exchange of energy sources based on seasonal availability

The dynamic of the city often asks for a much swifter response to acute problems; and for a response with a different reach. One design firm that pioneered the application of other than the traditional means of the designer is AMO, the research branch of Rem Koolhaas' renowned firm OMA. Their focus is not so much on buildings, but emphatically also on research, publications, and temporary projects. The new research branch was presented at the time when the firm was working on *CONTENT*, a magazine that reflected on the firm's projects since the seminal publication *S,M,L,XL* (1995). Especially in the beginning, it was the place within the larger firm where they reflected on how we are living together, and where, through cultural expressions, a debate was initiated about the role of architecture in picking up complex local tasks. Another interesting example in which the system of the city was mapped by OMA in an unusual manner is the project Roadmap 2050. It is, in essence, the report of a study about the possibilities of carbon-neutral Europe in 2050. AMO called it 'a practical guide'. It hopes to make an agenda and lay a foundation for the spatial task that goes hand-in-hand with the European climate ambition.

The initiatives outlined above are all attempts to forge new relations with a public outside of the design practice. 'Crowd building' takes this one step further by already giving the end users an active role in the design process from the beginning. In close collaboration with a group of initiators, designers devise a plan in which, in line with the wishes of the group of end users, all kinds of innovative concepts are included. A design firm such as Space&Matter has completely reinvented itself in the past few years by using this work method. While maintaining a very direct attitude as a player in creating concrete spatial impact and realizing housing complexes and living-and-working areas, they insert themselves into the process at a different time and continue to coach it from start to finish. From research in collaboration with future residents to developing a complete 'village', as the residents of a group of circular, carbon-neutral houseboats that was realized through crowd building like to call it. The by now internationally renowned Schoonschip project is a good example of how the process works and in what ways firms that are involved have to adapt in order to make it succeed. As a build-it-yourself project in Buiksloterham in Amsterdam-Noord, Schoonschip is the result of an idea of a group of friends who dreamt of living a sustainable life in the city and on the water. These were people with a creative network, but without any experience in architecture. In that sense it was a rather abstract dream in need of support and connection if it was to have any chance to bear fruit. The task posed an in essence even greater challenge because the group was aiming for a form of housing which as such did not yet exist: on the water, self-sufficient, and carbon-neutral. This immediately confronted them with the question how to obtain something that was not available. As co-creative coaches the designers of Space&Matter, together with the group, could gradually form an increasingly clearer image of how this new form of housing might look and function.

The basic principle of Schoonschip is modelled after another boat in Amsterdam-Noord, which initiator, and documentary film-maker Marjan de Blok had visited in 2008: the geWoonboot (a Dutch pun on 'houseboat'). This is actually not a houseboat, as nobody lives there, but a circular and to a high degree self-supporting boat that is being used as an office. It generates the electricity and heating it needs in a carbon-neutral manner and uses rainwater as the basis for its water management. The autarkic principle of the boat was copied as a core value in the development of the circular housing village Schoonschip. Other core values are friendship and community. This gives Schoonschip, especially in the rhetoric framing it as a project, something of the air of a commune, an island that tries to maintain itself independently outside of the organizational interference of the city. Circularity and carbon neutrality are, besides being evident intrinsic values, also inherently connected to those principles. They facilitate the wish to go 'off the grid'. In the case of Schoonschip, this is done in a very practical sense, thanks to a smart grid, a local electricity network that stores and distributes the collected solar energy.

Being self-supporting in a city, as is the ambition of the Schoonschip residents, paradoxically first requires a lot of help from outside, especially in a highly regulated city such as Amsterdam. The wish to be self-sufficient turns out to grate against the limits of regulation. It requires bureaucratic exceptions and a different approach by the officialdom. Realizing Schoonschip — which succeeded in early 2021, more than ten years after the plan was first conceived — therefore took especially a lot of planning and meetings. In order to guide that process, Space&Matter looks for another role than that of a traditional design firm. Normally, a design is made on the basis of a plan, after which buyers are invited and then a builder can step in to physically realize the project. With crowd building this process is reversed. It starts with buyers who want something, have relatively abstract ideas which then jointly have to be made concrete before a contractor can be approached. This means that the future users have the initiative and have a great say in the development of the spatial arrangements, the possible future uses, and the amenities. Because this group was known in advance, it meant that they didn't have to take into account a number of things. An agreement among the residents to forego private ownership of automobiles and instead use electrical cars that are shared, means there is no need for parking space. It was much more important to pay attention to the jetties that connect the floating homes. In and on the jetties, social and material flows converge as they simultaneously function as primary meeting places and as the grid for the circular flows in the neighbourhood.

The power of crowd building lies in the private efforts that are put into a project but it does not contain a mechanism to automatically also involve the outside world, or the surrounding neighbourhoods.

Schoonschip is not only an example of a process to arrive at a spatial intervention in direct collaboration with future residents. Other players can also have an active role in the crowd: those who in an earlier stage were not, or only in the background, or in a much later stage involved in thinking about the planning. Here, Space&Matter took on the role of guiding partner in designing the urban plan, Delva devised a spatial framework for Schoonschip and the entire surrounding neighbourhood of Buiksloterham. Metabolic contributed its circular experience and Spectral developed the smart grid for the electricity supply. Public and semi-public partners such as Waternet and the City of Amsterdam also had an important role. Still, the residents themselves were always present or even leading throughout the entire process. Together they wrote the Circular Buiksloterham Manifesto, which until now has been most concretely materialized in Schoonschip.

Almost by definition, crowd building results in experimental and idiosyncratic projects that serve as prototypes for possible later projects. This is also what makes it interesting for Space&Matter and their

research: via this type of project, they look for innovative urban prototypes that throw light on possible future forms of living and living-and-working blocks. The prototype is a full-fledged final product in this, for others to work with.

Schoonschip, Amsterdam: a sociospatial, sustainable bubble

There are however critical remarks to be placed about the process of Schoonschip and perhaps about crowd building in general. In the case of Schoonschip, they score high on circularity, climate adaptation, and greening, but the village separates itself from the rest of the neighbourhood and city district. Those who wish to come and take a look are reminded at every entrance that they are entering private property and do so as guests. And this is not a coincidental side-effect, but the result of one of the explicit goals of the initiators, whose aim was to have a sustainable village populated by friends. In an interview,[4] the initiators talked about this downside, when asked. For example, they would have loved to have some social housing in the village as well, but because they started talking about this too late in the process there was, in their words, 'no more room for it'. This may indicate a possible flaw in the process of crowd building. In its present form it seems to inherently lead to communities that run the risk of withdrawing themselves into social, and in this case also spatial bubbles. The power of crowd building lies in the private efforts that are put into a project but it does not contain a mechanism to automatically also involve the outside world, or the surrounding neighbourhoods. In this case this means that the newcomers completely determine how the place will be used, without any involvement from future neighbours and other residents. This outcome is not in line, by the way, with the goal of crowd building as defined by Space&Matter themselves. On the contrary, the platform explicitly speaks of the importance of accessibility and the feasibility of seemingly impossible wishes for living and working.

<table>
<tr><td>1</td><td>Participatory observation has met with severe criticism in science circles, especially since anthropologist Margaret Mead applied the method in her research in Samoa. In her study she claimed there was no period of puberty in the Polynesian community, a conclusion that did not turn out to be borne out by her data.</td></tr>
</table>

1   Participatory observation has met with severe criticism in science circles, especially since anthropologist Margaret Mead applied the method in her research in Samoa. In her study she claimed there was no period of puberty in the Polynesian community, a conclusion that did not turn out to be borne out by her data.

2   William H. Whyte, *The Social Life of the Small Urban Space*, New York 1980, p. 16.

3   Laura Burgers, Eva Meijer, Evanne Nowak, *De stem van de Noordzee*, Amsterdam 2020.

4   Johan Nebbeling, 'De duurzaamste drijvende wijk van Europa ligt in Amsterdam en is bijna af', *Trouw*, 18 February 2019.

DESIGN BY ORGANIZATION

A Conversation with David Gianotten

Eric Frijters is professor and research leader of Future Urban Regions. He is also a founding partner and director of FABRICations, the knowledge-intensive design practice he started in 2007, together with Olv Klijn. The Amsterdam-based practice has a research-by-design and metabolic approach to urban challenges.

David Gianotten studied architecture and construction technology at the Eindhoven University of Technology (TU/e). After his graduation, he gained educational and working experience in Japan. David joined OMA in 2008, launched OMA's Hong Kong office in 2009 and became partner at OMA in 2010. He has worked extensively in the Asia-Pacific Region, and has spent seven years working and living in Hong Kong. In 2016 he became a professor in the TU/e Architecture Design and Engineering department and recently he started his own chair of 'Transformation Architecture'. At OMA, he is responsible for the management, business strategy, and growth of the company worldwide. Before joining OMA, he was Principal Architect at SeARCH in the Netherlands. David now leads OMA's large global portfolio in the Asia-Pacific region, and he is the Managing Partner of OMA, overseeing the management, business strategy, and growth of the company worldwide. David has led the design and realization of the Potato Head Studios—a resort in Bali (Completed 2020), WA Museum Boola Bardip in Perth (Completed 2020), Prince Plaza in Shenzhen (Completed 2020), White Cube LIRCAEI in Lusanga (Completed 2018), MPavilion 2017 in Melbourne, and the Shenzhen Stock Exchange headquarters (Completed 2013). He was responsible for the end stages of the CCTV headquarters in Beijing (Completed 2012) and OMA's conceptual masterplan for the West Kowloon Cultural District in Hong Kong.

Frijters and Gianotten joined forces for the design of the Bajeskwartier, the transformation of the six towers that once formed the biggest Dutch prison into a sustainable housing complex that enhances the health of its inhabitants and of the city of Amsterdam as a whole. With the redevelopment of VDMA in the southern city of Eindhoven they worked on circularity and urban forestry in the city centre.

The two met up in late 2020 to discuss Gianotten's work at OMA and its research office AMO. Gianotten explains why he likes to curate interdisciplinary teams

Urban forestry at VDMA (Van Der Meulen Ansems) terrain in Eindhoven, Netherlands

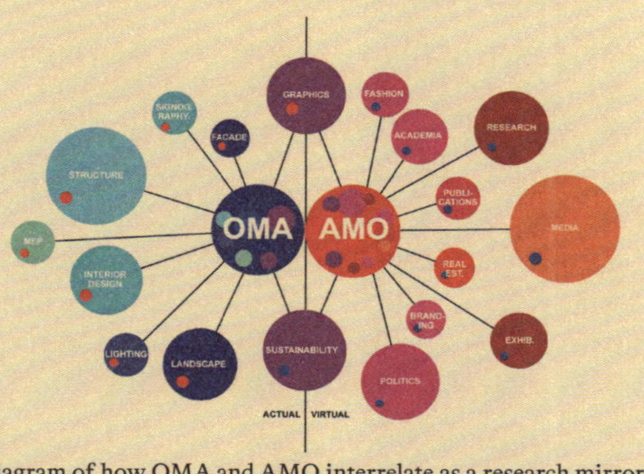

Diagram of how OMA and AMO interrelate as a research mirror organizations

for projects to gain important knowledge that informs his designing practice, and dubs it 'design by organization'. He talks about the importance of gaining deep local knowledge before he starts drawing and designing. He explores the importance of narrative to keep relevant partners aboard during a project. For Feyenoord City, he tells, that narrative was created around the so-called 'seven fields of influence'. In order to make sure these fields were all well serviced, he brought the most important stakeholders together in a group that reflected these fields of influence. That way he, and others, could manage and protect both the financial flows and the shared interests of the stakeholders.

They conclude their discussion with an exploration of the aesthetic consequences of metabolic design, about detailing and about how sustainable impact can be maximized while the aesthetic impact stays minimal.

Approaching the City as a System

ERIC FRIJTERS David, in the context of looking at the city as a system, I would like to discuss several topics with you: transition in cities, knowledge-acquiring tools, contours of a (new) design practice, working territories, new actors in the playing field, new typologies and aesthetics. In this conversation I'd like to emphasize that the notion of the city has a wide meaning to me. It represents the place where we grow our food, or we get our energy from. So, what we traditionally call countryside or what we call city belong to that same system. We are obviously not the first ones to look at the city in that way. In the sixties there was already a strong, growing new consciousness that understanding that system would be relevant for spatial design and spatial planning, mainly in the area of landscape design. People such as Abel Wolman in the sixties, Howard Odum and Paul Duvigneaud in the seventies and Robert Frosch in the eighties already considered cities as living organisms and talked about the metabolism of cities. In 1972, the Club of Rome already depicted the whole globe as a complex model, a system of interconnected black boxes, in which it became clear that if you change the content of one, you change the system as a whole. So, the idea is that under the bodywork of the city economic, social, cultural, ecological, political, environmental systems are in play and their interaction shapes the expression of a city. But if we look under the hood, we don't really understand what we are seeing. Contrary to our own bodies, in which 7,400 chemical reactions are taking place right now and that we have been able to map completely, we have a hard time describing what flows, processes, or any other kind of events are taking place in our cities.

This is a fascinating thought, right? We have been making cities for over 3000 years, but we don't have a single clue of how they actually work. We have been teaching and learning about designing cities only by word of mouth, but we never really checked if they functioned in the way we intended. Now, on the other hand, there is the good news that I think we have the technology to start really grasping this. We all have mobile phones. We can even have access to satellite images if we want to, so we can actually see the cities from above. Where Leonardo da Vinci could only guess how cities would look from the skies, we can actually trace high-definition satellite imagery. And now we finally make a start in understanding how that system responds to and interacts with our designing efforts. This is where we are now. We still cannot map all the processes that take place in cities, but we can explore our plan of attack to start controlling their design.

**Research by Designers:
AMO as Amoeba**

I'd like to start this conversation with the idea that there is a growing spatial interest of designers to be involved in understanding the city as a system. It is a given that many of the problems cities are coping with have a systemic origin. The spatial expression resulting from that, feeds into twenty-first-century challenges such as energy transition, circular material resources, and climate adaptability. All of which have to do with wind flows, hot and cold water storage, water availability, water quality, and so on. Would you consider the invention of AMO as an early attempt to be systemically involved in contemporary urban challenges?

DAVID
GIANOTTEN No, I think it's maybe not the first attempt to be involved in it, but it's the first attempt to make it part of the discussion that you would normally have with municipalities, governments and or clients. The things that

we encounter constantly as architects and urban planners, is that we are asked for a result and we're not asked for an analysis, or we're not asked for research while we believe that you can only come up with a proper result that would function well when you really understand the situation and the context. By inventing AMO, OMA put that on the agenda. It meant that we could formally reserve time for experimentation and a period of generating an understanding, before working towards a result. It was a first attempt to make clients in general aware that whatever happens in their systems and whatever leads to policies is one side, but the professional also needs to have a similar type of process to define, analyze, and understand the systemic context and the use and behaviour of people. AMO is empowering architects and urban designers to create a critical position towards their briefings and come up with their own agendas, not only related to architecture and urban planning, but also related to politics, economics, finance, and other topics we have to take responsibility for.

But what was totally new twenty years ago, would never work anymore in current times, I think. Now, a lot of very interesting practices and also small practices in our domain have these types of agendas. What we are currently doing is much more behind the scenes, trying to be some sort of amoeba that also involves itself in other realms without formalizing it, and then directing it back to AMO, directing it back to OMA. Or even trying to attract finances or help clients to set up the economics and politics around their project. Additionally, I think this is very necessary in order to address interference with the system while public clients are retracting from that realm. They don't have the knowledge, the people, the interest or the money to really do the research that is necessary to intervene through policies in a responsible way. Opposite to that there is the market. And there are very few people in the market that actually have a long-term vision, a long-term interest in results and even fewer in results that are not financially driven.

EF——Let's talk about your take on addressing cities as a system, or in other words how the task of planning and designing is becoming very complex within the forcefields that designers have to navigate.

DG   There's a huge gap, one that was never this big between these two forces with their own agendas and knowledge banks, namely the government and the market. So, the market knows very well how to earn, how to prevent having to spend for a very long time, while governments have ambitions for cities but they have a harder time controlling these financial flows. Moreover, they both don't seem to know how they can actually operate or spend money on knowledge and understanding. Governments just take it upon them to bring land to the market, enriched with ambitions and policies, and then leave it up to the market to transform it into something that is in line with that ambition. But they forget that the market is not necessarily interested in realizing their ambitions. Their real interest is in making money and then walking out as soon as they can. This is a big contradiction and there's a huge gap between the two. That's where we come in and try to operate as urban planners and architects to take some of the responsibility that historically was invested in the government and also some of the responsibility that we think the market should have.

Seven Fields of Influence in Urban Development

EF — Could you illustrate what kind of tricks you have up your sleeve to work in this gap?

DG   One of the best examples that I have in understanding that gap is our Feyenoord City project in Rotterdam. Many people think it's about the stadium for this legendary Dutch football team, but our original investment was not related to that stadium at all. The main aim is to revitalize Rotterdam South, bring jobs, bring educational opportunity and safe neighbourhoods. The club and its stadium turned out to be a great vehicle to create a place for a new ambition and a new state of mind for that part of the city. To reach those goals we combined the client and the government and created our own project, that in the end turned out to be much more a project about the city and its underlying system. There is something in it for everybody involved.

EF — So you are describing an engaging narrative in which the new stadium acts as a diversion for urban development: Feyenoord City. A narrative was created that behaves like a snowball. It has the potential to actually grow into a binding narrative that is flexible enough to engage everybody that has to stick to it or be involved in it. And you support this new initiative because it's a complex one?

DG   Correct, that is the idea. And at the same time, to make sure all the different viewpoints — a governmental point of view, a market point of view, or a healthy living point of view, in which sports obviously is a very important element which is Feyenoord's main interest — keep having their influence on the project we proposed to bring the whole organization under the umbrella of a foundation. This foundation acts as a closed system in which the money that is earned by building these houses is reinvested.

EF — This is a new idea.

DG   Yes, it's a relatively new idea. And it's something that we came up with because we felt too lonely as an architect and urban planner with the causes I had. I could table them, but I was very dependent on whether other people would like them or not, and then would support them financially. On the other hand, I felt that I couldn't get the right counter activity, counter knowledge, counter policies from governments and municipality that I needed to develop a system that is more responsible, that could really be readable and understandable by the people that actually use it. Because that is an important thing. As urban planners and architects we can invent everything and design everything. But if people don't end up using it or if they don't understand how to use it, it falls apart.

So we created this ecosystem. That's how I called it at the time, an ecosystem in which all elements are represented: political, policy-making, social, economic, financial, planning and design, documentation and information — all these interests play a role in the decision making in this foundation. We organized this ecosystem into seven domains. As such people would not be the client of it, or the policymaker of it, or the designer of it, but all these people would actually be part of that the same system. In that system they would represent one of these seven domains, or parts of these domains, and actually become as complicit as all the others to create a closed circle in which we would be able to address all domains and interests.

EF — What are these seven again?

DG   Political, social, economic, financial, policy, information, design and planning.

EF — How did that ecosystem administratively land in a foundation? And are all these seven items present in this foundation?

DG   Originally there was no foundation, because we came up with that idea only later on. In the beginning we just found three parties that gave us some confidence that we could do it, which were the football club, the local government, and some investors. We originally participated partly at risk because we believed it would work and after a year's time, everybody was aligned. And during that year, we came up with the idea of the foundation, since we needed a vehicle to work with.

EF — Currently the foundation is guide by a large consultancy team and is in the hands of three parties, being the soccer club, the local government, and the investors. And they all have a share in the foundation?

DG   Yes. But the return on the shares is zero.

EF — Yes. That's why it's a foundation. Otherwise, it would have been a company.

DG   That's crucial. Nobody is there to maximize their own profit. They couldn't. Everybody is paid for their work, but nobody is getting paid for profit.

EF — So, Feyenoord City keeps the machine running because it generates all kinds of money and extra research, but there is no money coming out of this vehicle?

DG   No, not at the moment.

EF — That is interesting, but why would for instance an investor want to be part of this construction anyway?

DG   Being part of such an ecosystem obviously gives you a lot of data. It provides knowledge, new insights, and gives you a lot of contextual understanding. Besides that, it gives you the possibility to not only contribute on a financial level, but also on a socio-economic level, which a lot of companies these days of course find extremely important.

EF — All right, so you benefit from generating data, there's a learning component in it, and it gives you a social responsibility profile. It strikes me that in the seven pillars that are the foundation of this ecosystem you mentioned, there are no sustainability themes in there. It is surprising, while every newspaper is full off it, but I assume you've hidden them somewhere else. How are you coping with the environmental issues that challenge our planetary boundaries I referred to at the beginning of this conversation?

DG For me sustainability is part of everything. What I'm really worried about is if you put sustainability as a separate pillar, which happens a lot, people might start to believe that there's a technical measure or solution available. But actually, sustainability is depending so much on behaviour, and therefore it is much more a social phenomenon than necessarily a separate pillar. At the same time, it should also be part of sustainable finance models, policymaking, as it is part of design. Therefore, we never separate it. I also never present projects based on their supposed level of sustainability. Or on claims that they create a sustainability awareness. I present sustainability as part of an ecosystem that is our responsibility as a whole. And that to me is part of this system I'm working on. It is not to profile myself in a sustainable way, but to profile the way we have to create cities nowadays, because it has become so complex. It is no longer a policy that you answer to and that you earn money with. That was the model just after the industrial revolution, but now cities, because of all sorts of inventions and the availability of large amounts of data, have become such complex changing environments.

Feyenoord City Master Plan

New Way of Working, Artistic Expression and the Sticky Story

EF — How does this way of working and collaborating influence the spatial and artistic expression in your work?

DG I'm invested in testing the system in different ways. We also have to pay much attention to context. Collaborating with a local team is very important, for that matter. I did a project in Indonesia, for example, together with Potato Head. We designed a 168-room structure, built from recycled bricks and poured concrete cast in reclaimed driftwood. The whole structure floats on stilts to minimize its footprint. Everybody framed it as a hospitality project, but what we actually were doing was trying to create an agenda for young Indonesians for how they want to live, how they want to interact with their own surroundings and actually how they want to build a community. And we could only do that because we were invested in our client, which was Ronald Akili.[1] Thanks to him we were able to work with people like Andra

Matin,[2] local architects, sociologists, artists, and environmentalists to create a new ecosystem to start another type of movement, which is based on similar pillars as Feyenoord City, but in a totally different context. In this approach we are completely relying on local investment and connections to bright minds. So, the aim was to shape a movement, even though the most visible outcome is the resort we built.

Potato Head Studios as the result of an intense working relation between local artists and OMA

EF —So, the quality and the impact of your projects become greater depending on the organization, and your curation of a team that is collectively invested in a compelling narrative? We both are and have been working on Bajeskwartier, the metamorphosis of a former prison complex in Amsterdam into a sustainable housing block. Was that project based on a sticky story as well? What glued the team together you think?

DG The stickiest part of the story about Bajeskwartier is marked by the big step in the very beginning of the project to mobilize an enormous knowledge bank that could inform the urban planning. I think we played a role, you played a role, and AM, the developer, also played an important role by giving us the possibility to actually involve a huge number of people early on. By accumulating the forthcoming enormous amount of knowledge, we, as the designers, try to channel this type of energy into a new way of looking at what is currently there and how to use this transition from information to knowledge into a plan of transformation and the central question: How can you fit it within the ecosystem of the existing city? We didn't physically work on programmes, but we worked on knowledge banks, not ideas. And then we translated that into a physical environment.

Your metabolism of the city, or in this case the metabolism of Bajeskwartier, is a good example of that. The trick here is to put a very strong proposal on the table. Of course, in pushing our circularity objective, the knowledge of for instance contractors and the people that did the demolishing played a crucial role. I remember that we said we wanted to reuse ninety percent of all materials already available on the plot and that they thought that we were totally crazy. By making that type of agenda part of design we were able to come up with something that is not necessarily looking alien or futuristic, but rather looks as the next iteration.

Design by Organization

EF — You said that the experiment should be avoided in aiming to have an impact to change our methodology. Can you explain that some more?

DG   I think there is a real problem in the debate about what role architects and designers can play. It's not about young, small, big, established, or iconic. Instead, it's all about the knowledge, the ideas, and the curiosities in that sense. One thing I really don't like in our field is how the needed change is blocked by a category of big and medium-sized offices that are established to a certain degree and control a large part of the market. I think they form a barrier for the type of development we just discussed. To create an impact and to deliver the necessary change we need to form large forces in order to change the methodologies that I'm looking at. I believe size matters. Research-by-design-based starting points start from the assumption that size doesn't matter. And very often when you say size doesn't matter, it means that it starts with something small and you don't need to be afraid of the small. But for me, it means you have to combine forces, large and small forces, very interesting forces with new forces, experience with curiosity, to combine all these in such a way that size matters. And that's why I always try to create new environments for empowerment on a project basis that relies on a force that is significant.

EF — To have impact in responsible change you created this role to compose a coalition of small, medium-sized, and larger voices that are a new, interesting, curious and experienced basis for that force, right?

DG   Yes, we take the role of research by design and transform it into design by organization, embedded designing.

EF — You spoke a few times about this idea of a knowledge bank. The assumption is that by curating a talented team you also shape an interesting knowledge set. So, part of a project's intelligence is outsourced and made productive within the organization of the project. Does this mean that you assume that the composition of profiles in your office will not necessarily change through hiring data scientists, for instance, in addition to designers, to be better equipped for the new generation of knowledge development and problem-solving capacity?

DG   No, it doesn't change the way the composition of our organization takes shape, but it changes the people within the system, and it especially changes the connections the office has. We see the office as an organism. This one has 220 bacteria in it. What we do is constantly accumulate small fragments of context. Do you know these things that you throw at the window and they sticks and then start running away? We are like one of those things. We throw ourselves to something that sticks, we gather everything around it. We bathe the whole team in locality. Everybody brings something back metaphorically speaking: the hairs, the dust, and the smudges that come down with the sticky ball. And then we have acquired what we need and then we jump to do something else. It is all to create this bigger window, which we want to be sticky too.

EF — So, in an way, the 'sticky story' we just mentioned is also applicable to your own organization? But how does that change the DNA of the office?

DG   Not much, because I think everybody has multiple interests. Many in the office are multiply trained. Everybody has an inherent curiosity. What it does is it changes the people, but it doesn't change the process, or the methodology, or the organism in itself. We have always been this sticky, uncomfortable practice. Our practice is one hundred percent based on curiosity and empowerment.

EF — Curiosity and empowerment are actually the fundamental ingredients to discover new territories to work in, right?

DG   Precisely. And all we do is feed that curiosity and nourish that empowerment. I think that is the strength of the practice. Everything else, like our finance department, the business operation, or our human resource policies, needs to be in service of that. Everything is the feeding ground for these two things.

EF — This strategy of being informed, and acquiring knowledge, seems to automatically lead to a vernacular approach of design. I believe you call it contextual. What do you mean by 'contextual architecture'?

DG   The main bulk of my work is within this urban complex or urban complexity, as I call it. That is where I feel most at home. I always try to operate in such a way that I am one step ahead and that I can control of where that complexity is going. That is where I feel most happy as a designer. When I look at my design portfolio, I find it extremely contextual indeed. I tend to work mainly on material details and application. It is a very solitary process when I work on shoes, desks, and chairs. That's where I work as David and let go of my own personal insecurities and design wishes. My architecture is similar to that, and shows itself as a control freak type of architecture, which needs to be extremely contextual.

      The basis for that is to work with local knowledge. I also like to work with local materials and to collaborate with local designers and artists. And I always try to invest myself in the context of a project. At the start of a project, I always go to the location and stay there for a longer time. I never just do a site visit and start my project. When we

Embedded designing, Bali, Indonesia

worked in Bali, for instance, I stayed there for many, many weeks with my whole team to really understand what we could do, before we even made the first sketch. And that's why it came out so differently.

EF We did not discuss this 'being there' as a knowledge-gathering strategy yet. This is a way of data collection, that has a completely new dimension. Could you describe what's happening?

DG Yeah, I think it's mainly experiencing and making connections to find out where the real knowledge is. For me that is not reading about it in books, but actually making the human connections, making the environmental connections, trying to understand that knowledge and not trying to make it my knowledge. I'm not necessarily a knowledge guy, but rather a process guy. I do not want to be a specialist; I just want to understand. In that way I can gather much more, without putting all of it in my head and recognizing all of the possibilities. I work simultaneously on fourteen different projects in fourteen different environments. It is impossible to keep all that knowledge in your head. So what I do is, I make this framework of mental sticky notes. I make these connections. If I then have a design problem in which several of these react, I take one of the sticky notes and the whole thing comes together. This type of knowledge gathering may sound a bit superficial, but it isn't. I just focus on the knowledge that I need to be successful in the project.

Aesthetics

EF —Let's go back to the topic of aesthetics. I believe that new processes result in new products and therefore new looks. We talked about Bajeskwartier, where we try to achieve fifty percent of innovation in terms of the metabolism of the building, in this case supporting, for instance, a radical increase of physical health of the inhabitants, of circular material use in the building, and a boost to the local ecology. But while aiming for that we decided to be willing to deal with only ten percent of aesthetic change. If we agree that in the near future new ideals will result in new design outcomes, how will this relate to the aesthetic quality of architecture and urban design?

DG I think aesthetics will become more contextual again, instead of industrial and generic. I also think that because of the introduction of new materials. Not only bio-based or recycled materials, but also materials that can be harvested in a much more responsible way. We will create new details and therefore trigger new processes of production and of building and therefore aesthetical innovations. I foresee that we'll be able to create details that we are currently not able to. And I

Contextual aesthetics: WA Museum Boola Bardip, Perth, Australia

think the aesthetics will be steered in a way where precision is high on the detailed level. To do that we want to infiltrate an industry that really locked down the way it operates. We have to approach it in a factual matter, not in an experimental way, approach the industry with huge force and in large quantities. That will have an effect on aesthetics. But we as designers should be ready to break through the dominant conservative mentality of the building industry: 'It is always done like this', or 'this is how we always do it'. When people use that argument, by the way, it is often really done first no more than two decades ago.

EF — I guess your design for building with wood at Bajeskwartier is one of the most concrete examples related to this detailing as well, right?

DG Yes, it is. It is the expression of persistence to invest in specific and local innovations for material treatment to produce interesting and relevant architectural images. I hate the broccoli, as I always call it. I hate broccoli architecture where you see that it is extremely green, but you have no idea what it actually means and does. I think it's successful when you show that sustainability is a responsibility and a normal thing. Something that everybody understands. I believe that we were sustainable by nature, before we learned all kinds of bad habits.

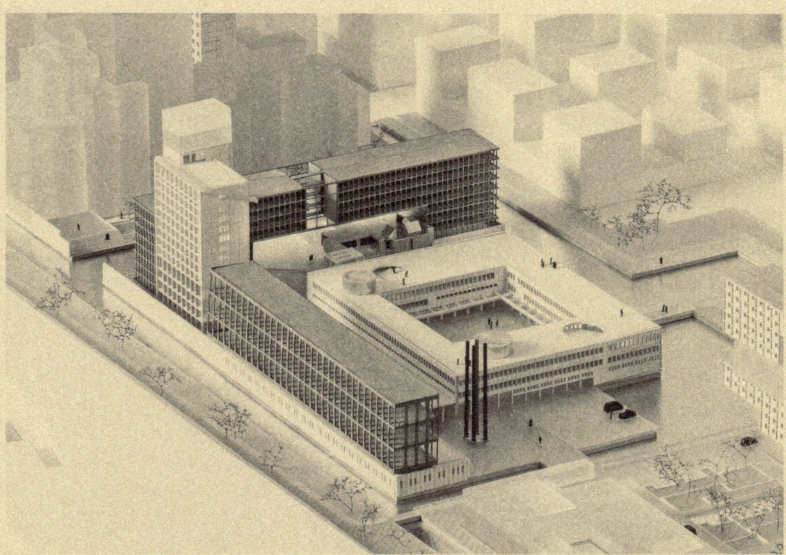

Relevant architectural images appear through local innovations for material treatment. Bajes Kwartier, Amsterdam

1   Indonesia's hospitality industry has thrived immensely in recent years owing to the entrance of entrepreneurs such as Ronald Akili. He opened Potato Head in Jakarta as a side project, but the recognition the restaurant received prompted him to eye the business more seriously. Now, Potato Head serves hip foodies in Singapore and Hong Kong, and the restaurant has even become a destination for vacationing gastronomes. People flock to Potato Head Bali to take in its architecture, as well as the food, identifiable by its iconic, colourful antique window shutters.

2   Andra Matin is an architect renowned for his clean and modern creations and use of space that is environmentally conscious. He founded his own architectural firm in 1988 and won several Indonesian Architect Association awards, including those for his works on the LeBoYe graphic design office building and the Dua8 building.

New Fields of Activity for Spatial Design

Artist and designer Jalila Essaidi operates on the intersection of art, design, biology, and technology. Like an inventor, she searches there for unseen solutions to complex problems, solutions that are actually right in front of us. And we don't always have to develop new and advanced techniques for this. Quite often, these techniques are already available in nature and we only need to recognize, translate, and apply them. For example, she managed to apply the silk of spiders as raw material for a bullet-proof skin; she invented a method to make fabric from cow dung; and she adapted a way to use trees as transmission towers for distributing internet. Also, a new board structure modelled after the shield of a desert beetle was made in her development lab, to help buildings retain moisture and thereby fight dryness. To find such innovations all she had to do was take a better look, she concludes. The techniques are actually just waiting for us in nature, but in order to identify and apply them it is necessary to fuse fields of knowledge and activity. Essaidi's innovations serve as a prelude to what the philosopher Glenn Albrecht has called 'the Symbiocene'. In his attempt to change our relation with the Earth Albrecht looks for a new conceptual framework and a new idiom to force this change. He uses the term Symbiocene as an antithesis to the Anthropocene. In the Anthropocene, humankind is the decisive factor in the geographical development of the world. By contrast, the Symbiocene predicts an era in which the decisive factors lie beyond the pure human and where humans will start blending with nature and technology.

We, albeit with a different focus and different jargon, also propose a change of perspective in the light of the enormous task of optimizing the contemporary urban environment. By looking not primarily at the space, but rather also at the system of the city, we choose an integral and metabolic approach to the city. In addition, this approach is projective, in line with the 'metabolic urbanism' of Daniel Ibañez. Starting from this change of perspective, we look for and (re)discover situations and places that will have to start playing an active role in the urban system to make it healthier. This chapter deals with these new places, linked to national, regional, or local tasks that result from a metabolic approach to addressing complex issues. Although we try to structure this chapter according to the various scale levels on which the tasks are primarily defined, the translation of this into

Essaidi's rain harvesting panel 'aquatecture', modelled after the shield of a desert beetle

new places shows how a metabolic approach cannot be restricted to a single scale level. In light of the broad definition of the city we proposed in the introduction, we see this as a confirmation of our attitude, rather than as a discovery.

There's nothing new about the fact that the list of demands we put on the urban system does not fit within the spatial borders of the city. For instance, the food and energy need of urban dwellers has always been larger than could be produced within the available urban space. And so this space has always been found outside the city. The growing need for space for new infrastructure, for example for new energy sources, does however make designing the city more pressing and leads to a constant compromising and looking for unused space, both within the city's boundaries and beyond. The needs of us humans therefore puts the city in a continuous spatial dialogue, and sometimes even in conflict, with its surroundings. The structural imbalance between the available space (and raw materials) and systemic demands (and population growth) was clearly articulated for the first time in 1972. Graphically illustrated by a steady downward trend representing the amount of raw material on Earth and by a rapidly upward trend representing population growth, the imbalance mentioned above was put on the agenda in *The Limits to Growth*. In this publication, the Club of Rome mapped the so-called 'system of the world', the whole of complex connections that make up the world, based on the logic of structural growth. By doing so the international, multidisciplinary collective of scientists described, for example, the impact of growing emissions, pollution, erosion, and use of raw materials on life expectancy worldwide. The researchers came to the inevitable conclusion that exponential growth was finite, no matter what, simply because the supply of raw materials needed to realize such a growth is so limited. How limited the supply of natural resources has by now become, is demonstrated every year on Earth Overshoot Day. That is the day on which, according to calculations of the Global Footprint Network, all raw materials that the Earth can regenerate in a year have been used up. From that day in the year onwards humankind is living on credit, as it were. In 2019, Earth Overshoot Day was on 29 July. The temporary effects of the Covid-19 pandemic gave the earth some respite: in 2020 humankind only started living on credit on 22 August, almost one month later than in the

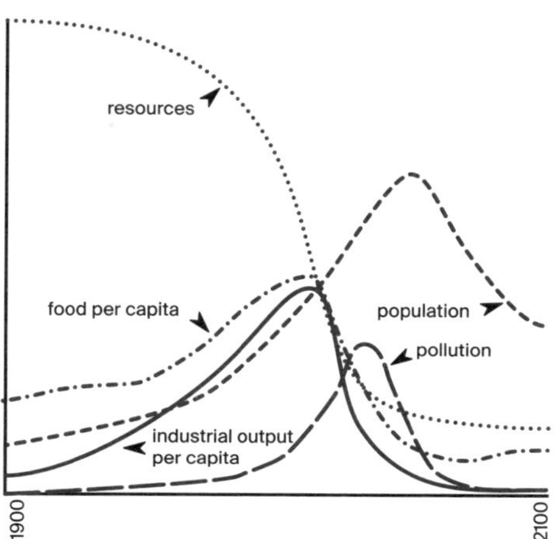

Diagram predicting the exhaustion of resources due to population growth from The Limits to Growth, 1972

previous year. However, in 2021 humankind was already heating things up to the previous level. In an alarming diagram the researchers of the Club of Rome showed already in 1972 what our excessive demands on the supply of resources might mean for life on Earth in the long run. Without radical change, the lack of raw materials will lead to a dramatic food shortage during this century, leading to mass unemployment, migration, poverty, ecological damage, and death.

The Limits to Growth made it painfully clear how the present system overflows the boundaries of the available space and is in need of a major overhaul. That process has meanwhile started up under the pressure of climate change, but is far from completed. The question also is whether humankind really fully realizes that the present critical situation will require quite real, and in some respects radical changes. The necessary systemic changes will also have a very concrete impact on the functioning and look of our surroundings.

Tasks on a National Scale

The changes in Dutch food production provide a clear example of this impact. In spite of the lack of space in a very urbanized region, the Netherlands is at the same time, surprisingly enough, one of the most important food exporting countries in the world, measured in financial value. And even though Dutch agriculture is technologically highly developed, realizing a huge yield from a relatively limited use of resources, it still undeniably has a negative impact on local water and land usage, among other things. As the research in the previous chapter already showed, the Dutch food landscape is on the eve of a number of great challenges. For one thing, the number of farmers is dwindling, dry summers are becoming more and more frequent, and eating habits are changing. Products, and therefore also production methods and transport, have to meet different requirements. This change in demand for food will have a strong effect on the structuring and use of the landscape, which is still dedicated for 40 percent to agriculture and horticulture at the moment.

Another big national task that requires more space is the energy transition. The transition to new sources of energy also requires innovative infrastructural solutions for storing and transporting the generated energy. The current infrastructure can take care of part of this, but we will also need a new type of building for organizing the optimal functioning of these new flows. For geothermal heat, for example, one can think of heat hubs. And interventions are needed in the urban fabric in order to collect and reuse heat and energy that is now leaking away. This could be done by creating public heat networks and connect them to major heat generators such as industrial buildings or data centres. Their redundant heat can be collected, redistributed, and reused. However, these are only temporary solutions as the expectation is that with more efficient production processes and better technology these places will be producing less redundant heat in the future. The soil in the Netherlands in large parts of the country facilitates the economic application of geothermal heat as a heat source. An infrastructure for geothermal heat needs distribution stations, new buildings with a function that was hitherto unknown and that will have a far-reaching effect on the experience and functionality of cities and neighbourhoods. We will further clarify these effects when we discuss the local scale level.

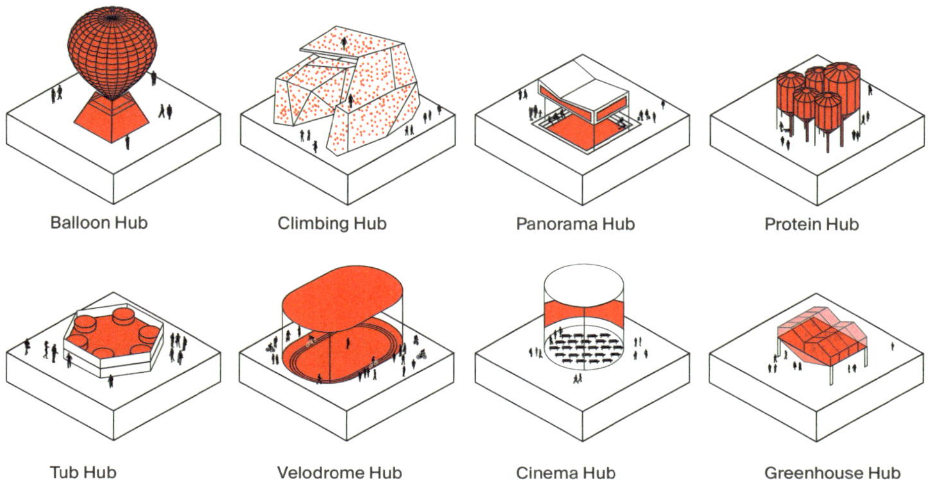

Various potential forms for proposed heathubs: a new form public urban infrastructure designed to assist in energy transition

Making our economy circular also requires spatial innovations. The amount of copper applied in cities nowadays by far exceeds the supply we can dig up from copper mines. So, the necessary innovations will partly involve smart tracking and reusing of existing building materials. Material passports and local reuse to minimize the transport of materials can help to economize on the use of resources but also of energy. Even far better would be to construct buildings in such a manner that it becomes unnecessary to demolish them and build new ones. By making the structure of buildings more spacious in both floor plan and storey height, spaces become more flexible in use and can be more easily adapted to new functions. For another part the transformations will be more visible, noticeably changing how the city looks. In order to promote the reuse of building materials it is also smart to start building in a modular way (at least partly) so that future changes will require less radical interventions. In that regard we are already seeing large-scale experiments with service concepts: parts of the building remain the property of the supplier. This development started with 'leasing light' but by now 'elevator systems as a service' and even 'façades as a service' are provided. The idea behind this is actually quite simple. If the supplier remains the owner of the light fixtures, the elevator system, or the sliding doors to the balcony and therefore also remains responsible for their maintenance, then it is to be expected that the supplier will be using more sustainable products that need little or no maintenance. Also, the same supplier takes back the elements he owns at the end of the building's life cycle and can install them again somewhere else. This is also the idea behind the circular business model of the start-up company Ciskin. They sell façades that are sold with a guarantee that they will be taken back after use for either recycling or reuse. Customers are given a service contract for maintenance and monitoring of the façade. In addition, Ciskin collects and analyzes all sorts of data about their façades in order to improve the quality of their product. The service model requires a different attitude of real estate companies, which will have to assess the value of the building in a different way. Because of the new demands being placed on the qualities of façades, designers will also have to adapt and start designing parts of the building differently, since a façade-as-a-service system is preferably modular. The façade modules must have sizes that fit in elevators and can be transported to the individual apartments in the building. After all, replacing and/or sevicing parts of the façades when the building is already in use must be possible. In this way, an as-a-service concept therefore influences the appearance of architecture, but also its spatial plan. In short: the great transition tasks in the areas of climate adaptation, energy transition, and circular application of materials will continue to require new work methods and strategies, and generate new fields of activity.

Tasks on a Regional Scale

One of those new fields of activity that stands out is utilizing space on water for, for example, generating energy. The development of the North Sea as a solution space for the lack of space in the Dutch and European urban systems on land is a good illustration. As the space on land is limited and the ambition to generate sustainable energy is big, it looks as if there is nothing for it but to seek the solution on the North Sea. The energy potential of the North Sea was already explored in 2010, in the *Zeekracht* report, and at the International Architecture Biennale Rotterdam 2018 a further elaboration of this, *An Energetic Odyssey*, was discussed with politicians and other stakeholders. As the Netherlands face a huge energy transition, we are looking more and more at the sea as an area for exploration. However, in doing so we also see more and more clearly how complex the colonization of the North Sea for our energy supply really is. After all, we may be able to solve part of a large problem at sea, i.e., the lack of renewable energy, but at the same time this creates all sorts of new challenges. A wind turbine at sea catches wind, but what is happening under water at the same time? How does such a wind turbine affect the biodiversity on the sea bottom? Does it mainly result in damage or are there also opportunities to be found for the environment? And what about fishing? Are generating energy and harvesting food at all compatible and are there perhaps other possibilities for producing food? Perhaps a wind turbine may be the start of a new method for cultivating shell food at sea.

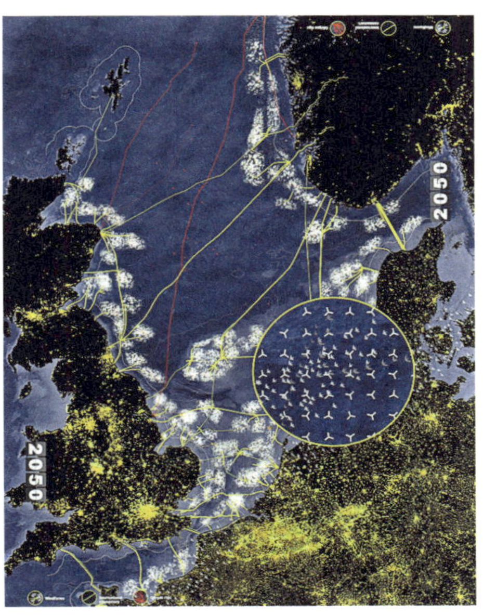

The connecting power of research by design is illustrated by An Energetic Odyssey in which 27 Ministers of European countries gathered around the idea of a large electricity network in the North Sea

Taneha Bacchin regards the North Sea as the largest national public space. On behalf of the Technical University Delft she headed a study into the possibilities of carbon sequestration and coastal safety. The basis of the project is hybrid land use. The assumption is that the current use of space will increase wherever possible. This means that the amount of vegetation and variety therein — what we call the ecological density of location — increases. In her research, both land and sea are regarded as elements of the same system; as one whole. This gives rise, for the first time, to a perspective that defines how to approach the space at sea as an object of spatial planning.

Our conclusion is that the 'escape' to sea provides not one, but rather a whole cluster of new design tasks, challenges, and opportunities. In 2019 the Amsterdam Academy of Architecture and FUR did studio-research on what opportunities there were for ecological conditions in the North Sea as a result of the advent of wind parks at sea. The wind turbines were regarded in this as a means to generate energy but also as vehicles for improving the ecological conditions on site which in addition could be linked to other possible opportunities for growth, such as tourism, recreational purposes, and food production. In other words, instead of regarding the wind turbine as a threat to local ecological conditions, in this study we chose — in the words of studio teacher Marieke Timmermans — to see the feet of the windmills as breeding grounds for ecological improvement, and also for growing food, artificial reefs, as well as recreation and art.

Within this context, the young designer Inga Zielonka elaborated in her project how a windmill park cannot only help to reduce CO_2 emission by generating carbon-neutral energy, but also help to sequester CO_2. She does so by creating an undersea forest in which biodiversity receives a boost, water is purified, seafloor quality is restored, and scuba divers have a new and interesting recreational destination. These divers are also tasked with maintaining the forest by sowing seaweed. Seaweed cannot grow on the loose soil that was created by large-scale fishing in large parts of the bottom of the North Sea. Also, seaweed forests need sunlight to reach the bottom in order to flourish. This afforestation therefore has to take place in stages. In the plan, the feet of the wind turbines first serve as the substrate on which crustaceans can grow. They help fight sedimentation, thereby helping sunlight to penetrate. In the next phase, ropes are strong between buoys for the first line of seaweed to grow, which in turn helps with purification. As purification progresses, the seaweed will be able to grow deeper and deeper to finally reach the sea bottom where it can form the bedding for a recovering ecosystem. Finally, even fishery will benefit, according to Zielonka, when they find a healthier fish population thanks to the fertile living environment provided by the seaweed forest.

With her metabolic approach to the task Zielonka shows how the arrival of wind turbines need not be a threat to the ecological situation at sea and can even go hand-in-hand with improving and restoring local biodiversity. At the same time, her plans provide new educational and recreational functions around wind turbines.

Designer Anne Floor Timan's approach is totally different. She too wants to plant seaweed forests to increase biodiversity but she combines this with a study of new opportunities to live and work at sea. Her research uses the fishery-free zones created by the wind parks to realize sustainable saline agricultural areas. She does so by placing the wind turbines in a large circle on a hard substrate that works like an embankment. The substrate itself becomes the foundation for houses, allowing the farming families to settle inside the embankment, the walls of which have been treated to accommodate sea creatures. Timan outlines the possibility of an entirely new human living community that will settle the North Sea, not as a colonial intruder or an invasive exotic species to drive off local residents, but rather as caretaker and stimulator of a recovering ecosystem. In her inspiring new sea community, the new human residents of the North Sea join forces with the environment in order to strengthen it and make it grow. In doing so, she implicitly also revives the almost forgotten image of the farmer as keeper of the landscape and the natural environment.
Designer Lola Sheppard of the Canadian Lateral Office explores a completely different landscape for spatial planning and regional design. She and her partner Mason White focused the research in their design practice on the relative wilderness of the Arctic region. Their goal is to study how design can improve and protect the social and ecological living environment of people and animals. Like the North Sea, the Arctic region has a long history of exploitation of both raw materials and food. Unlike the North Sea, the region they study is also inhabited

by people. In the project Boom/Bust, for the Oslo Architecture Triennale of 2019, Sheppard and White went looking for an alternative relation that the people of the island of Newfoundland could have to their own environment within the new economic context, on the basis of a number of spatial speculations.

As shown by Anne Floor Tilman, there is a need for an underwater master plan for the seabed, whereby all future use, on top and below the water's surface, is carefully considered

Newfoundland is built on a boom/bust economy (periods of sudden explosive growth, alternated with periods of shrinkage) the foundation of which is the exploitation of raw materials. The island is used as a production area for fish, fur, grain, wood, minerals, and oil. This impacts the natural resources, the landscape that is being exploited to serve the needs of the urban mainland, and the people who live there, whose culture is being pushed aside, as is their local smaller-scale economy, and who as a result of the economic situation find themselves in a constantly precarious employment situation with alternating periods of prosperity and crises. The spatial planning policy of Canada on the edges of the Arctic area is to an extent driven by an 'if-you-don't-use-it-you-loose-it' mentality. The various activities undertaken from that mentality often lead to curious spatial expressions and buildings. It is in this context that Sheppard and White study possibilities of replacing nine spatial types that carry the old exploitation economy with nine sustainable alternatives that are more inclusive and focus more on the region itself. In this region, which now functions as an exploitation area to feed the Canadian mainland and provided with energy, their research looks for economic opportunities that are based on other value models and the spatial typology that comes with them. Research by design is applied here to explore the possibilities for creating alternative frames of thinking; design perspectives that enable a new relation to the environment. Instead of economic growth and exploitation, they posit an economy of degrowth, which presupposes another attitude with regard to labour, resources, and concepts such as collectivity, care for the environment, and stewardship. In this way they try to create a spatial foundation for interrupting the disruptive and hype-sensitive 'boom-bust cycles' and ban the real estate investments in those hypes. Instead, there will be a more sustainable form of spatial development that is more in line with the local urban metabolism and diminishes the waste of important resources.

As designers move into new fields, new typological solutions also emerge.

The spatial types they are developing are tributes to the rural power and indigenous culture of the region. The old industry has resulted in a landscape with characteristic, obsolete types of buildings, such as a drilling platform, a fishing port, a plant for processing seal skins, and a shipyard. Sheppard and White come up with nine proposals to convert these places into buildings and complexes with social functions that form the basis for a sustainable economy that is founded on agriculture and tourism. Where once a highly expensive greenhouse complex stood that was built for growing cucumbers — a product for which there turned out to be no market at all in Newfoundland — they propose to build a large-scale composting station. Where, until 2015, there was a rubber production company — founded shortly after World War II thanks to generous government support, but it never functioned properly and went bankrupt after two years — Lateral Office proposes to create a large maker space. The former shipyard becomes a water treatment plant connected to a fish farm. Where once mining was king, they propose a market hall with a community centre. They also make room for a knowledge centre and cooperative living and working areas. All these proposals points to a different relation with the area. A relation that, according to the designers, is founded on what will perhaps be a less robust economy but one that will be less stressed, more diverse, and therefore a lot less vulnerable to ups and downs with all the job insecurity that brings.

These designers demonstrate how multi-layered the metabolic tasks are at new scale levels. Because they are concerned with the underlying system, one could also say that they increasingly have to manifest themselves in the domain that was traditionally the work field of engineers and planners. This means that designers no longer only respond to changing systems by making a spatial translation of that change, but that they just as much manipulate or influence the systems themselves. Design activity here also means political and economic analysis, cultural criticism, and the spatial illustration of a changed system proposal. They actively relate to the three moments that Ibañez distinguishes in the metabolic design research into the city: urban metabolism (analysis), metabolic urbanization (criticism) and metabolic urbanism (projection). As designers move into new fields, new typological solutions also emerge. Which we will discuss in more detail below.

Local Tasks

This new design space is not only situated outside, in the periphery of the urban region. The city itself often has a variety of un-used places that lend themselves to a more intelligent and more versatile use. For starters, under the ground. Here, out of sight, the always growing infrastructure of cables and pipes competes with the roots of trees for room to expand. Here too, space is becoming scarcer and solutions still have to be found for connecting old infrastructures to new ones in a smart way. As natural gas is being phased out, a very extensive network of pipes is also decommissioned. Depending on the choices made by local governments this network can either be used for clean alternatives, or a new network (for instance, a heat grid) may be installed, which will claim more subterranean space for other pipes and hubs. Earlier, we already talked about heat from renewable or rest sources as important options for feeding a heat grid in urban regions. Giving more thought to the location of these sources makes this heating task of not only local but also regional interest. A metabolic approach cannot be restricted to a single scale level.

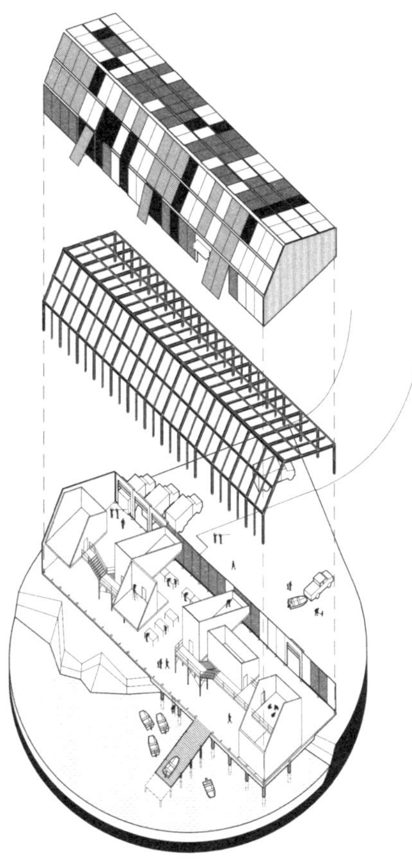

Proposal to convert an obsolete building from a boom-and-bust economy into a sustainable market hall

The rivers Rhine and New Maas determine various flows through the Rotterdam region, like goods, people, waste products, energy, water, local flora and fauna, energy, food, sand, and air. They connect the sea with the city and hinterland through the harbour. When we zoom in on the flows of energy, we see that the amount of residual heat leaking from the harbour is often many times larger than the entire demand for heat in all of Rotterdam and the Westland combined. This shows the potential for a heat grid in the region, although we should take into account that when the harbour will become more sustainable — also urgently necessary — the heat residue will probably decrease over time. This means that other heat sources must also be connected to the network to keep it functioning in the long run as well. The image below shows a proposal for a heat infrastructure for the Westland region with a main structure and also a series of heat distribution points, hubs that take the heat from the main structure and distribute it locally to homes and businesses.

In an in-depth study that was the result of the above analysis, commissioned by the International Architecture Biennale Rotterdam, research was done for a strategy that uses the potential of residual heat and geothermal heat as heat sources for urban surroundings.[1] Again, Rotterdam and the Westland region were chosen as case. The Rotterdam harbour is the obvious starting point for the analysis. The industrial activity there generates much CO_2 emission and residual heat. Both these flows can be captured. The residual heat can be reused for heating buildings, and the CO_2 can be used as raw material in the greenhouses in the Westland. Together, they make for a sizeable reduction in emission. By no longer generating heat themselves but only reusing it, connected homes can save up to seventy or eighty percent of CO_2 emission. Such an intervention also results in a sizeable economic surplus value for residents, as the cost of energy could be mitigated for those with lower incomes. In addition, it creates jobs and, finally, air

Harvesting urban waste and distribute it through out the region with a ringshaped regional heat infrastructure

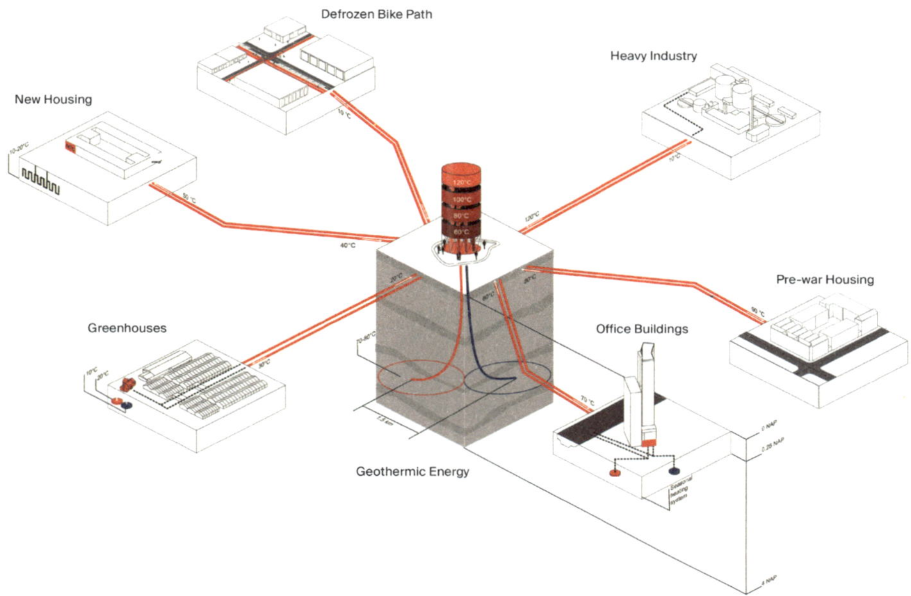

The heathub delivers water of varying temperatures to the sites where it used,
each with a different temperature requirement

pollution is reduced, which benefits the health of the local population.
    Such an intervention could mean an enormous sustainability jump
in many areas, but it also has important consequences for the regional
infrastructure and therefore cannot be undertaken lightly. Also,
because it will have a significant influence on the location future of
urban expansion and economic activity. In addition, such an intervention requires thinking about the future supply of heat and the
possible decrease in demand for it. On the supply side the question is
whether in the future industry will still be generating the needed residual heat. Industry is also becoming more and more sustainable and
so less and less residual heat is produced. To make the system resilient on the supply side, it should be able to easily switch to renewable
sources when the time comes. At the same time, the demand side is
becoming more and more sustainable as well. For example, houses have
to meet stricter installation requirements. This brings up the question of whether there will be sufficient demand in the future to justify
the infrastructural investments needed today. Choices like these have
consequences in the long run that may transcend the initial sustainability agenda and could limit and partly determine the choices of future
generations.

Such a new regional infrastructure subsequently also requires local
design interventions on a different scale level. These interventions must
facilitate the new flows introduced into the city and also bring them in
line with other urban social needs. After all, a metabolic approach does
not end with concluding that we should be more frugal with residual

flows but also knows how to intertwine that knowledge with other themes and issues. Increasing sustainability should also provide opportunities for increasing spatial quality.

How a regional heat grid can result in a new use of space locally, is illustrated by the example of a design studio about the Amsterdam 'westerscheg', also known as De Bretten. The 'wedges' of Amsterdam are a good example of spaces that are already partly interwoven with the urban infrastructure but whose function is not really clear either. This concerns strips of green that come into the city from the rural edges and are surrounded on both sides by industry and residential neighbourhoods. Jasmijn Rothuizen used this assignment to create a new type of buildings that optimally fits in the surroundings and meets the demand for distribution stations in the heat grid. She designed a series of possible heat hubs, each one linked to a different heat source and a different function for the surrounding neighbourhood. The hub at the train station also serves as a car park and charging facility for electric cars, while another hub retrieves heat from open water. It provides the adjacent neighbourhood with heat, and also with food that can be grown inside the hub. A third hub captures residual heat from data centres to heat the neighbourhood and the stands of a nearby sports stadium, while also serving as a heated club canteen. A fourth hub is a power station that uses waste. The CO_2 it emits is captured and used as a nutrient for the food grown in nearby greenhouses. Food that can eventually be eaten in the in-house restaurant.

Apart from providing specific solutions, with her designs Rothuizen demonstrates how innovative energy and heat winning can be easily integrated with various circular, social, and healthy functions for the neighbourhood.

Exploring and designing the integration of sustainable urban energy resources in the city. Heathub by Jasmijn Rothuizen

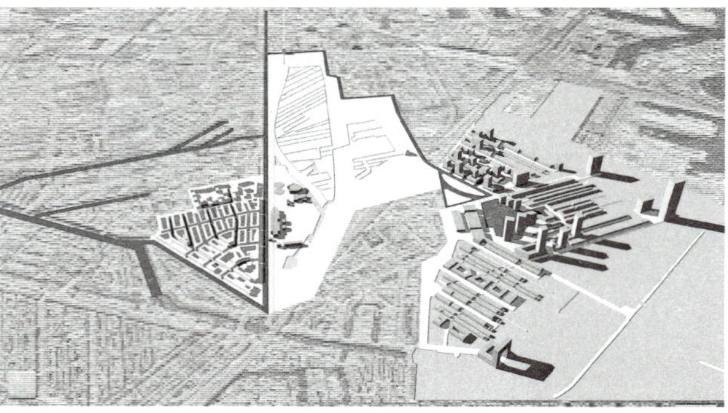

Defining new roles and spatial expressions for water infrastructure in the context of the city by Wieger Postma

This is important, as installing a heat grid — whether it is in the westerscheg of Amsterdam or in the Westland — requires buildings that have an aesthetic and functional value; buildings where users feel at home and that they can make their own. By adding leisure or social functions to the hubs the resulting design proposals not only produce sustainability in a quantitative sense but also a huge quality boost to the immediate environment.

More young designers tackled the question of what the function of this area could become. This resulted in a layered series of designs in which the green of the 'wedge' is connected to other parts of the city, some of which are yet to be developed. An interesting design proposal is that of Wieger Postma, who devised a study of the current and still to be added flows of water as the basis for the design of a completely new city district. For Postma, the green wet wedge represents an opportunity to create a new adjacent neighbourhood where water is the primary infrastructure and the element that shapes things. In doing so, his research anticipates a systemic change of the area in which the water flows define transport but also become a weapon in the fight against dryness and heat islands in the urban environment. The wedge itself remains intact and becomes the primary source for the network of canals that structures the new city district.

Both projects are an attempt to think through the consequences of climate change for a dense urban environment such as Amsterdam. They look for answers to existing problems in order to tackle these within the city itself, while also researching how interventions on the urban scale could contribute to solutions for the climate problem. In doing so, they not only look for the periphery around and outside the city, but also within the urban fabric itself, in the unused spaces one can find there.

A quite different example on the local scale in which climate change demands a renewed look at places is a study about the development of Ningo Prampram,[2] a fast-growing city in Ghana, in the Greater Accra district. Ningo Prampram is located on the south coast and is constantly threatened by flooding. At the moment, the city is growing more or less spontaneously without any structured plan for its development. Because of climate change the risk of flooding keeps increasing, also in places where people are now building houses. The local communities that have formed in the danger zone are becoming more and more vulnerable. Ningo Prampram, in other words, urgently needs a planned city extension that can steer the present spontaneous urbanization in a safe and future-proof direction. The plan conceived by the city administration together with the designers leads to a natural infrastructure in which economic chances and opportunities for growing food determine a more structured urban growth. The starting point is a study of the flood lines. These currently especially pose a risk to the city's survival, whereas they might also be used as an opportunity. By structuring these areas for producing food, they provide constant irrigation near the city, which can then take shape around it. In a second step, other flows such as energy, waste, and fresh water can be captured via this route. So, the spatial ordering of the city here becomes a direct translation of the various flows that match the natural infrastructure.

A metabolic view leads to two interesting things here. The building blocks of the city extension for water, energy, and food systems are designed by looking at the daily routines and habits of the end users, the local population. In addition, the design of the framework of the city is such that the accompanying infrastructure for the systems can be upscaled when routines and habits of the residents increase. The masterplan for the city and its intended expansion is adaptive, and rather a framework than a plan. It takes the dimension of time into account and provides a lead for the growth of the city at different speeds. This means that the design is founded on an analysis of the urban system, includes a critical view on the process of urbanization, and takes both the underlying structure and the spatial aspects of master planning into account.

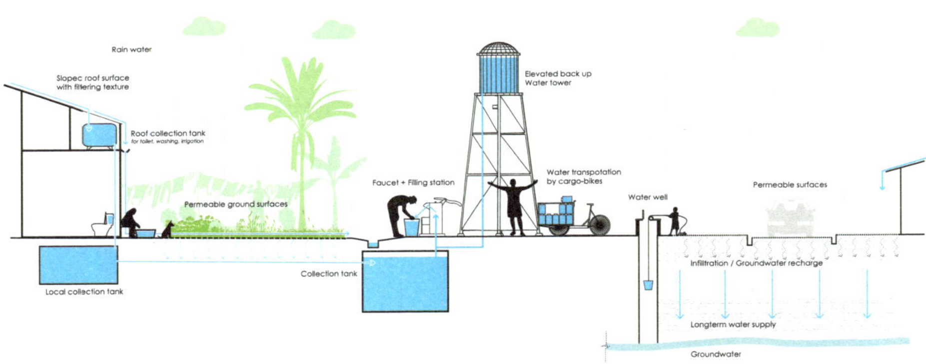

Designing the city through metabolic understanding of daily urban use. An adaptive Master Plan for the planned urban extension of Ningo Prampram near Accra, Ghana

New Players

So, to arrive at a more sustainable use of the city, more knowledge is required about how the city performs on a multitude of aspects. Such an overview is needed if we are to assess the actual performance of the city on various themes and to be able to project that performance in the future. It can also provide an impression of the spatial effects of a specific ambition at various scale levels. One way to gain new knowledge about the city is by collaborating with new players who bring new knowledge and expertise and can help create a healthier city. Also, other parties can be helpful in exploring a different perspective. One example of such a player with a broad, long-term perspective is the World Wildlife Fund France. The WWF played a decisive role in the development of a new residential neighbourhood in Lyon. As an organization that protects nature the fund also cares about green in cities and promotes urban sustainability and carbon neutrality. By acting as co-initiator of Lyon Confluence, it takes this urban involvement one step further. The organization co-wrote the Sustainable Action Plan, which defined ten sustainability principles that should be the hallmarks of a carbon-neutral future of cities. These principles focus on sustainability in the broadest sense. Carbon neutrality, circularity, accessibility for bicycles and public transport, water adaptation, and biodiversity are important pillars, but so are a healthy economic climate, a robust local culture, and physical health and well-being. These principles would not only have to be applied to the design of the Lyon neighbourhood, but the WWF also devoted itself to monitoring and reporting how the neighbourhood performed in the first ten years after it was built.

The WWF's focus is primarily on biodiversity and nature, which are the organization's principal areas of interest. In the case of the restructuring of the former industrial area Lyon Confluence these elements presented a number of huge challenges. The unfortunate history of the area with regard to nature and biodiversity — which led to polluted soil — is being compensated by its favourable positioning exactly between the river beds of the Saône and Rhône. This meant that the project managed to realize sixty percent of greenery in the form of parks, water gardens on the banks of the Saône, as well as a large square around a water basin that directly connects to the river. These biotopes guarantee a huge revival in biodiversity and are constantly being monitored by various associated environmental organizations. The facilities help to retain water and let it flow back to the river, combating heat islands and improving air quality. The result is a healthier living environment for both the animals and people that inhabit the neighbourhood. These different groups of inhabitants are also taken into account when building homes and offices in the area. For example, much attention was spent on safeguarding the space for the animals to move around in the environment.

The involvement of a party such as the WWF demonstrates how the different look — in this case specifically aimed at biodiversity — can have a decisive role in the structuring of an urban area, sometimes unexpectedly putting other values at the top of the agenda. This results in attractive neighbourhoods with mixed functions, frequently leading to new forms and organizations. In the next chapter we survey a number of such new buildings, neighbourhoods, and structures and we take a look at the shape and values of the city of the future.

New Products and Activities
The changing work field and the desire to gain knowledge about the system of the city leads to new players, but also leads to a whole new

Adaptive Master Plan for affordable housing based on the growing systems for energy, food, water and waste as a resource for the planned urban extension of Ningo Prampram near Accra, Ghana

Bosame
Amlakpa
(Amlankpo)
Polipolo
Oda Open
Kponkpo
Nuntuso
Butsakor
Kpohe
Akraba
Salem
(Salom)
Dormanya
Lakpleku
(Dainahara)
Dam
Tekpanya
Dam
Mataheko
NEW NINGO
(NEW NUNGO)
Zeba Ar
OLD NINGO
(OLD NUNGO)
MOYO AHWIAM
(LAGOON)
MOYO
(LAGOON)
Kponkpo
GULF
OF
GUINEA
GULF   OF   GUINEA
0   0.5   1km   2km

La Confluence district in Lyon, France

range of activities, commissions, and products for designers. Often a building is not the right answer to the sustainability requirement of a client. Sustainable development of an environment often requires, in the first place, thoroughly grounded strategic plans at various levels of scale. Such plans make an appeal to other aspects of the profession and often even require completely new manifestations of the spatial understanding of designers. On the regional scale, designers are expected to relate more and more to regional energy strategies. On the local level, masterplans for sustainability are becoming a crucial step in metabolically responsible spatial organization. One of the first instances of this is the sustainability masterplan for the Cadix neighbourhood in Antwerp, in which the designers quantify the neighbourhood's sustainability. They then propose improvements, which can also be quantified, complete with financial advice. To express sustainability in scores they use ten indicators, including biodiversity ('natural environment'), water management, flows of raw materials and waste, and energy. Health, liveability, economics, and mobility are also taken into account. The researchers address global goals with regard to environment, well-being, and justice and say that these require a translation into the local situation. The masterplan provides a number of clear and quantifiable perspectives for policymakers and developers. A number of scenarios outline what results are feasible, desirable, and realistic in both a financial and sustainability perspective with regard to these aspects.

Their quantification of the initial situation showed that performance was especially low in the area of sustainable energy, water usage, health, and liveability. An optimal scenario could improve the situation from a general sustainability score of forty-six to eighty-one percent. That score quantifiably juxtaposes material and immaterial values and indicators, allowing policy choices to be based on and assessed by actual spatial measurements and analyses. The complete analysis can be superimposed on the map of the neighbourhood as a layer that visualizes the social, circular, and climatological effects of policy and design choices.

Layered Designs

The above examples show that the profession of the designer is broadening and changing. The need for sustainability in the city leads to other products, other research projects, and other spatial designs. Another example of this comes from a competition for space that is on the rise in heavily densified urban environments. It results in dilemmas about the use of all sorts of urban places that are currently being rediscovered as multifunctional spaces. Take, for instance, the rooftops. At the moment, the question is whether we should use them as green spaces or for generating energy. Rooftop greening not only provides food, but also heat resistance, more biodiversity, and it combats dryness. All valuable and necessary, but it doesn't solve our energy problem. Such a spatial competition is illustrative of the reluctance we observe in embracing the layered complexity of the sustainability issue. It leads designers to 'wicked problems', problems for which simple and final solutions cannot be found by deduction. Our inability to do so makes it seem as if we would have to choose between different necessary solutions. But in reality the answer seems to lie in smart combinations, in new hybrid forms that can combine the various problems and challenges. In this case an integrated, combined approach yields the best return: solar panels provide energy and also shadow on hot days; plants reflect sunlight and provide cooling, which in turn increases the efficiency of the solar panels.

Such competition for space occurs at all scales of the desired transition. On urban rooftops space is obviously scarce, but on the North Sea space cannot be indiscriminately given to wind turbines for providing renewable energy either. The North Sea is a complete world in itself with an extensive and important nautical biodiversity. It is also a field of activity of various sectors such as fishery, international shipping,

In the search for multiple uses of roofscapes in urban areas, Swiss coalitions of Universities and private parties are testing PV-panels that work on front and back sides in combination with different kinds of vegetation that cool the roof and whose colours should increase the performance of the panels

and the military. All of these functions play a crucial role in our food supply, trade flows, biodiversity, or national safety. The North Sea is not some fallow terrain waiting to be explored. It is also an important natural environment full of original inhabitants, as well as a prominent economic and political space. Here too, various interests and agendas need to be reconciled. The same goes for rural areas, by the way, where many farmers are currently facing the question whether they should continue to harvest food or would be better off if they were to use their land to produce energy. Or would growing wood be a good alternative? That seems like a realistic option if more wood is being used in construction and the demand for wood — and with it its price — will strongly increase, which is not too far-fetched if we are to take Daniel Ibañez's words elsewhere in this publication seriously. It is inevitable: if we are to accommodate the various interests that are present in urban systems in the limited available space, we will have to embrace layeredness and complexity. In the next chapter we present a number of interesting examples of designs at various scale levels that do exactly that.

1   'A New Metabolism for Rotterdam', FABRICations, IABR, Rotterdam (Kunsthal), 2014.

2   Planned urban extension for Ningo Prampram by FABRICations, Mixed Urbanism, MLA+, MORE architecture, OKRA Landscape Architects, commissioned by UN Habitat.

NEW TERRITORIES, NEW SOLUTIONS

A Conversation with Lola Sheppard and Mason White

Lola Sheppard and Mason White are Toronto-based architects and educators. Lola studied at McGill University and then Harvard University. Mason studied at Virginia Tech and then Harvard University. They are the founding partners of Lateral Office. Lola is Professor at the School of Architecture, University of Waterloo, and Mason is Professor at the Daniels Faculty of Architecture, Landscape, and Design at the University of Toronto. Their work at Lateral Office is research-driven and experimental, both in terms of the spaces and places they explore, and in the choice of issues they take on.

Many of Lateral Office's projects are rooted in rural and Arctic areas. Lateral Office seeks to connect local culture and practice with designs that increase sustainable living conditions for Indigenous peoples. In other contexts, they explored new typologies, as in Newfoundland, where their work was focused on the creation of a sustainable economy that is less vulnerable to sudden collapses and breakdowns. More recently, the project Contested Circumpolar: Domestic Territories, in collaboration with Arctic Design Group, is an inventory of narratives from the eight Arctic nations: Canada, Finland, Greenland, Iceland, Norway, Russia, Sweden, and the United States. The stories take off from domestic life in these countries and connect the home to the underlying infrastructural typologies that support and interconnect them.

Sheppard and White's practice also addresses topics that are often overlooked by designers. Their project, States of Disassembly, for instance, imagines an alternative attitude towards e-waste. They define Western capitalist society as dwelling in a sphere of consumption

Contested Circumpolar: Domestic Territories

that is carried by spheres of extraction and dumping of waste elsewhere. These latter spheres, and the communities that are created around them, aren't visible from the privileged position of the urban consumer and are consequently often left out of sight of the public, and untouched by the designer. Lateral Office reacted to this by envisioning seven new typologies that deal with e-waste and the communities around it.

Lola Sheppard and Mason White virtually met up with Eric Frijters to discuss their work and what their metabolic approach to design means for their working methods and research practice.

The City in its Context

ERIC
FRIJTERS

FUR's investigation is about the appearance of the city and its underlying system. We want to show that the new upcoming urban challenges — being related to the energy transition or circularity in cities or maybe the rising water levels in the Netherlands, for instance — are asking for a different response of urban spaces and require them to become more sustainable. In that sense, manipulating shape or form of urban spaces is not enough to cope with these new challenges. We have to start understanding the system of the city in order to design healthier urban environments, while we are producing a new urban or architectural aesthetic.

Therefore, I would like to talk about the work you do: looking into the periphery, both literally and metaphorically, to understand what happens when our cities become more circular. What kind of new typologies do we need to facilitate that transformation and how will it change the face of the city? When I use the word 'city', I include the most remote places. The city is not only a dense collection of buildings, but includes its systemic functioning as well. The place where the food is produced that is consumed in the city, is part of that city. All these places belong to the same system.

LOLA
SHEPPARD

It's interesting how the hinterlands act as an extension of the city. Sometimes that system reaches a point where it is no longer only serving the city, but is, in fact, a new entity in its own right. These hinterlands might form islands, chained together by shared systems or infrastructures.

MASON WHITE

These urban systems may be invisible or only temporarily visible. They may be shipping routes, or data lines, or military systems. And those systems do start to form a different scale of urbanity that is unlike the urban scale. Some have called this territorial urbanism or regionalism. Like the city, this condition can support the possibility of new typologies. It also asks the question of who practices here, who can participate, and who can discuss new possibilities for this kind of space.

LS

Architecture is inherently defined by its cultural and environmental context. From the challenges of the climate crisis and rampant exurbanism to architecture's colonial role in rural and remote communities, conditions broader than the city itself shape how we design. Embracing these dynamics through critical interventions, an architectural response opens up that directly complies with the demands of the twenty-first century through new typologies.

The Performance of Cities

EF — If we agree on how systemic dimensions of cities relate to their spatial expression, is it without a doubt that this expression is about to change? As you just acknowledged, the origin of our contemporary planetary challenges can be traced back to the way we plan, build and use cities. But before we can effectively intervene as designers, we have to understand the systemic dimensions of the object of intervention. So how do we gain relevant knowledge on the city to create insight that can lead to an action plan? But let's start from the beginning: do you have any thoughts on the interrelationship of city spaces and the underlying system, and do you believe there are interesting opportunities there?

LS It is easy to forget all the infrastructures that enable modern urban life to happen. We don't necessarily see the electrical, energy, or water systems that sustain us. And we're only reminded of their existence when they fail in a kind of cataclysmic moment. A key question, which I think you ask in your own work, is how do we make these city infrastructures legible, visually, spatially, and culturally, in ways that they are not today? How can we learn from the urban periphery, where some of these infrastructures are less sophisticated, but more legible?

EF —That is an inspirational thought indeed. There is a tendency to make our cities more complex and increasingly sophisticated, but what can we learn from the periphery? Can we improve that process, by focusing on the performance of those urban systems, instead of copy-pasting the conditions that make a city? Because currently the performance of the city is not really helping the environmental issues that the planet is dealing with.

MW You raise a good point with the idea of performance. Although it's not one Lola and I use very often.

LS We discovered that in small, dispersed communities, whether it's rural Newfoundland or the North, singular and one-dimensional solutions are not applicable. That it isn't feasible to build a single school, a single hospital, or other mono-functional infrastructures in these small, distributed communities. So, the question emerged how to share and pool resources, whether by making distributed social infrastructure or mobile infrastructure or by combining functions? I'm thinking of one project we envisioned for Newfoundland, where libraries are shutting down because many small towns can't afford to keep them open. But libraries are so important to cultural life, especially in a small community. In that project we explored a sharing and pooling strategy: the library operation is paired with a teaching space and a workshop. Bringing multiple programmes together enables or justifies the investment. Technical infrastructure, whether it's mobility or energy in these rural and remote communities, could be approached in a similar way that demands a kind of programmatic rethinking.

Periphery and Urban Behaviour

EF —What appeared to me as very authentic is your focus on the rural. While the whole world was obsessed with globalization processes, dense cities, and big urban centres, Lateral Office has been exploring the periphery.

LS The romantic notion of wanderlust, and having the ability to freely move away from the familiar with minimal possessions, is a desire that almost everyone has experienced at some point in their lives. The nomadic lifestyle is appealing because it represents the possibility of rebelling against symbols of stability and permanence in favour of exploring the natural environment and being able to adapt to a variety of living conditions with ease. For instance, in our Making Camp project, this nomadic architecture features a new way of living on the go. It recognizes that people are re-creating the suburbs and re-creating semi-urban conditions in 'wilderness'.

EF — Why are people re-creating suburbanism and forms of urbanism in these contexts?

MW   In some ways, our project on camping started with Reyner Banham[1] and his observations on environment, architecture, and envelope. The simplicity of envelope, with the water-wicking capability of the tent and the thermal capacity of the campfire, offers an essential notion of environmental control. No architect is needed in this understanding of the camping concept. However, when you look at current practices of camping, and one sees recreational vehicles gathering in suburban cul-de-sacs, at the foot of some remarkable landscape, creating huge amounts of waste and garbage, one realizes there is a gap between the aspiration of camping and the reality. This was an important discovery, to realize that the problem is not the tent. An opportunity emerges in how to arrange and gather people that are seeking to get away from everyone, yet are together with others.

EF — So the city has grown into us; urban behaviour takes over our intuition. We take our cities for granted and apply their design as a standard in any condition. We have lost the connection between the purpose of design and the reason that design was needed. For instance, we developed street profiles to create safe places for pedestrians, bicycles, and cars. We reproduce urban solutions in rural contexts because we cannot recognize how rural communities have organized themselves as distinct social, cultural, and spatial entities, which carry a much more direct relationship. We are urban by nature and that is why we re-create a cul-de-sac typology while camping.

The Architect-Detective and Serial Thinking

EF — To be able to read and understand urban regions or cities, we look at them as though they were living organisms. This analogy leads to the metaphor of urban metabolism. We have been able, in the recent history of humankind, to create a detailed map of how the metabolism of our own bodies functions; we can diagnose and pinpoint metabolic malfunctioning of the human body and cure people. However, it is very hard to cure the city. We really don't understand how the metabolism of cities is structured; how people, material resources, and energy flows exchange between different stocks, is largely unknown to us. So it makes total sense to start mapping these flows, and that is also a way to start looking at cities to try and aggregate that new knowledge into a practice that is done by designers. Lateral Office set a new standard for making maps. The map is a simple but important tool to start documenting knowledge, noting insights, relationships, pinpointing specific ideas on activities of people, or the cultural meaning of places. In a map, information spatially aggregates to become a resource for knowledge. Could you describe your process of investigation?

MW   Our preferred description of how we begin any project or inquiry is the idea of operating like a detective. All our projects begin with some form of map-making, drawing, and revealing of hidden influences. It doesn't always produce a traditional map, but we are usually trying to chart and visualize the connections that have been obscured or forgotten.

Henri Lefebvre[2] talked about the idea of the user as 'spatial practitioner' and saw this as a bottom-up practice of resistance to top-down political and spatial structures. We like to think about the architect working in the realm of spatial practice. Indeed, we see ourselves as spatial practitioners more than architects, because that gives us agency to look at spatial ideas across scales without feeling caught in the roles of urban designer, landscape architect, or regional planner. The mode of 'detective' allows us to move across all scales and find a way to synthesize them and recognize how they are all complicit with each other.

EF —How does this work? I assume it is not as simple as picking up any architect from the street to say: 'Start researching this.' It's more than that; you have to learn how to look. How do you do that and what kind of tools do you use?

LS   Our first entry into a project begins with knowledge gathering and map-making, at various scales. There's always a phase before design, which can be several weeks, or may last one or two months. During that time, we are observing, reading, talking, and making drawings. And then we often transition to serial thinking for the design response. We try to develop about five to nine ideas that are radically different from each other and bias the programmatic relationships between the elements. In this process we ask what hierarchies are forming between different stakeholders, energy, materials, and economies. The seriality procedure helps finds several possible responses for a single, albeit complex, question. It is perhaps similar to Cedric Price's understanding of architecture as a sort of theatre of relationships portraying the scenography.

MW   Our approach to serial design is similar to iteration, but even broader. Iteration is often tied to form-finding, such as building and testing a series of architectural massing models: the famous blue foam model form-finding iterations. But we don't do serial thinking as form-finding, we do this for a deeper cultural understanding of connections between things. To get away from the visual bias, we try to think about what architecture can do — what its social, economic, and ecological impact is. We ask what the relationships are that people are having with their things, or what patterns are emerging.

The way to describe our process and findings is similar to Howard Odum's concept of emergy[3]. Using the notion of emergy, sunlight, fuel, electricity, and human service can be put together in a common basis by expressing each of them in the emjoules of solar energy that is required to produce them. Odum developed a kind of a diagrammatic language of communicating energy inputs and outputs. The diagram serves a similar role when Lola and I, or other team members, are communicating, or enjoying the misunderstandings of each other. In that case, we will try to frame these relationships among occupants and elements into a diagram. That sort of conversation helps produce this range of possible serial projects.

EF —Could you give an example?

MW For instance, Making Camp is a serial project developed across five ideas. Each one of them is critiquing the conventions of domesticating wilderness in a different way. The projects explore the relationship between temporary occupants of nature and the infrastructures they occupy. The five proposals we envisioned each offer a different possibility, none are necessarily better or worse. It's just about difference. But the difference is compelling enough to generate conversation and critique, rather than the singular, the one idea. We are also influenced by John Hejduk,[4] although he was never my professor, in his architectural narratives and their intimacy. I think there's a version of Hejduk's

Serial projects offer a kaleidoscopic insight in critiquing societal conventions through a spatial lense

masques hidden in this approach. I recognize a trace of Hejduk in the way we are telling stories and pursue a multiplicity of projects and typology. And Hejduk's approach to typology opens up the discipline's possibilities of architecture's relationship to people in a different way. Working through scales and on the future.

EF — It is interesting how you position design in a research framework and how the basic posture of design could be applied at different levels of scale. Is

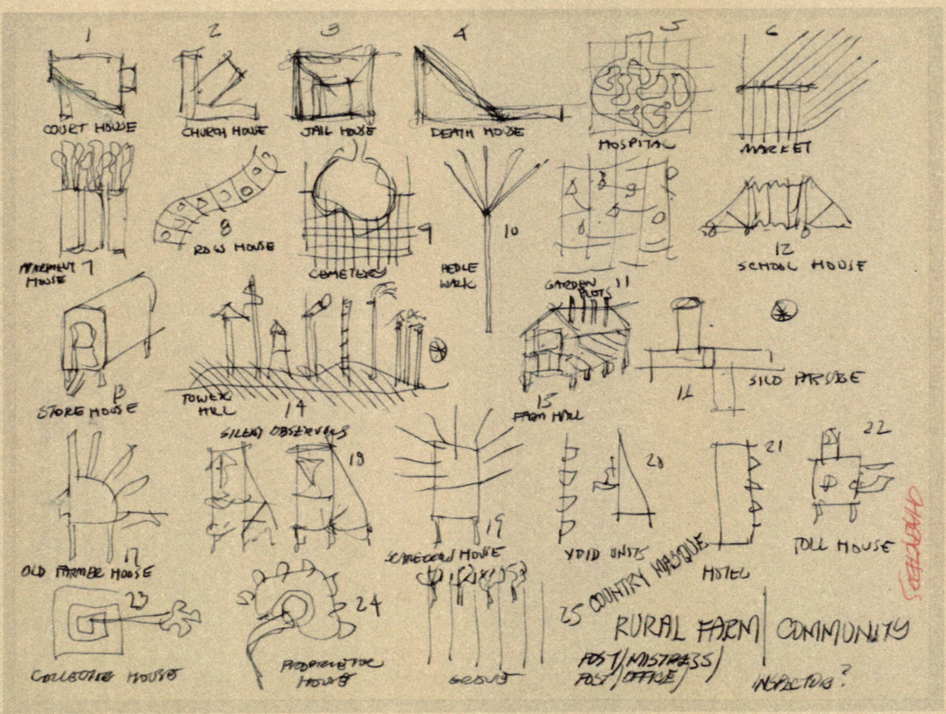

Sketches by John Heyduk for characters from the Lancaster/Hanover Masque

the freedom to go through all the scales and start understanding how these little details in many houses change, a very big thing on a regional scale, or the other way around? Would you go as far as defending that what you describe as a detective-mode, could be another kind of spatial discipline, a profession that is learnable? Maybe we should start training people as being these spatial investigators, these detectives in scales?

LS   It's an interesting question, whether spatial practice should be its own discipline or whether this skill should actually be embedded in each of the various existing design disciplines. The human scale includes both physical and sensorial dimensions. Designers create spaces and objects such as stairs, doorways, and chairs that are closely aligned to human measurement and how we see the world. But as we look beyond the human scale, new ideas and typologies emerge that help us rethink how we conceptualize architecture and build for the future. It makes sense therefore to consider different scales. It might be challenging for each discipline to always relate to other scales. It would mean that a planner needs to look at regional food systems, but also has to document what the local food market looks like. And conversely, the architect, even if they're only going to design a building, need to zoom out to consider opportunities at the larger scale. So, I could imagine it as a new department in a university in terms of research methods. But I would not withhold any designer from shifting across scales in his or her working methodology as well.

EF —I would say this new department could be a very useful complementary approach to scientific research. Since the latter never allows itself to do any future predictions, research-by-design could be a very useful tool. Whereas science is focusing on things that have happened, giving meaning to historical events, design can do both. It is not only capable of describing the past and the current condition, but it also proposes future conditions.

LS   I think this question of telling stories is really important in our research. It provides understanding prior to design. Moreover, it is also uncovering an existing story about a place and the project becomes an alternative, or new, or an overlaid story about that place. I think for me, that's why the multi-scaler research is so important, because the 1:20,000 map only tells you one part of the story, while the eye-level experience provides a crucial additional insight.

MW   Exactly. Usually, we wander off into unexpected and destabilizing spaces where we're not experts and we can revel in the discomfort of realizing how little we know about something and how much knowledge and awareness we still need to gather. And then a panic appears and we ask ourselves: what can we do with what we have so far and what might be our contribution?

Circular Typologies

EF —I am triggered by this panic mode. I guess part of it is sourced in the security that we are engaging a problem for the very first time in a domain of knowledge unknown to us. In that sense working in the Arctic or on circularity both represent a territorial niche. A place where we as designers have not necessarily been before. What is the impact of design and design thinking in these peripheral spaces?

LS   Maybe we have to look at it from another perspective. How do we reimagine existing infrastructures, whether of health, or mobility, or energy, from engineered solutions to a social and cultural inventions? Many of our projects consider environmental resilience in tandem with social and cultural resilience. In early projects such as the Arctic Food Network (2012) and in the Salton Sea (2010), we wanted to rethink the systems of food and water in those regions. Certainly the Salton Sea project was a direct critique of standard engineered 'solutions', which tend to overlook opportunities across scales and disciplines.

EF —How does your States of Disassembly project fit in this collection of rethinking systems? There are some intriguing conclusions coming out of this research. The teachings from it could be applied, both in the methods and the outcome, to other problems.

MW　You're right, electronic waste and the idea of waste cycles more generally is in need of urgent reconsideration. As with extraction, we have become disconnected from our waste systems. Plastics is probably our most harmful form of waste, but electronic waste is not far behind. The intention of the project is to make it more evident in our immediate realms. And to ask, what would this presence look like and how would it be experienced? Could we participate in that? The project offered a different kind of market and engagement with e-waste.

LS　I think that States of Disassembly also reveals a hidden global toxic colonialism that is tied to global capitalism; how the West extracts from other countries, consumes electronics, and then sends its waste to other countries. This is happening on a national scale and to some extent the urban bias is also a legacy of this colonial bias. This perpetuates the notion that the country is there to serve the city and to serve the global forces at play in the city. Rural and remote places are often colonialized and subservient to global companies and industries, such as mining.

EF — Well, that project is actually analyzing and connecting global practices into fairly local expressions. That's what your project does in the end; it leads to new typologies that we do not currently have, that are, or could be, part of the solution of addressing this idea and it has, in my opinion, a fundamental impact on what architecture in the end is and how that relates to our training, right? If the origin of spatial design disciplines, like architecture branches of the study of arts, in which the idea of authenticity and originality in structure, form, and material expression are part

This new scheme for the Salton Sea seeks to revitalize the site on economic and ecological levels

of the main objectives in any proposal on any specific place, then the challenge of transforming linear construction processes for circular buildings defies these very foundations. That's a dialectic that we have never had to solve before, because originality is now confined to the boundaries of the existing city, which holds all the material resources for construction and waits to be mined. That is a completely different task than what we were trained for.

MW   Absolutely. The electronic waste project is one of the few projects where we decided that being specific about where it was located was less important. We never describe a physical location.

LS   It could have been in Korea, in Canada, or New York. The project is less about specific sites than about intervening in specific moments in the programmatic chain of consumption, reuse, and assembly. Some of the building types were about reselling electronics, others were about the celebration of disassembly and the potential for education or entertainment, and others yet were about disassembly to extract the resources again. And so, seriality shapes programmatic specificity.

EF — In the way you perform research by design, you behave like a detective trying to avoid specific disciplinary characteristics. It is fascinating how you describe the discipline as able to design solutions, without a connection to a specific place. It is offering solutions, sometimes in the chain of events, sometimes in storytelling, sometimes in putting new topics on the agenda. Do you recognize a new generation of stakeholders appearing, forming new transdisciplinary alliances in developing urban areas and challenging the twenty-first-century problems?

MW   A project I had a lot of hope for but that did not materialize in the end, was a project called the Arctic Food Network. We worked with a hunters' organization, a nutritionist, an infrastructure and planning department head, and an economic development officer. This was an interesting collaboration from which you would never think design could emerge, especially interesting design. We talked to people and we discovered that the classical kitchen or food hub, as we know it, is maybe a very successful typology in New York or Toronto, but not in the Canadian Arctic. Here, we needed something completely different, a disconnect of all these activities that were until now centred into one thing: the kitchen. The project deconstructs the idea of a food hub into different parts: there was a kitchen, a freezer, a greenhouse. These structures were going to form a network, or a kind of constellation, connecting traditional ways in which hunting was taking place among people. It was intended to be a way to celebrate the deep history of hunting practices in the region. This way of approaching problems, examining existing practices, but finding new relationships or structures for them, inevitably leads to new typologies.

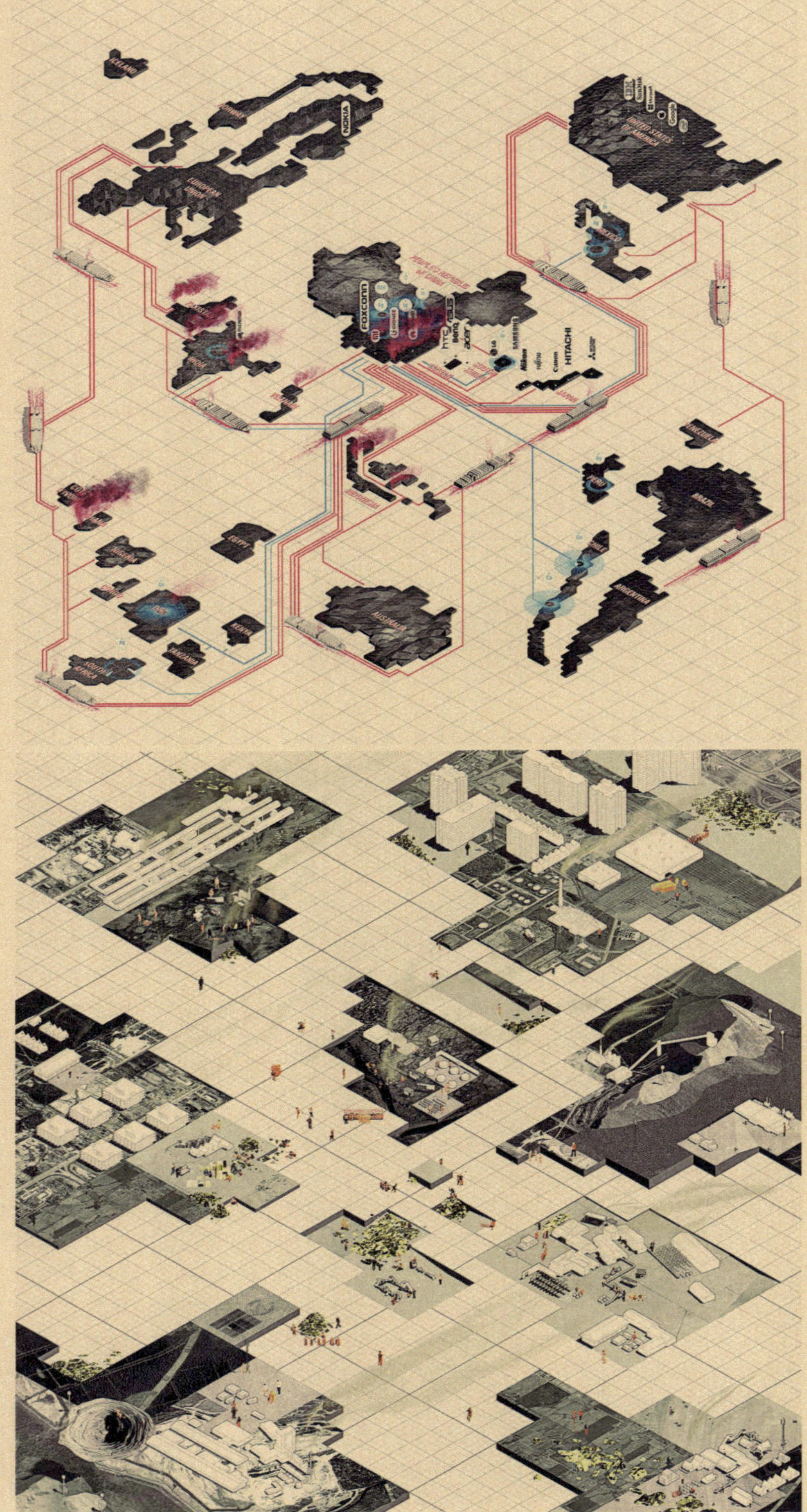

States of Disassembly: The geography of electronics material extraction, its subsequent product manufacturing, and ultimately its disposal reveal a fragmented globe

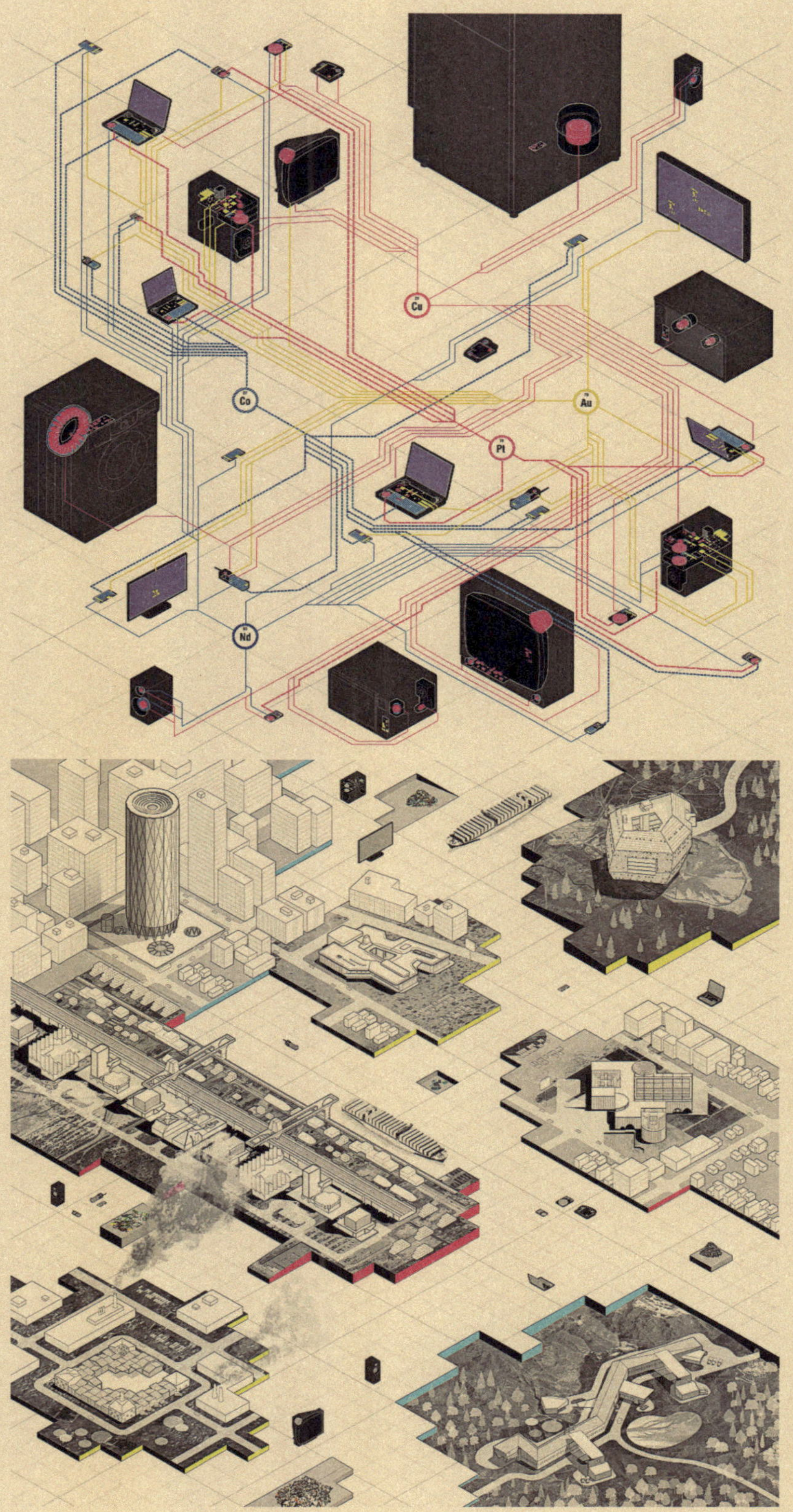

Exterior Hub of an Arctic Food Network

EF Are there some analogies in terms of design approach between this Arctic Food Network project and the Water Economies project we talked about earlier?

MW Yes, they both use an approach of soft systems. They both generate a logic not of a singular large intervention, but of an accumulation of many small interventions. This accumulation can be increased or decreased to find a regulatory planning system that is lower risk because it can be modified and adapted without completely changing the system.

LS As the forces that shape our built environment shift to include technology, economics, ecology, and complex systems, architects need to envision more than the physical space. We need to produce narratives on how to best operate within this new societal landscape. In this context, speculative architecture seems to have never been more critical.

Vernacular Aesthetics

EF — Could you hint on what this shift would mean aesthetically?

MW Well, we're trying to reveal new vernaculars, which is an interesting contradiction. New vernaculars don't just appear, so what might this mean? I don't mean a new vernacular in the post-modern sense though. North America, under Venturi and others, was more interested in the vernacular as image or as sign. However, our interest in the vernacular is more through use and how it emerges from, and reflects, local practices. Have we assumed too early that the vernacular is something from the past? Why are we not acknowledging that new vernaculars have yet to emerge? I think that the modern bias of the twentieth century has created a dogmatic understanding of design among architects that views the vernacular as dumb, or even as an excuse to not design anything. But this idea of new vernaculars offers possibilities that have been overlooked and probably relates also to the idea of being a spatial practitioner.

LS The very definition of a vernacular architecture is that it isn't designed by an architect. I'm thinking back to our very first self-generated project, entitled Flatspace, which was close in spirit to the States of Disassembly project. It was also siteless, and examined building types that proliferate across North America and that aren't designed by anyone. Architectural vernacular has its roots in people like Rudofsky or Oliver, where it's about indigenous materials and building form but less about morphology, building type, and building programme. However, we have vernaculars in the modern age as well, whether it is the air terminal or the warehouse or the big box store or any number of building types, that are not specific in their materiality, nor their geography, but start to be specific programmatically. We find the same big box to some degree in Holland, in New York and in Toronto. One might argue that these, too, are forms of vernacular.

MW   Ikea vernacular, vernacular of Ikea. That's a new vernacular right there.

Proposal to thicken the exurban 'Flatspace', combining the highway off-ramp system with the parking lot logic, leaving an abundance of larger spaces for co-habitation with nature

1 Peter Reyner Banham was an English architectural critic and writer best known for his theoretical treatise *Theory and Design in the First Machine Age* (1960). He was a frequent visitor of the United States from the early sixties on. It resulted in the publication *Los Angeles: The Architecture of Four Ecologies* (2009), in which he categorized the Los Angeles experience into four ecological models: Surfurbia, Foothills, The Plains of Id, and Autopia. He was often seen on his trusty Moulton bicycle on the streets of London, inspiring thousands of hipsters. He prioritized services over style with 'A Home Is Not a House' (1965) and focused on building performance in the analytical *The Architecture of the Well-Tempered Environment* (1969).

2 Henri Lefebvre was a Marxist and Existentialist philosopher and a sociologist of urban and rural life. He theorized on international flows of capital and of social space and is best known for pioneering the critique of everyday life. He was a witness of the modernization of French everyday life, the industrialization of the economy and suburbanization of its cities. In this process, the rural way of life of the traditional peasant was destroyed. He moved back to Paris where he developed his critique of the alienation of modern city life, which was obscured by the mystifications of the consumerism and the mythification of Paris by the heritage and tourism industries. These critiques of the city were the basis for Lefebvre's investigation of the cultural construction of stereotypical notions of cities, of nature and of regions. Accorded international fame, he questioned the over-specialization of academic disciplines and their 'parcellization of urban issues into many disciplines such as planning, geography, surveying, architecture, sociology, and psychology, which dealt with space and other human geography issues.

3 Howard T. Odum was an American ecologist. He is known for his pioneering work on ecosystem ecology, and for his provocative proposals for additional laws of thermodynamics, informed by his work on general systems theory. Odum left a large legacy in many fields associated with ecology, systems, and energetics. He studied ecosystems all over the world, and pioneered the study of several areas, some of which are now distinct fields of research. Odum published one of the first significant papers in each of the following areas: Ecological modelling, Ecological engineering, Ecological economics, Estuarine ecology, Tropical ecosystems ecology and General systems theory. He was one of the first to discuss the use of ecosystems for life-support function in space travel.

4 John Hejduk was an American architect, artist and educator of Czech origin who spent much of his life in New York City. Hejduk is noted for having had a profound interest in the fundamental issues of shape, organization, representation, and reciprocity. He established his own practice in New York City in 1965 and is associated with several schools, including the New York Five (with architects Peter Eisenman, Richard Meier, Michael Graves, and Charles Gwathmey) whose early works are described in Five Architects and the Texas Rangers, a group of innovative architects and professors at the Texas School of Architecture, Austin, whose other well-known participants include Colin Rowe and Werner Seligmann.

Other Types of Buildings, Neighbourhoods, and Landscapes

Cities will inevitably start to look different in the years to come, as changing demands to the system will find spatial expression. From the previous chapter we learned that the complexity of the city compels us to bring together and mix the various functions and interests both systemically and spatially. Through the expansion of available research methods our knowledge of the functioning city will increase, which will make it possible to improve its performance. That improvement of the performance of the city will also drastically change our experience, view, and use of the city. And not only in the city itself, but also in the near and less near periphery, in the urban fringe around more densified areas, in the infrastructure that supports the city and in the ground carrying it, these changed values and system requirements will become tangible, visible, and evident. It is not just the way our bread-making machines or ovens will be powered, but the way the wheat is grown for baking that bread will also radically change. The city's transition thus also forces a transition in thinking about the city and its boundaries, possibilities, and limitations. It necessitates a big metamorphosis with all the functional, aesthetic, cultural, intellectual, and emotional consequences this brings. In most cases, the spaces in which that metamorphosis must take place are already in use now. A different, sustainable use will render part of the existing spaces unusable. At the same time, as we illustrate below, this new use also provides opportunities for developing new (types of) spaces in which multiple kinds of use are combined. The enormous complexity of this task lies mainly in the hands of the designers that will shape this metamorphosis.

In some cases, this will amount to a leap into the unknown, and the current concomitant value models, forms, and functions will still be unknown. In other cases, the new typologies that come with the transition will follow the logic of existing organizations or build on time-honoured traditions. Sometimes they will become possible because of a technical innovation, sometimes because of a new organizational structure or a different field of activity, or they will be started by other initiators with different demands and wishes. Almost by definition, these typologies will have to find ways to combine functions of a varying nature.

Old Uses, New Applications

One example of an old use that may find a new application is 'alley cropping'. This form of production in which wood and food are being produced simultaneously has been in existence for centuries in extensive agricultural areas, but new interpretations provide renewed opportunities in the current search for mixed structuring of the landscape. A metabolic view of food production and the need for an optimal and preferably multifunctional use of all available space has given rise to new studies into simultaneous cultivation. This has all sorts of potential advantages. For example, some forms of large-scale

Alley Cropping: cereals between rows of walnut trees

food production do not profit at all from a continuous exposure to sunlight. Planting rows of trees between long strips of crops then provides sufficient and all-around light for the tree so that it can grow straight up, while at the same time guaranteeing a healthy strip of edible plants on a scale that allows mechanized cultivation. Both forms of cultivation thus benefit from each other.

Landscape architect Hanna Prinssen's project, A Fire Scape, also finds inspiration in old techniques. Her design was inspired by an old method of the indigenous population of North America, who use fire to maintain the landscape. By burning down parts of woodlands in a specific and controlled way they created open landscapes for the hunt. The knowledge of these techniques was lost following the British colonization of the continent. Instead of controlled application of fire, fire prevention programmes were put in place that drastically changed the organization of the landscape. Forestation increased considerably since then, changing the ecosystem in the process. Another effect is that with the Earth warming up, forest fires are more and more frequent and these fires rage freely and mostly out of control, with dire consequences for both humans and animals. This observation — that fire prevention projects have actually backfired in that sense — has made Prinssen revive these old indigenous techniques. She does so by analogy with the changing Dutch relation to water, which is no longer exclusively aimed at holding back the water with dikes, seawalls, and dunes, but rather advocates to admit the water again into the landscape and the ecological system in a controlled fashion. This means looking for a new, more resilient landscape where the water is welcomed as a guest instead of feared as an intruder. This principle is the leitmotif for a new fire landscape, where safe living areas are created by constructing a topology called 'fire dike'. This is a line along the edge of the mountain ridges where the top layer of soil is dug off to expose the underlying rocks. As no inflammable material can grow there, future fires can no longer pass this fire dike, which protects the built environment. The fire dike also has aesthetic value and constitutes a valuable new addition to the landscape with specific recreational possibilities. Within the dikes forests may grow, helping to meet the growing demand for wood as raw material, without endangering the communities there.

The above examples speculate on the future transformation of the landscape as a result of a changing use. They illustrate the search for innovative synergy between old and new systems functions in an

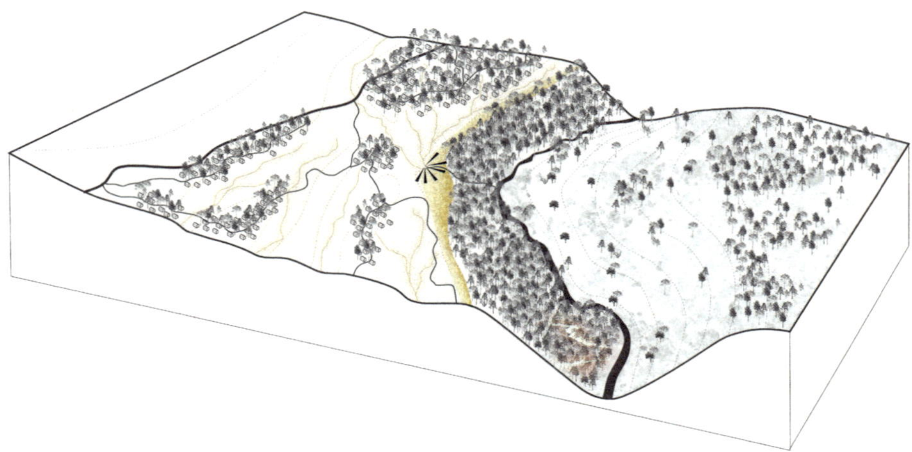

Speculations on landscape design based on future change of use, A Fire Scape by Hanna Prinssen

increasingly scarcer space. In addition, we see that producing wood, growing food, or generating electricity do not necessarily have to compete for space at all. Both examples also show that a different use promotes the development of new types, both in urban centres and outside them. The heathubs described in the previous chapter are examples of buildings where various functions may possibly be combined in a smart way. One already realized example is BIG's waste power station in Copenhagen, where energy production, sports, and recreation come together in a new type of building. Not only in terms of mixed use, but also in making the exchange of material flows productive. The building is a direct expression of its role in the metabolism of the city.

In many cities the various administrative bodies are currently heeding the call to create neighbourhoods that are equally focusing on living, working, and learning. Here, working means a lot more than opening up a laptop at the coffeeshop on the corner: it's about facilitating production processes and the accompanying logistics infrastructure. This leads to a much more mixed street view than we are used to, with different plinths and adapted buildings. The changes in the space around us can also be strongly felt in the more rural areas, the places where the energy transition manifests itself most prominently and creates new types of landscapes. In spatial terms, generating energy has always been a not very subtle and discreet activity that demands much space. This is true of

Waste power station Copenhill

exploiting fossil sources with the accompanying chimneys and plumes of smoke, but just as much of energy based on renewable sources, which may translate spatially in, for example, the form of wind turbine parks and solar panel fields. Also, this changing energy mix requires an infrastructure that has a gravitating and structuring effect on environmental planning. But it's not just the energy production that defines the identity of our landscape to a large degree. The growing popularity of wood as a construction material may potentially have serious consequences for how the landscape is organized and how it looks. The question here is how compatible these new functions are with the existing programme of the landscape. Will agriculture and dairy farming be replaced by large-scale production of wood? Or will new hybrid forms of production landscapes emerge that will define the look of the landscape in the future? Again, the question here is whether we really need to choose between different purposes or that we'd better clear a path for a new, combined use of space.

Are Cities the Effect of Use or Just Facilitating It?

The fact that cities develop out of a change in use is as old as the phenomenon of the city itself. Belgian historian Henri Pirenne places the birth of the modern European city in the late Middle Ages. In the ninth and tenth century AD, they often formed as settlements around ecclesiastical or secular power centres. Or around markets, where people gathered and became active in settlements that were founded by merchants, often on strategic points of existing trade routes. In the early Middle Ages, cities were also the home of the manufacturing industry. Craftspeople would settle in cities to busy themselves with the production of furniture, pots, and other utensils, not only to satisfy local demand but also using surplus production to trade beyond the city walls. In the eleventh century AD, this transformed cities from organizations based on feudal relations and religion into places that had to provide room for a different economic practice. Cities grew in size and economic productivity thanks to the rise of the guilds, which meant a change in the city's function. With the guilds came a new structuring of the space on the edges of the city. Not only did they organize the sale of goods in the marketplace; they also controlled the production and distribution process. And as such, cities, besides being places for trade, evolved into places where makers manifested themselves. Throughout the late Middle Ages crafts became more and more specialized, giving rise to evermore specific guilds that kept up small-scale production in their own specialist niche within the city walls. Only in the course of the nineteenth century, as these physical city walls begin to disappear, was the production process also pushed out of the city, not least because the optimistic promise of growth and flourish made by the Industrial Revolution turned out to come at a price. It is therefore the

Guilds in the city

metabolism of the industrial capitalism that can be named as the cause of the spatial separation of living, production, and commercial functions.

In 1852 William Wyld painted his *Manchester from Kersal Moor, with rustic figures and goats*. For present-day viewers this is an almost hallucinatory image. From the pastoral, peaceful foreground we look out on what must have been intended as an image of promising progress: a vista of happily smoking factory chimney stacks. Modern viewers may be forgiven mistaking it for an image photoshopped by climate activists, instead of the intended optimism. The view of the city is painted as a hopeful look at prosperity. Wyld himself could not possibly have been aware that he had so accurately depicted its downside. The first disadvantage to appear was that such large-scale industrial activity had severe ill effects on public health. This insight resulted in factories being gradually located outside of cities, where they could be connected to an infrastructure that facilitated large-scale trade. During this time, the city itself transformed from a place of production into an environment primarily for living and consuming, leading to the modern version of the shopping street. Until then, shop functions had been directly linked to the locations of the guilds. In the second half of the nineteenth century the increasing desire of consumers gave rise to another phenomenon: the first department stores were built in Paris and London, two cities competing for the best reviews of their modern consumer paradises.

The typology of the shopping street is a still relatively new phenomenon in our cities and not as obvious as many people tend to think. London's Regent Street, one of the oldest shopping streets of Europe, recently celebrated its 200th birthday. The oldest shopping street in the Netherlands, the Lange Hezel Street in Nijmegen, is only 140 years old, whereas the city of Nijmegen itself has been there for more than 200 years. Such spaces within the urban fabric started to function as intermediaries for products, whereas not long before these would have been picked up at the craftspeople themselves. The distance between the place of production and the market became even greater in the next century, when as a result of growing globalization many production processes were moved to low-wage countries in the second half of the twentieth century. The ever more efficient international traffic and trading facilitated by computerization, automatization, and robotization continues this process. The scale of production also increases.

William Wyld, *Manchester from Kersal Moor*, 1852

Mass production means a lower price per unit and makes it profitable to transport products over great distances.

The history of the rise and possibly imminent demise of the shopping street as an urban innovation is illustrative of how the use of the city determines the advent and disappearance of specific urban forms and types. In order to facilitate the systemic changes of commercial processes, the city needed to start behaving differently, or: allow for a different use. To bridge the spatial gap between the industry outside the city and the consumers in it, the shopping street was a fitting invention. However, the changed consumer behaviour of present-day city dwellers no longer requires the shopping street to obtain products that are made far away. It means that an iconic urban image is now endangered and a different layout of the city is looming; one with a different aesthetic and cultural identity.

A Different City Because of a Different Use

This process of increasing mass production will not come to an end anytime soon, but there is a tentative trend towards smaller-scale producers who are returning to the city more and more often. As mentioned, the shopping street as an important urban space is under pressure because of the changing market, which is moving more and more online. At the moment it is not production but rather also trade that is moving from the city into anonymous boxes. At the same time, the fringes of the city are transforming once again: here, residential functions and production processes are starting to emerge again side-by-side. The ever-faster development of high-quality computer technology in production processes not only makes industrial applications more efficient but also cleaner and quieter, which makes it easier to integrate them into the urban environment. This creates jobs and layered, interesting neighbourhoods that enrich the urban landscape with new functions. This is necessary, as not only our cities and production sites are changing, but our lives and especially our relation to work are also constantly subject to change. If one's working life used to consist of a more or less linear career path following an applied education, in the twenty-first century careers tend to evolve in a less straightforward fashion, with frequent and varying intervals, career switches, and additional schooling along the way. Permanent contracts are becoming scarce and the running time of a career is less fixed. More and more often, people work in varying collaborations with shorter running part-time contracts or on a project basis. At the same time, the labour market in Western cities, especially in Europe, is shrinking, a trend that is only reinforced by increasing robotization. This economic and social reality requires a different urban environment with a more extended mix of economic activities.

One effect of this is that in various cities experiments are currently undertaken with stacking and combining places to live, work, and produce. For example, in the mixed London neighbourhoods of Caxton and Faraday, commercial activity, small-scale manufacturing, and residential units come together in a new urban mix. Or, take Brooklyn Navy Yard, a new working-class neighbourhood where many business functions are being stacked on top of each other, with production and logistic functions on the lower levels and small-scale manufacturing and office functions on top. In Paris, the excellent network position of a former marshalling yard at Porte de la Chapelle is used as a starting point for keeping large-scale logistic functions within the city and combining them with a new mix of offices, apartments, public facilities and greenery, and food production.

Such a varied urban mix not only results in an attractive living environment, but its location also provides opportunities for sustainability, as illustrated by a number of large-scale harbour transformations in the Dutch context. In Rotterdam, for example, attempts are made to translate these changes into the development of Merwede Vierhavens; in the Amsterdam Hamerkwartier similar plans are being made. Also, in Eindhoven the former Philips sites Strijp-S and Strijp-R are being transformed into a new urban development for 'multiple use'. In all these projects the aim is to arrive at a mix of living, working, and learning, which should result in a more dynamic city scene. It should not be underestimated how important it is to keep the distances between these various forms of using the city at a minimum, for the exchange of — residual — flows of energy and raw materials and for diminishing the materials cycle. Simple examples of this are sharing parking spaces that support economic functions in the daytime and can be used by local residents at night. The proximity of producing and living also has energetic benefits: residual heat from, for example, data centres can be used as heat source for adjacent apartments. In view of a better understanding of urban metabolism such neighbourhoods provide important opportunities for developing circular cities, by organizing living, leisure, sports, education, and economic productivity immediately above, below, or next to each other.

Mixing Living and Working in Residential Neighbourhoods

The two London neighbourhoods of Caxton and Faraday were developed by Studio Egret West and both are a reaction to the changing economic landscape of the city where the smaller industry has disappeared in the interest of housing development. In the former industrial area of Caxton in Canning Town, East London, 336 apartments were built above a high plinth for light manufacturing businesses. This plinth is made of wood and steel and faces a street where space has been cleared for easy loading and unloading at the commercial space but where pedestrians still have priority. On the roof of the car park between the four living/working high-rises a communal garden was realized.

Faraday has a similar aim, but on twice the scale. Here too we are talking about a former industrial site, in the south of the city, in a neighbourhood that once provided jobs for 6000 people but where the warehouses now all stand empty. The designers' aim is to create an extended mix of apartments next to studios, exhibition spaces,

Caxton Works is an example of Urban plinths used for light manufacturing purposes in Canning Town

Faraday Works by Studio Egret West: a partial transformation of a former Siemens production facility in Westminster, London creates many new homes and jobs

bars and restaurants, workplaces, and industrial activities. Unlike in Caxton, the industrial function has been concentrated in one building. The proposed street scene, which again gives a clear space for pedestrians and bicyclists, is somewhat reminiscent of a late-mediaeval guild street, where craftspeople are literally working in the street. Faraday Works aspires to a vital mix of living, working, and retail, dressed in an attractive street scene that preserves the characteristics of the heritage that lends the place its identity. The ambition is to create a diverse community from a rich mix of 380 different apartments, both rented and owner-occupied. In addition, at least 800 new jobs will be created. What makes both developments so special is that they have found a way — in spite of potential nuisance and inconvenience from small-scale industrial activities — to create a mixed neighbourhood with space for manufacturing. This greatly enhances the variety in the neighbourhood and it not only increases opportunities for sustainable exchange of energy and sharing facilities, but it also strengthens social cohesion.

Another striking element is that in both cases a former industrial area is now also providing space for living functions. Living is often a rather dominant function in the urban fabric. But perhaps the transformation to an urban area with mixed functions is easier to accomplish when the focus is more on working instead of on living? Whatever the explanation may be, the result is a lively street scene in which a great diversity in the use of the space fuses organically: working, playing, parking, walking, bicycling, and parading.

An Ecosystem for Making, Thinking, Innovating, and Learning

One of the largest and most ambitious projects in which urban functions come together in a new way is to be found in New York, where the old harbour area of the Brooklyn Navy Yard is gradually being transformed into an innovative hub for both big and small, more traditional, and highly innovative makers and start-ups. The goal is to build a vital ecosystem for working and learning for a wide range of businesses. Fashion companies have their design department here, but so have a production facility and a flagship store. The entire chain from design to production is thus combined. Opportunities for exchange and cross-pollination become even bigger as a wide range of companies and branches are located in the same place. It comes down to an active policy to provide a flourishing industrial base and to retain and attract a mix of production companies. This also boosts the strategic growth in other important sectors such as technology, design, crafts, and film/media.

The development of the Brooklyn Navy Yard is a reaction to traditional industry pulling out of the area of 120 hectares (300 acres) in all. In its stead, all sorts of new producers are now based in the harbour. There's also large-scale cropping as one of the largest rooftop farms in the world was laid out on a number of roofs. Agriculture literally moves into the city. Together with the ecological benefits of greening the city, the constant supply of local food products of course scores well on the metabolic balance sheet of the local catering industry. Both small-scale and large-scale industrial production is also being pulled into the old harbour area, as are large office complexes. In Dock 72, the company WeWork has realized an office building of more than 20,000 square metres (215,000 square feet) of flexible workspace. WXY Studio, who made the masterplan for the Navy Yard as an innovation hub, speak of a 'renaissance of urban manufacturing'. The plan sketches a perspective on 30,000 jobs in 2050, housed in half a million square metres (over five million square feet) of vertical production space. seventy-five percent of that space will consist of manufacturing, twenty percent of creative office functions, and the rest will be facilities and services. The former harbour activity still has a home in the Brooklyn Navy Yard: three of the six dry docks are used to repair and restore ships.

Brooklyn Navy Yards is the answer to the question:
'What is the future model for urban manufacturing and innovation?'

In order to create and facilitate this ecosystem the design of the area needed to meet new requirements. Industry, including the clean industry within the city limits, needs space and requires a specific logistics infrastructure. As in the London neighbourhoods, the plinths of the buildings in Navy Yard are therefore high and designed for loading, unloading, and parking, to accommodate the logistic wishes of the producers. Large industrial elevator shafts facilitate the creation of vertical factories that even accommodate heavier industry within the urban environment. Allowing for logistical functions and heavier forms of production involving large machines places special demands on the design of the street profiles in the area. The plinths must have strong floors and be adaptable, which means they cannot have too many constructive obstacles. Because the ground floor of the area is reserved for the heavier production processes, which also involve much heavy traffic, it is obvious that lighter business activities are housed on the higher floors. This mixed activity again promotes social interaction and mobility and makes for a more dynamic city profile in which economic productivity, leisure activities, and sports come together directly above and beneath each other. Within this structure the district attempts to be in line with the same dynamic in contemporary urban life.

Besides accommodating offices and industry, the former harbour also provides space for urban agriculture. The rooftop farm in the Navy Yard is an initiative of Brooklyn Grange, the company that already developed a roof farm in Long Island and, most recently, on top of the Liberty Bklyn building in Sunset Park. The Navy Yard farm occupies 6000 square metres (1.5 acres) on top of Building 3 and grows vegetables for local supermarkets and restaurants. Especially leafy vegetables and tomatoes do well on the rooftops of New York. In all, on three roofs in New York, of which the one in Sunset Park is the largest, Brooklyn Grange produces some 50,000 kilos of herbicide-free vegetables. The city farmers also collaborate with a number of social and educational organizations. For example, they provide training and therapy for traumatized refugees and bring young people into contact with their farms. They also organize events that make tens of thousands of visitors aware of their activities each year. It is one of the ways to involve the surrounding residential neighbourhoods in the activities in the harbour, where no one actually lives. The rooftop farm also helps to make the city more resilient against storms and flooding — a vital contribution, evidenced by 2012 Hurricane Sandy. It is one of the reasons why the project was partly financed by the local government within the framework of the Green Infrastructure and Stormwater Management programme, as the farm retains half a million litres (over a 100,000 gallons) of water during heavy rainfall. It helps to unburden the sewage works in such situations and prevents the dumping of unfiltered wastewater into rivers. It thus makes the connection between mixed urbanity and its underlying metabolism in an obvious and natural way.

Brooklyn Grange rooftop farm in New York City

The Future of Urban Logistics

In Porte de la Chapelle, one of the northern access gateways into Paris on the edge of the 18th arrondissement, the focus of the new neighbourhood is on logistics. The aim here is to find a new mix of office buildings and logistic functions, in combination with a thousand apartments. Sports facilities are given ample space here, just like education in the form of branches of the École nationale de commerce, Paris' business school, which traditionally also trains technicians. The heart of the organization of Porte de la Chapelle is *l'hôtel logistique*, the place where an urban railway terminal for repairing trains is being combined with flexible office spaces, educational functions, fitness spaces, urban agriculture, a data centre, shops, and a heat production facility. This compact mix of living, working, and learning also affects mobility: the various needs of the city dweller can be satisfied within walking distance, which gives rise to a healthy culture of walking.

As a pivoting point in the logistical chain, the neighbourhood is very favourably situated. It lies alongside the tracks, near the train hub of Gare du Nord, the logistics gateway into northern France and therefore also into northern Europe. The enormous scale of shipping containers one normally finds along highways has been integrated into a residential area in an almost natural way. Houses surround a company hall, the roof of which has become a new base for urban living above the plinth. This logistical plinth is completely hidden from view for regular urban life. The advantage of including such functions in the neighbourhood is that the so-called 'last mile' of urban logistics can be organized very sustainably. The packages are already in the city, although not yet at the right front door. This final stretch can therefore easily be covered on bicycle and no longer requires delivery vans. In the plinths of the residential high-rises room has been made for small offices and studios with a layer of accessory apartments above them. At the centre of the high-rise one floor is designated as a collective space.

Porte de la Chapelle produces a very real economic surplus value, while another extremely substantial advantage is obtained from concentration, and thereby limitation, of freight traffic circulation. In practice this means that thanks to the new logistic hub 44,000 truck movements can be avoided, as freight trains can be used instead. This results in ninety-nine percent fewer fine particles and in a more than eighty percent reduction of CO_2 emission in Paris, formerly caused by logistics. At the same time, 7000 square metres of urban agriculture will be created, enough for an annual production of 45,000 kilos of lettuce, herbs, and edible flowers, as well as 4000 square metres of sports facilities. Not only will the neighbourhood be healthier, but it also helps Parisians to become healthier.

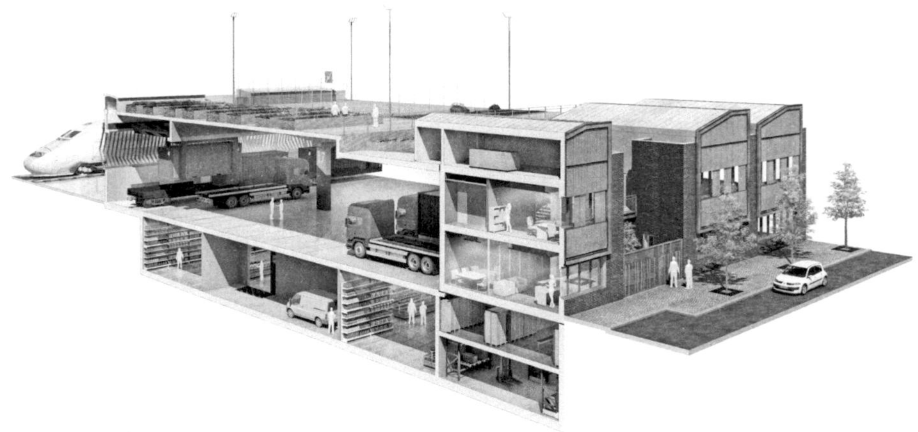

Mixed-use Urban Logistics Centre, Chapelle International, Paris, France

Not just the neighbourhoods in cities and villages and landscapes we live in will gradually change their appearance now that we can experiment with new spatial functions thanks to a better understanding of the urban metabolism and the involvement of other players. Also at the scale of buildings new forms will emerge. An interesting initiative in this respect is Vechtclub XL in the city of Utrecht. This complex is a reaction to a changing economic dynamic in the city. Most striking in this is the way in which the site originates and is being organized: organic and bottom-up from a collective, rather than being managed from the top. Vechtclub XL is a multi-tenant building for applied creative businesses, located in Utrecht's Merwedekanaal zone. It is the result of a process of organic redevelopment. These origins are linked to a current challenge: keeping and expanding work functions in the city by creating affordable new workplaces. Vechtclub positions itself as an alternative developer as opposed to market-driven project developers who produce high real estate prices and often show no interest in creating meaningful value chains among the end users. At the scale level of the complex the initiators took control of managing and developing an empty factory hall with the aim of making better use of the economic and cultural potential of the local creative industry and giving it a chance to scale up.

Important in this is a careful selection and managing of tenants. Selection of tenants is done on the basis of personal interviews about ambitions and the willingness to collaborate with other tenants. This leads to an increasingly rich ecosystem of producers and service providers. Like in the Brooklyn Navy Yard, Vechtclub actively looks for users with complementary disciplines and aims at forming value chains, for example those of designer, maker, and sales representative in circuits such as interior and product design, fashion, and software. If a crucial link is missing, external companies are invited to join. When tenants leave or grow within the location, Vechtclub remains in charge and safeguards the quality of the ecosystem. Meanwhile, the system is informed by practical support and financial advice, facilitated with catering and meeting spaces, and reinforced through matchmaking and both formal and informal programming to promote cross-pollination. Here, the activity of designing has taken on the more abstract form of designing and organizing urban ecosystems.

Vechtclub XL, Utrecht, the Netherlands

**A Sustainable Link for
a Healthy Urban District**

The Green Tower in the Amsterdam Bajeskwartier manifests itself in
a quite different domain. It is a fine illustration of the type of building that primarily results from an emphatic vision on a healthy urban
metabolism. The building is part of the redevelopment of the former
Bijlmer prison in the Bajeskwartier, an area that used to house a pen-
itentiary and is now being transformed into a neighbourhood of the
future. The Green Tower plays a crucial role in facilitating the sustainable performance of the area and in maximizing this performance in
the six domains that determine a healthy urban ecosystem.

In many respects the Green Tower is an attempt to develop and innovative building type from a metabolistic starting point. The tower
is the physical translation of the sustainability masterplan of the
Bajeskwartier and is also the direct result thereof. The idea is to lay
the foundation for a healthy urban metabolism in this neighbourhood
of the future. A metabolism that allows for circular flows of material
and the exchange of energy flows and mitigates the effects of climate
change. Also, the building promotes a healthy lifestyle, safeguards the
vitality of the local economy, and promotes cohesion and inclusivity.

The Green Tower is the only one of the six original prison towers
to remain standing, taking on an important cultural function of
cementing the memory of this place. The transformation of the former
women's tower provides space for both green nature and green technology, making the building a fine location for leisure and sports, catering,
and a number of technical innovations that support the neighbourhood in terms of energy and cicularity. As a building, the Green Tower
is in essence a smart vertical version of a city park, programmed with
functionalities that help the entire neighbourhood to become greener
and more sustainable. In order to achieve this the Green Tower is made
up of different functional layers, each one providing performance
improvements that benefit both the building itself and the surrounding
neighbourhood. The first layer consists of the green façade, the park,
which is made up of floors with observation posts, a climbing wall, an
air-purifying wall of plants, a food garden, a herb garden, and an open-
air recreational garden. Through it all there is a long yellow pedestrian
bridge that starts at street level and then meanders through the garden
to end at a panoramic terrace on the top floor, where a café serves the
food produced in the tower. In addition to food and cooling, the garden
also provides a basis for healthy ecological conditions in the neighbourhood, with a balanced mix of plants that attracts and houses birds and
insects. A second layer regulates water storage to combat both drought
and flooding. The water is captured in the upper open garden and distributed from there to a water treatment plant. The purified water can
then be used to irrigate the other gardens. Unpurified water is stored
in a basin below the building that is directly connected to the existing

canal. In the third layer, the tower functions as a circular hub. Waste flows that cannot be locally processed, such as plastics, glass, and general waste generated in the restaurant and café are carried off to be processed outside the tower. The organic waste from the catering is processed within the tower and used as compost for new food production. To properly manage the various flows one of the existing elevator shafts has been reserved for the supply and removal of waste flows. Another elevator shaft has been specifically designed for the logistics of the tower catering and the climbing hall. The maintenance of the machinery of Waste Transformers — where organic waste is converted into electricity, heat, and nutrients — is also facilitated by this shaft. In a fourth layer, the Green Tower also manifests itself as a heat and energy hub for the surrounding Bajeskwartier. Heat is partly obtained from the inner garden, which retains the heat of the sun in the greenhouse that is then used to heat up the rest of the tower. The tower also stores heat that is captured as residual heat from the datacentre and the surrounding neighbourhood. This is augmented by the energy flows from sun and wind from a power nest on top of the tower. These flows are then all redistributed across the neighbourhood, providing it with green power and heat. And so the Green Tower functions as food garden, recreational park, catering facility, electricity and heat hub, and as a recycling centre — a mix of functions that here is geared towards the local situation and possibilities but may be differently configured in other contexts. The building translates all kinds of large-scale performance agendas into a local level both around themes such as health and biodiversity and sustainability of energy production and use of resources.

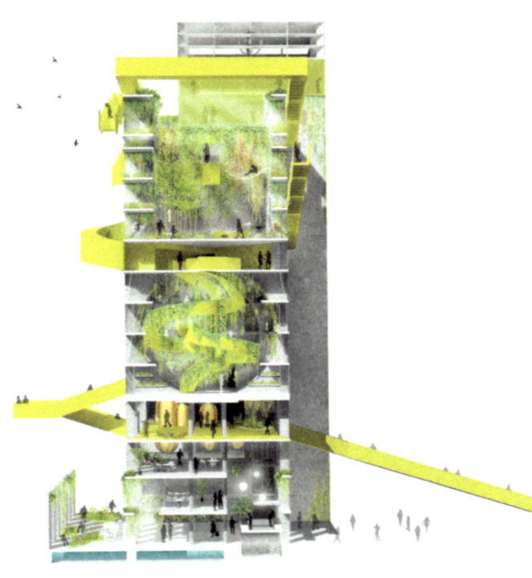

The Green Tower is a circular hub and a new urban typology, capable of producing energy and compost through the transformation of organic waste flows into plants

Also outside the busy urbanized environment design with an eye for the underlying system produces new typologies. Agriculture will have to change considerably in the light of the nitrogen problem and climate goals and this leads to different organizations and technological innovations that create an adapted rural image. The towers of Carbyon for instance, can be placed in the landscape for air capture of CO_2 to clean up our atmosphere, by means of a continuously rotating drum that consists of activated carbon fibers.

Livestock population will inevitably have to shrink in the years to come, but the demand for protein will not change. In a provocative

Rotating drums for capturing CO2 as will become fixtures in our landscape

Those Vegan Cowboys produce milk from grass, without the need for cows

projection of a future animal-farming-without-animals, Those Vegan Cowboys — a start-up company with the purpose of designing affordable and scalable technology that can be used to turn the corner on climate change — envisions a sort of robot cow looking more like a tower than a benign grazer in the landscape as a new producer of our cow milk products

Less provocative is the realization that fewer farm animals will inevitably lead to even more vacancy of farms. In Tilburg, a group of young designers formed a study group about the issue of this vacancy and the possible answers to it. Interesting in this regard is the project by Siddhartha Gautam, who thought hard about the growing possibility of robotic applications in agriculture and came up with a proposal for a more focused, less large-scale, and more effective agriculture that anticipates in a more direct and flexible manner the needs of local consumers. To this end, an agricultural area in the south of the Netherlands is restructured and drones, robots, and autonomous vehicles are used to work the land in a local-demand-driven way, catering to the market in a very focused manner. As such, it is an exponent of what is called 'precision farming'. The idea is to create a local circular agriculture that minimizes waste and matches supply and demand practically seamlessly. This also means renouncing large-scale agriculture in favour of a much more precise alternative with far less overproduction and waste of resources. Such a structure requires a landscape plan that is also determined by other parameters than those that apply to large-scale agriculture. As drones are the logistical bases in this design, the range of this means of transport is a determining factor for the scale of the operation. In addition, the plan assumes a production that is driven by the demands of individual households in the surroundings in terms of size and type of crop. This means that the monoculture in the landscape is replaced by a large variety of crops in the fields. The use of drones and robots also requires new technical devices in the field: charging stations, solar fields, and wind turbines. Empty farmhouses will be used as the base for automated agricultural workers and for storage, but also for educational purposes and social meeting places, giving the farmland a mix of functions.

Precision farming: the blue circles around vacant buildings represent the 200m coverage radius of agricultural drones

One alternative answer to the question of a different use of agriculture compared to the current mono-cultural production landscape is the project of the hidden island IJsselmonde near Rotterdam. This project addresses a number of landscape related challenges all in one go: subsidence, salinization, and producing food for the world market. IJsselmonde, better known as South Rotterdam is the most densely populated island in the Netherlands, but it doesn't feel like an island at all. In addition, the area is under threat. Its special location in the river delta makes it vulnerable to climate change. The sea level is rising, the Maeslantkering that is supposed to protect it needs to be replaced, and the salt water is increasingly penetrating the groundwater and freshwater sources. A projection for the year 2120 transforms the island of IJsselmonde in a group of islands: the IJsselmonde Archipelago. In this future scenario, measures to adapt to climate change will make the hidden islands of IJsselmonde more visible. Each island has its own character and identity and together they reinforce each other as a whole. The islands will be connected by ritual transitions, experiential connections that make the island dwellers aware of their 'islandership'. The newly created edges of the islands will be developed into various types of places to stay where contact with the water takes central stage. For example, one place will be densified with new houses on a super dike, while in another place a soft fringe is created with space for recreation and biodiversity. The new amorphous dam around the archipelago protects the islands from the rising sea level and the water buffer between the islands increases the archipelago's capacity for storing freshwater. People live, work, travel, and enjoy leisure activities on and near the water. This actively integrates the water into the daily lives of the residents and the project connects, in a smart way, the systemic challenges to the spatial ambition of enhancing the currently lacking island feeling.

In order to develop such projects effectively designers have to engage in a number of additional activities that, again, are closely related to analyzing, critically evaluating, and innovative imagining metabolic urban systems. Initially, this comes down to adding an analytical layer.

In making an urban plan it is obvious to thoroughly understand and include the surrounding spatial system, to make sure that streets line up neatly, cables and conduits can be connected, but also to make sure that daylight can enter into apartments and that space is made available for work, commerce, living, and education. In the future, designers must not only inform themselves of the various principles of generating and distributing energy, but should also be able to translate waste production profiles into local processing techniques and learn how urban extensions cannot only be *built* in a circular way, but can also be *used* in that way. This includes an analysis of waste and residual flows, but also, for example, knowledge of measures for mitigating the effects of noise pollution, air pollution, and flooding. These are challenges and required skills that must be added to the initial task in order to realize the goal: designing spatial quality on a whole range of systemic tasks.

While addressing the systemic challenges of land subsidence, salinization, and food production, the IJsselmonde group of islands will attempt to mitigate the effects of climate change, as well as provide spaces for people to live, work, and play

HERE I STAY, TRACING, CHANGING

Photography by Roosje Verschoor

HOFOR

BLOMDAHL
THAT FEELING
AAG
A WORLD
GULD KÖPES
AURORA BOREALIS
IN LAPLAND
Handla
med omtanke
PETER RO

D
MENS JEWELLERY
BY AAGAARD
C. O. Persson
SCHALINS
RINGAR
SCHALINS
OF SWEDEN
NYHET
LARS
WALLIN

SAMPLES AVAILABLE
IN THE SHOWROOM

9995AN000 029
9995AN000 029

lding

€ 9   935 DOP 004   (218,5 x 81,5cm)
€ 9   935 DOP 004 (218,5 x 81,5cm)
999 DOP 676
2 B (220 x 82 cm)
€ 61   999DOP592 B   (220 x 82 cm)
(224 x 85 cm)
€ 59   999DOP534 A   (224 x 85 cm)
€ 59   999 DOP 615   (223 x 87,5 cm)
(223 x 87,5 cm)
€ 99   946 DOP 006   (209 x 88 cm)

ding

TOTAL

MIDDENEN

METABOLIC BY DESIGN

A Conversation with Daniel Ibañez

The Forest City project, near Libreville, Gabon, Daniel Ibanez, Vicente Guallart and Ali Basbous, 2019

Daniel Ibañez is an urbanist and architect. Originally from Spain, he is now based in Cambridge in the US. He is a Doctor of Design from the Harvard University Graduate School of Design.

Daniel is director of the Master in Mass Timber Design and co-director of the Master in Advanced Ecological Buildings and Biocities at the Institute for Advanced Architecture of Catalonia. In addition, he is senior consultant at the World Bank on sustainable construction and urban development and research associate at the Urban Theory Lab Chicago and the Harvard Office of Urbanization. Daniel's overall research critically seeks to frame the design disciplines in relation to broader socio-ecological interdependencies through cross-disciplinary studies in the field of urban metabolism. In his publication *Wood Urbanism: From the Molecular to the Territorial* (2019) he and his co-authors explore the broader metabolic implications of the growing interest in timber as a building material: what it means for forestry regimes, for landscapes in harvesting areas, or for climate adaptation, among more.

Ibañez stresses the idea that all building presupposes an unbuilding, an extraction, elsewhere. His research thus has a global lens and follows, and critiques, the full cycle of building materials, from mine to building to dump. He is a strong advocate of biobased building in a mono-material way as an important tool of dealing with the effects of climate change.

In the following conversation, Eric and Daniel discuss these issues in some depth, touching on what they mean for design practices and for architectural aesthetics. In their discussion, Daniel critically reflects on the understanding of the urban area as a system, as a machine or an organ, and tells us what can be learned from trees in our approach of the city.

ERIC FRIJTERS Hi Daniel, great to have this conversation. We have to talk about a lot of things. As you know, studies on urban metabolism are very diverse and there are many approaches to it. Maybe we can talk a little bit about the idea of the city as a system. A critical understanding of urban metabolism has always been recognized by design disciplines to shape spatial strategies. You've referred to Patrick Geddes' Valley Section, or to the megastructures of the Japanese Metabolists. Confined to the regional scale historically, today's generalized urbanization is characterized by an unprecedented complexity and planetary upscaling of metabolic relations. To do this, designers need new ways of acquiring information and then transform this into relevant knowledge to be made productive in

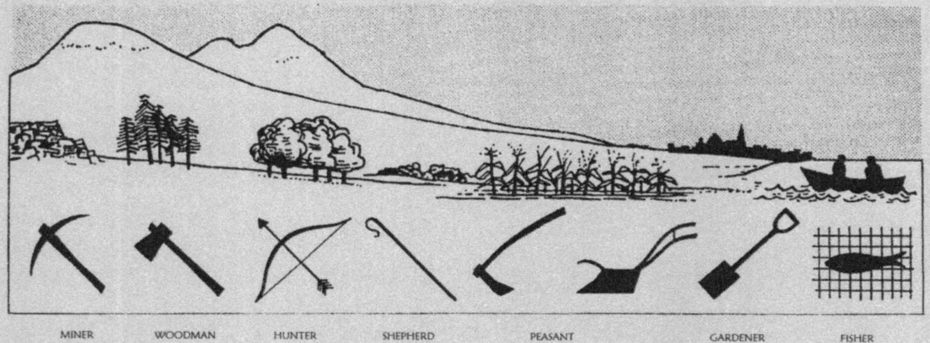

Patrick Geddes, *Valley Section*, 1909

the context of making city. I see a new type of practice emerging, as well as new working territories. In other words, the city is literally invading areas that it could not invade before, and we need spatial planning to guide that process. An example of this is the urbanization of the North Sea. Since there is no space left on land to build entire urban systems, some parts are now projected on sea. Where before this space was only used for biota and fishery, now it hosts the production of energy and agriculture as well. Besides new working areas, designers are also involved in developing new products. In order to frame the performance of 'spatial masterplans', we now also need 'sustainability masterplans'. And to be able to mine the city for circular design, we need to have insight in what's in store. This is where material passports appear. These transitions expect new expertise in designing buildings, cities, and landscapes. And with these new insights new actors are required and probably new aesthetics as well. But before we go there, let us start with introducing you and your area of research.

DANIEL IBAÑEZ

In general, in my work I try to understand the interdependencies that are associated with the way we build. Basically, I try to examine what is the role of design in regulating how materials and energy flows circulate, metabolize, and in turn, produce the urban. In my practice and research (I can't detach those two things) it is impossible to think about design and construction of a building in one particular location, without considering, what I call the 'metabolic interdependencies' of design. In other words, all the material (and energy) processes that are involved in the production of buildings and cities. This requires working at the intersection between two fields of knowledge: design and urban metabolism. But instead of acting like a designer who moves away and tries to become an urban ecologist fascinated by these 'upstream' interdependencies, my role has always been to learn from this field of knowledge to articulate a project for the design disciplines. Furthermore, I research the disciplinary implications of these metabolic interdependencies for the methods, boundaries, aesthetic propositions, and typologies of design.

Planetary Urbanization

EF — From a theoretical perspective, may this also be nested in contemporary discussions on planetary urbanization?

DI   In order to understand the world, you need to have a theoretical framework to look through. The way you look at things affects the way you operate and intervene in the world. Indeed, the theoretical framework I have embraced is this idea of planetary urbanization. This framework has been fundamental in my work as research associate at the Urban Theory Lab. This framework proposes something very simple and radical at the same time. When we talk about urbanization processes, we normally refer to very specific typologies of agglomeration, a.k.a.

'cities', when in reality, urbanization is a much bigger process that involves the operationalization of landscapes of production, infrastructures of connectivity, that are as important as the moment of agglomeration.

I am not sure if you are familiar with the work of Inostroza and Zepp.[1] These urban geographers have been working on connecting 'urban metabolism' to 'planetary urbanization'. Basically, they are saying that, today, planetary urbanization recognizes five types of urbanization patterns from a metabolic perspective. Their work depicts planetary urbanization as a vascular movement of material and energy flows in one direction with capital flows circulating in the opposite one. First, 'extended urbanization', which consists in all the territories we need to activate to extract the resources to keep cities running. These are agricultural fields, forests, mines, and so on. Another type of urbanization fabric is 'differential urbanization', which consists in those types of urban agglomerations that are created in relation to an extended urbanization pattern. For instance, a mine would be the extended urbanization pattern, that is supported by a mining town nearby, mostly for workers that go to and from the mine. In their view, it has some basic ingredients of a 'city', but not all: differential urbanization is a type of pattern that is specifically supporting extended urbanization patterns. Third, Inostroza and Zepp define 'accumulative urbanization', which is what we typically refer to as cities. It refers to relatively dense urban centres, that bring all the different resources, flows of materials and capital together. It accumulates and recirculates them, as a central hub in the metabolism of planetary urbanization. This is what I like to call a metabolic vortex, the place where all these materials and capital flows are orchestrated and circulate through. Two other types of urbanization patterns are relevant in their account. One is 'cascade urbanization' which are highly specialized urban patterns that are in service of mostly one sector of the economy. Think, for instance, of car manufacturing. In order to fabricate cars, you need specific types of urban factories associated with the manufacturing of tires, steering wheels, or window shields. This urbanization pattern is created and characterized by the manufacturing of this particular commodity. That is very unique from a metabolic standpoint, as the type of material and energy flows in and out of those types of urbanization patterns is very specific. And then they also signal a fifth one, which is 'speculative urbanization'. These urbanization patterns are simply a way of fixing surplus capital. This considers all the speculative, and in most cases uninhabited, developments that we find in the Middle East. These are 'cities' not characterized by a specific function in the overall planetary metabolic system, but just accumulated capital in the form of buildings, and urban infrastructure. This view helps to explain the different metabolic roles of very distinct planetary urbanization patterns beyond the undifferentiated and generic notion of 'the city'. It is important to highlight the dialectics in the work of planetary urbanization between these areas of intense urban agglomeration and the vast landscapes that are operationalized in support of, and as a result from them. In simple terms, this view helps us understand that every time you build something, you are unbuilding something elsewhere. Every time you are constructing a landscape, you are destroying another landscape elsewhere.

Every time you are constructing a landscape, you are destroying another landscape elsewhere.

EF — Does this dialectical relation install a theoretical lens only?

DI   No, I want to use it as a generative aspect for design. I want to make sure that as a design teacher, I also train a generation of designers that are enabled to understand the way the world operates today. I teach them to use this knowledge as generative material for their projects. I think that's going to fundamentally reshape practice and the way we are thinking of cities. One example is how many metabolic functions with their associated buildings and urban patterns that once abandoned 'the city', will return. For instance, contemporary urban debates call for more productive cities that incorporate energy and food production, manufacturing, waste management, and so on, within the city fabric. All of a sudden, this return of metabolic functions to the urban front stage will end up with a series of new typologies. One project I personally like along these lines is the New Corktown project by Albert Pope and Jesús Vassallo, presented at the Venice Biennale 2018 and featured in the Wood Urbanism book. This project for Detroit provides multiple density housing solutions made fundamentally out of mass timber. As a carbon storing material, mass timber creates an interesting metabolic relationship with the environment by removing and sinking atmospheric carbon in the form of buildings. However, it is particularly interesting that these carbon deposits are inserted together with the plantations and industries required to produce them. The overall urban proposal brings back some of those external landscapes

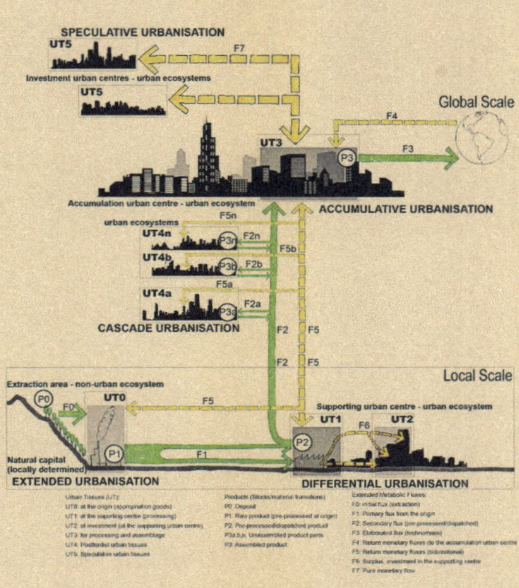

A metabolic urban network by Inostroza and Zepp

supporting construction that are typically located elsewhere. So, the interesting thing here for me is, that the urban design proposal combines, very effectively, landscapes of metabolic production, transformation, and consumption as a new form of urbanism.

EF — It would be great to see more factories, more Fab Labs, more decentralized technologies, more laboratories.

DI I think this is obviously something that is emerging, and it will happen more and more. Modernity brought us separation and upscaling of many metabolic functions: infrastructures of pipes went underground, and all the factories and production territories were moved away from urban agglomerations without accounting for the deep environmental consequences of a globalized planetary metabolism. In this sense, I think we are in a moment of scaling down many of these global processes, bringing factories a little bit closer, bringing those productive landscapes closer together.

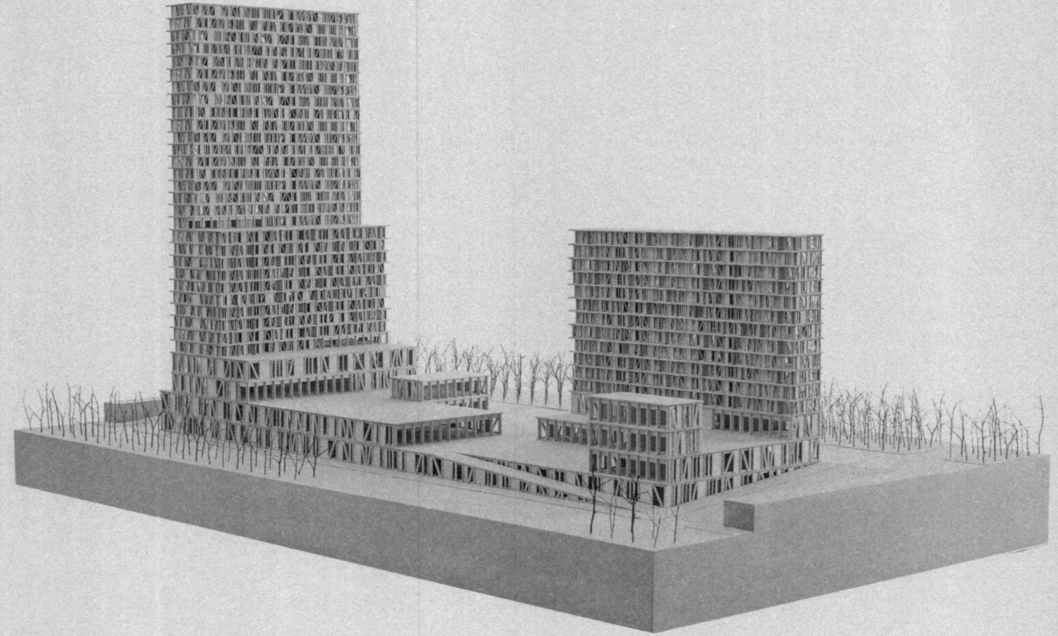

Model of a superblock using cross-laminated timber construction. A speculative project by Present Future for Detroit's riverfront, New Corktown, 2016

Marx and the Fundamentals
of Metabolism

EF — So now we have set the table, let's return to the idea of the city as a system and the field of urban metabolism.

DI I think designers have been quite good at using analogies and metaphors in order to describe the complexity of the built environment and the complexity of cities. There are many metaphors that we have historically used to this end. We have the city as an 'organ', the city as a 'system', the city as the 'machine'. What I found very interesting was the tension between the organic and the more systemic approaches to understanding the city. The first organic metaphors appear from biology and ecology trying to depict the city as an organ. In later evolutions of the metaphor, the city was subdivided in particular functions becoming multiple organs: the lungs, arteries and heart, the stomach, and so on. And all those processes depicted cities as organic superbodies taking huge amounts of resources, metabolizing and generating all kinds of outputs. In this organic notion, every piece of the city and its functions plays a fundamental role for survival. However, it was Howard T. Odum who moved this metaphor from an organic to a systemic conception. In his view, the city as a system means that each of its different components can self-regulate. As such, each one has a certain autonomy despite being nested within a larger system.

EF — So, cities are not collapsing after removing one part of it. But why is this tension between the systemic and the organic so relevant to you?

DI   This revelation is particularly interesting because architecture and any urban intervention have their own metabolic agency as opposed to being a particular function within a larger body. In all cases I'm more inclined to understand that tension as an incentive to articulate this as a combination of both organic and systemic. There are certain things that have autonomy and are self-regulating but they also all respond to the organicist principle of metabolized resources and energy, and transforming them into products and waste.

EF — I like how you make us understand the city as half organic, half systemic. This cyborg version of the urban analogy between the city and the human body tells us that they both have infrastructures, and every flow has its own infrastructure, and every infrastructure facilitates a different speed. But besides this similarity, there is also a huge difference. We know that our body hosts a metabolism of approximately 7400 chemical reactions. We have completely mapped it. But in cities, we cannot explain even one of the processes and completely describe them as a flow from source to stock. The question is, would this not be a good time, since we now have the technology, to start understanding cities in a similar way?

DI   I love the challenge that you are posing in the sense that, now everybody is carrying a phone, everybody is tracked. We have sensors to measure almost every material and energy flow. In this era of massive digital data there are a huge number of 'particles' emitting information everyday through cities, which could be providing data to us to fully map out the metabolism of cities and urbanization processes. It is going to be exciting times from that perspective...

EF — Besides the argument that we finally have the technology to understand cities more thoroughly, there is also a more intrinsic motivation to work on mapping the full complexity of metabolic pathways: a new layer of challenges dropped on top of our cities. We are not only supposed to live, work, and recreate in cities, but we now realize that these places should perform in a way that produces sustainable energy, that they are built within a circular framework and that they mitigate the effects of climate change for instance. In *New Geographies 06: Grounding Metabolism* [2014] you aim to trace alternative, synthetic routes to design through a more elaborate understanding of the relation between models and concepts of urban metabolism and the formal, physical, and material engraving of metabolic processes across scales. Could you take us there from the beginning and start with the introduction to this idea of Marx's metabolic rift?

DI   When writing *Das Kapital* Karl Marx was basically starting to realize that cities were importing a lot of materials from the countryside, and that basically all the waste regenerated was going elsewhere and not returning the nutrients back to the soil where they came from. This situation, in his view, was creating a rift in the metabolism between the countryside and the city. A process that is still at the core of the metabolism of cities today. The consequence is that cities now rely not only on the nearby countryside, but on a 'planetary countryside' that is situated all over the planet. In order words, the metabolic rate of urbanization is now upscaled, becoming faster and growing at a high pace. This accelerated and far-reaching metabolism is directly responsible for the ecological crisis of our time. So, leaving aside the more political aspects to it, what can we do as designers to address those metabolic rifts of urbanization?

As McKenzie Wark would say: 'The city layer is one continuous planetary city. It has a doubled structure. For every shiny metropolis there's an anti-city of warehouses and waste dumps.'

EF — Every time I use resources, I extract those at another place. Additionally, any metabolic perspective needs a moral compass to find the right balance in defining and deciding what parts or our planet should be optimized, and what parts of the world should be compromised?

DI   Urban political ecology is a field of research looking at urban metabolism in a radically different way. Building upon Marx earlier conceptualizations on the metabolic rift, these ecologists state that the capitalist mode of production is basically a process investing in extracting profit at all costs and, as a by-product, it generates systemic uneven development. As McKenzie Wark would say: 'The city layer is one continuous planetary city. It has a doubled structure. For every shiny metropolis there's an anti-city of warehouses and waste dumps.' I think that when we use metabolism as a lens to look at the urban, we are shown the complexity of an ecological-like system, together with the mediation of power. Designers should be aware of this and really try to engage with power, with politics, with the political as a way also of attempting to fix many of the rifts of contemporary urbanization processes.

The Need for Urban Feedback-Loops

EF —Can you give us a few ideas on how designers can tap into this?

DI   If you take a natural organism like a tree, it will tend to do three things. First, it will maximize energy intake absorbing as much nutrients and sun radiation as possible. Second, it will do it in the fastest possible way. Thus far, if you think about it, it is very similar to what cities and urbanization processes in general tend to do: use as much material as possible to build and grow as fast as possible. The big difference is the third component. Natural systems try to create the best feedback reinforcements possible. That means that the tree takes all that energy at the fastest rate possible to reinforce itself: the tree grows even taller, has more leaves, has more ramification, in order to get more energy and have a more powerful metabolism, which in the long term is going to enable that tree to have what is called a maximum power design. In other words, to reach a point where the tree maximizes the material and velocity of intake and generates the maximum amount of reinforcing feedback loops. Cities are very good at doing the first two but not the third one. As designers involved in the orchestration of a city's material and energy intakes, we should learn to move away from engulfing materials and energy flows in a non-reinforcing feedback loop, in favour of ecologically powerful ones.

EF —And that is what you want to illustrate in your book *Wood Urbanism: From the Molecular to the Territorial* — these feedback loops?

DI   Yes. The promise of wood as a construction material resides in this possibility. If properly done, wood becomes a material to build cities, and build them fast, but most importantly, it can do it while creating reinforcing feedback-loops. For instance, according to scientists and ecologists, the more timber we harvest from the forest and store in buildings (in a sustainable way), the more CO_2 we are removing from the atmosphere, again creating a powerful symbiotic feedback loop. Through harvesting we enable the forest to keep growing and optimize the capacity of forests to capture CO_2. At the same time, we create housing solutions with the biomass extracted from it for people to dwell. So, again, the more material we use in an appropriate manner, the better it could be for the environment, the better for us. So, this to me is a good example of this feedback reinforcement logic.

But there are other variations of feedback. The type of forest could be another one. By using multiple wood species in buildings, we ensure a diverse demand too. The risk of building with one or two species of trees might only create monoculture plantations. A good example of this specification process is the High School in New Haven by Gray Organschi.

Common Ground High School in New Haven, USA

Yet another interesting feedback loop comes from this idea of the pulsing cycles. This was also developed by the Odum brothers. They said that in a natural system we don't tend to a steady state, rather it operates through a combination of equilibrium and disturbance. For instance, a forest fire that partially destroys some trees enables a new generation to regrow. So, pulsing cycles are actually the norm. One of the research questions on the book was: can we productively design with this pulsing cycle in mind? One example: due to climate chance, British Columbia has been suffering from a pine beetle infestation. This bug infests the sap of the tree and kills it. While trees are dead, their structural properties as a material remain intact. What can be done? Not harvesting these trees means letting them decay and release the CO_2 stores back into the atmosphere. Conversely, it can trigger a response to build as much as possible in the fastest way possible before it decays, thus creating a reinforcing feedback loop between wood buildings and their material sourcing landscapes, the woods.

EF — So, this way of disaster mining is somehow a way of dealing with setbacks. Are there other ways for looping feedback and do you have examples where they are put to practice?

DI   Disaster mining is a beautiful expression of a creative and ecologically powerful feedback loop. There is an interesting project by Tezuka Architects in Japan, also featured in the book, who talk about disaster mining. Among the tsunami effects of 2011, a series of centenary trees got their roots flooded, and consequently they died. However, as in the case of the infested trees of British Columbia, the timber, as a material structure, remained uncompromised. Rather than being apologetic and letting these magnificent trees decay, these architects decided to use them to create a kindergarten nearby. The beauty of this feedback loop was both ecological and social. On the ecological side, by using these trees as structural material it provided them with a second life while retaining the CO_2 previously stored by them. On the social side, it provided a space with double use, as a kindergarten for kids and a refuge for the community from future tsunamis. To me, this symbiotic approach is a brilliant way of dealing with the inevitability of human- and non-human-made pulsing cycles.

EF — Does a feedback loop in this process of three stages always involve wood?

DI   In addition to maximum power design, which involves these three

Disaster mining: a chapel and a kindergarten by Tezuka Architects in Japan. An example of circular building

stages you mention — maximizing intake, velocity, and feedback reinforcement — I have articulated another line of thought derived from cell metabolism studies: autophagy. Which is a very different process. Any organism looking to survive must sustain its metabolism. This applies as much to cells as to cities. A surplus in this metabolic process generally results in the opportunity for the organism to grow and reproduce. However, under periods of starvation (caloric restriction/energy intake), cells switch to the metabolism of repair and internal autophagy. They invest in recirculating and 'feeding on' already stored energy and cellular debris to increase metabolic efficiency. As a survival machine, individual organisms are 'designed' to sustain, at all costs, their metabolism. And they do it by switching from one profile (growth) to another (autophagy). This is why, these days, some people are fasting, in order to activate that process of cleaning their body and losing some weight.

These days, you can find more copper in cities than in any other place on the planet. Which means that cities have become huge markets and huge stocks of materials that they now accumulate. Rather than relying on the harvesting of virgin materials from faraway geographies, why not use the materials that we have accumulated? What if we can truly shift from a linear metabolism of external extraction, transportation, production, accumulation, and waste generation to a circular metabolism of internal repair and retrofit? And what would that involve for designers? What would it mean to design in a way that whenever the obsolescence of that building has to occur, we disassemble the components and reassemble them elsewhere? I think it is an exciting set of questions that should be fully embraced by design. But this shift requires to be aware of the full material ecology involved in the process of building a building or a part of a city.

Any organism looking to survive must sustain its metabolism. This applies as much to cells as to cities.

EF —Daniel, you just provided three ideas about how to create these larger feedback loops considering carbon footprints, the idea of pulsing cycles, and the idea of internal metabolic feedbacks, that I think could change the paradigm of building at the expense of unbuilding, or demolishing elsewhere. In that sense, I learned that things have changed over the last few years in the Netherlands. Cities are organizing tenders that promote circular buildings and neighbourhoods that are not only built in a circular fashion, but are triggering circular behaviour with end users as well. That means designing environments that create opportunity for inhabitants and entrepreneurs to feed on residual flows, for instance.

DI   The important point here to me is that we need to transition from a paradigm of efficiency to a paradigm of creating powerful and symbiotic relationships with the environment. Most efficiency-driven paradigms are based on a very narrow system boundary. In other words, only considering a small set of 'externalities', and generally creating efficiencies only at one point of the process (the building, at the expense of other geographies). This is a big oversight. This is why we need all these different approaches we discussed above. Because they are embracing the full breath of 'externalities' by casting a large system boundary at multiple scales. There is no other way of making truthful claims about circularity.

Let me give an example of the importance of accounting for the full metabolism of design. In Barcelona, I direct a Master's programme that is called Master in Advanced Ecological Buildings and Biocities, at Valldaura Labs campus, at the Institute for Advanced Architecture of Catalonia. The final project of this programme entails the construction of a small advanced ecological prototype in our forest campus near Barcelona. Last year, we developed a small mass timber house to function as a quarantine cabin: where an individual could live off-grid in isolation for fourteen days. The uniqueness of this project is that, as opposed to just create some drawings and renderings as most architectural schools would do, our students go through the entire design and building process, from sourcing the materials to construction and the management of waste. They are responsible for the wood harvesting: selecting, cutting down and processing trees, dimensioning and drying the timber and creating their own custom-made cross-laminated timber (CLT) panels to be later assembled into the final building. The same process applies for most of the design components of the cabin. Our students design not just an architectural object, but the full metabolism of forming that object. For them, the so-called 'externalities' of the project become 'internalities.' In other words, the phases of extraction,

Solar greenhouse: a prototype for self-sufficient farming

processing, transportation, and waste management are integral parts of design as much as building per se. The nice thing about our projects is that students can pinpoint and correlate each panel of the cabin with the tree and its previous location in the forest. Or create powerful feedback loops by using offcuts from dimensioning timber into beautiful parametric rainscreen envelopes. For us this programme provides a representation of the full metabolism involved in doing any project, but at a small scale. Teaching a generation of architects who design having this metabolic mindset is critical for the challenges of our time.

Metabolic Footprint

EF — Why is that kind of precision relevant?

DI — In my research, it is of importance to measure the full metabolism from the emissions to the material traceability associated with construction. We can only manage and design what we can measure. I think that knowing where things were harvested, what tools and machinery are needed, how energy-intensive is to process them, who was involved, how far away did they come from, are all relevant. Modernity has been very good at hiding these processes. It is our responsibility to be mindful about them now that we are aware of the environmental consequences of not accounting for them.

EF — Is this a demasking of modernism in your opinion?

DI — In my view, modernism has exacerbated two things: the complete fragmentation of all the commodities associated with a building and black boxing of the processes that support urban life. How many types of material can a building have? Imagine a section of a generic building and ask yourself: how many layers does the wall have? You'll find the rainscreen, the insulation, the air gap, the water barrier, the structure, the interior cladding, the finishing, and so on. Now imagine how each of those layers translates to larger geographies with their associated factory, sourcing landscapes and transportation distances. These construction commodities travel through vast metabolic networks in order to accumulate in one place. Besides how good or ecological these commodities are, which is crucial, we also know that the multiplying transportations and upscaling distances are environmentally problematic. Therefore, I wonder if it wouldn't be better to build with less materials that do more functions in a more powerful way. A good example discussed in the book is, for instance,

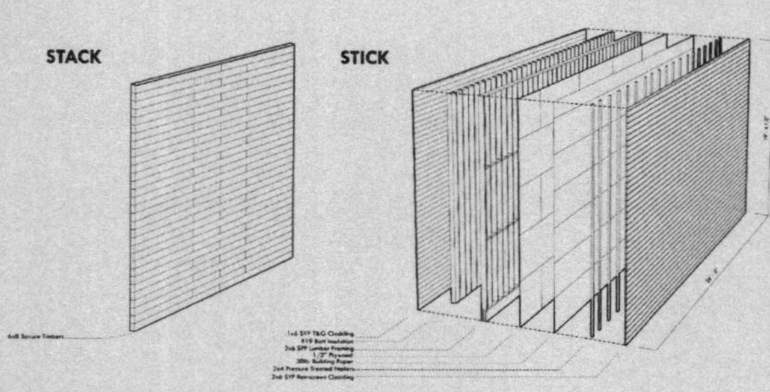

Wood as a monomaterial

the potential of wood as a monomaterial. A piece of mass timber can function as structure, insulation, interior finishing, furniture, and exterior cladding, all at once. You can potentially have all the functions required in a wall section covered with one thick layer of this material. A good example of this approach featured in the book is the Svartlamoen housing building in Norway. You see a CLT wall bearing the loads, helping to insulate, being the interior finishing, the counter. From a metabolic perspective, it is a powerful design. Somebody can argue that from a thermal perspective performance may not be optimal. And they may be right. But a design fully accounting for the overall metabolic power of a monomaterial building versus another one made with a multitude of layers that are contaminating through long and multiple transportation chains and built with fossil-fuel intensive materials, is going to be orders of magnitude worse. In that sense, for me, measuring and mapping the geographical specificity, metabolic networks, and emissions associated with the materials and components with which we build is extremely relevant. Another example, a bit nostalgic, is the project of Peter Zumthor for the Swiss pavilion in the Hannover Expo of 2000. Do you know that he was making a massive accumulation of timber, designed for disassembly and future use? I think that project points towards this logic of mono-materiality too, one material that is able to do a lot of work, rather than relying on multiple ones.

Svartlamoen residential building in Trondheim, Norway

EF — You mentioned two pillars related to modernism, right? The first one is critiquing the fragmenting of resources, but what about black boxing?

DI   Yes, if the previous helps to explain this schizophrenic multiplication of worldwide commodities, the black boxing refers to the fact that modernism has created a bubble that prevents us from understanding these metabolic interdependencies. Modernism is black boxing. It is based on a metabolic rift. Paradoxically, while it feeds on more materials and energy flows, at higher rates, and coming from further and further away, citizens live in eco-bubbles (ecologically premium enclaves, as Marvin and Hodson would say) that obscure the dirty, smelly, undesired, uneven, exploitative processes that, for the most part, support urban life.

Vernacular Design

EF — This leads me to all sorts of questions that would distract us from our goal. Because I'm now wondering, how would people in the Arctic build? They probably build with snow, right?

Architecture without architects: windcatchers in Hyderabad, India

DI   I think you are right! I want to note that the work I'm doing with wood is, for the most part, regionally specific.

EF — I think a metabolic approach to making a city has this unique quality to amplify local identities. Because if it's really metabolic, you'll probably make use of local ways, local resources, local partners, local habits, and consequently more local characteristics, I suppose. I sometimes use this image from Bernard Rudofsky's.[2] *Architecture Without Architects*, which is basically a book about design solutions that are very vernacular and extremely regionally specific. The image shows the old city of Hyderabad, where the skyline is dominated by hundreds of air chimneys, that give the place its unique characteristic. The roofscapes in the lower Sind district, where temperatures range from 35 to 50 degrees Celsius, channel the wind into every building, street, and courtyard. Since the wind always blows from the same direction, the position of the 'bad-gir' or windscoops is permanently fixed. The chimneys reach all the way down while transforming the wind to become an urban air conditioning and doubling as intramural telephones. Well, that city you can only make in that specific place, and that is truly metabolic to me. So, next to metabolic construction, you can also use the environmental characteristics of a city to create this very specific climate.

DI This is one of my favourite images, Eric, and brings back this super relevant point to me. I sometimes am asked whether I'm suggesting that we should return to nature and retreat into primitivism. I always reply that it is not really about retrenchment or a return to nature at all. Quite the opposite. I'm defending a maximal approach towards what we do. Maximal, but in a very mutually reinforcing way, not maximal at the expense of other things. It is maximal because it's really doing those three things that I was mentioning: intensity, the velocity, but also that reinforcement, those three dimensions are crucial.

Endesa Pavilion, Institute for Advanced Architecture of Catalonia (IAAC), Adria Gorta, 2011

We once did this prototype in the port of Barcelona. It was not only using one material, being wood, but also answered the question of how to apply design in a way that we could do a façade that was both active and passive. It was active because this façade module of timber enabled energy generation through the PV panels all year long. And it was passive because the geometry of the module enabled shade in summer and sun penetration in the interior in winter. In the context where we have forgotten many innovations that architecture developed for centuries before modernity, this simple design gesture is thermodynamically powerful, like the chimneys of Hyderabad that you were describing. We need to recuperate all this vernacular expertise; it's going to be crucial for the challenges lying ahead.

EF — What about the concept of aesthetics? I think any metabolic project requires a cultural change in order to be successful. It cannot be sustained only on basic strategies and proposals, but has to percolate through the citizens. This has to generate a new Gestalt, a new collective cultural project that really is one that triggers change.

DI   One of the things I've been very critical about in general is the simplified and generic statement that using timber equals being ecological. As expected, the timber industry is excited about the mass timber movement. At the end of the day, the systemic shift will benefit largely this industry. However, I think we cannot stop at simply swapping one materiality for another without a socio-ecological and socio-cultural change. Take for instance the example of SOM's Dewitt Chestnut Apartments project in the sixties in Chicago, a reinforced concrete building. The one you see on the right is the exact same building as the one of the left, but built completely as a timber structure.

Despite the fantastic engineering exercise proving that the technology is ready to build high-rise towers with timber, why does it look completely the same? Are we just really replicating the same cultural aesthetic paradigm of modernity despite the massive metabolic change it can offer? This makes no sense to me. As a provocation, I like to use radical antithetical examples. For instance, the project Spekulatius from my friends Yasmin Vobis and Aaron Forrest at RISD Ultramoderne where they propose these landscapes to be inserted in cities, as completely solid towers. This is not a tower of housing, it's completely filled with timber, a solid block, solely intended to store CO_2

SOM Dewitt's The Timber Tower Research Project and Dewitt Chestnut Apartments

from the atmosphere. A similar provocation applies to Anders Berensson Architects with their one km³ log pile called Bank of Norrland.

EF — That is rather provocative.

DI   Exactly. Now, I'm not suggesting this must be the way, but this is a provocation that really embraces those metabolic concepts and really triggers a different state of mind and a new aesthetic paradigm.

RISD Ultramoderne's Spekulatius project: a carbon storing skyscraper

The world's largest timber structure and the largest man-made carbon dioxide storage facility: The fictional 1 km³ log pile, Bank of Norrland by Anders Berensson

1   Luis Inostroza and Harald Zepp study urban ecosystems that perform a distinctive metabolism, appropriating fundamental materials and energy resources form other ecosystems. This appropriation enables a productive circularity, which sustains the material production of urban space. Upon entering the urban ecosystem, the material fluxes are processed by human labour to be consumed. Luis Inostroza and Harald Zepp, 'The Metabolic Urban Network: Urbanisation as Hierarchically Ordered Space of Flows', *Cities* 109 (February 2021).

2   Bernard Rudofsky was an Austrian American writer, architect, collector, teacher, designer, and social historian. His most notable work is *Architecture Without Architects: A Short Introduction to Non-pedigreed Architecture* (1964). He was most influential for organizing a series of controversial MoMA exhibits in the forties, fifties and sixties. He is best remembered today for a number of urban books that still provide a relevant design insight, concealed in entertaining, subversive sarcasm. His interests ranged from vernacular architecture to Japanese toilets and sandal design. Taken together, his written work constitutes a sustained argument for humane and sensible design.

The Changing Look of the City

Designers who start designing from the focus discussed in this book will come to new conclusions, which can take surprising forms. Those who start working on the physical content and design of the urban body with their sights set on the system will inevitably create a city with a different look. To illustrate this, let us compare two extremes: Michelangelo's *David*, and Graham from the Australian Transport Accident Commission. The Italian Renaissance grandmaster's marble sculpture is seen as the ideal of beauty and bodily perfection and as such as an imagination of the ideally designed city. The slender hero from the Old Testament radiates both force and intelligence and depicts the triumph of the minimally armed and armoured body over the annihilating force of the giant brute Goliath. Let us contrast him with Graham, who presents a quite different aesthetic experience. Graham was designed from system thinking. His head is large and almost as wide as his shoulders, to which it is directly attached. At the front, his ribs are protected by meat pockets that function as airbags. His skull is many times thicker than that of his pretty opposite and clad in a thick fleshy layer. Graham's legs not only bend backwards, but to all four sides, greatly reducing the risk of broken bones. Rather than slenderness and force, Graham projects an image of robustness and resilience. It is doubtful whether he would have been able to use the sling as forcibly and flexible as David to bring down Goliath, but he certainly would not feel much impact from David's sling himself. Nor from a blow by Goliath, for that matter. But then Graham was not designed to radiate strength himself but to be able to survive big physical blows. Graham is what human beings might look like if their bodies were completely adapted to survive serious traffic accidents. He is a visual thought experiment, and an example of how different a design will look if you start from a different type of question and let that question consistently prevail in all your design considerations. In Graham's case this question is a simple one. Graham's system is very good at one thing: taking blows. The system of a city is infinitely more complex and versatile and therefore more difficult to shape adequately. A body that can effortlessly process infinite amounts of water is of little use if it implodes when it catches a simple cold. However, Graham does demonstrate what the result of a different approach to the city could be and he illustrates perfectly that that city will look quite differently, feel quite differently, and will highlight quite different things than we are used to in a city.

Any design that takes a metabolic approach to make the city more resilient to the effects of climate change, use less materials and energy, and make it a better place for people to live, must do more than is currently being done. To keep the city healthy, it is not enough to cover it with a protective layer. A David with knee pads, a helmet, and boxing gloves will still not be able to deliver what we ask from the city. Yes, such a protective layer will definitely make the city a bit more resilient

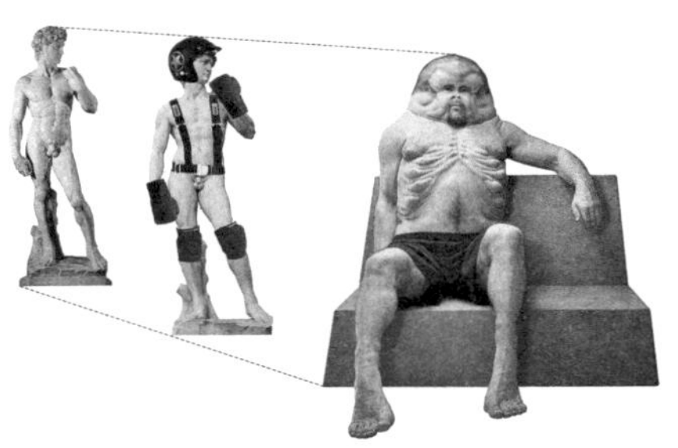

Michelangelo's *David*, 'David 2.0' and Graham

against blows to its own body but does not provide an integral approach, devised from the systemic structure of the city. And it will therefore not help in facing the big transition task either. A truly healthy city requires a different starting point, takes into account the whole system of flows, and is designed from thorough knowledge of all the six pillars of a healthy urban metabolism: the cycles of materials, a vital economy, healthy living, sustainable energy, flexible infrastructure, and sociocultural solidarity. Such a city must be both resilient and versatile and also perform as best it can on a constantly changing list of demands, values, and wishes of a great variety of residents, businesses, administrators, and users. On the one hand, this requires us to recognize and embrace the complexity of the city as a system and the hard to disentangle layers of the transition task. While on the other hand it requires openness with regard to the shapes and forms that are the result. That last aesthetic requirement may be even harder to stomach than the first one. Everyone wants a better performing city, but the aesthetic changes in our living environment may also cause quite a shock.

Function-driven Aesthetics: Clear Reason and Beyond

The fact that the look of the city changes because of the desired performance is of course not new. It is rather a constant since the eighteenth century. In the history of European cities, the ideals of the Enlightenment have been an important catalyst for architecture and city planning based on functionality. Providing houses is no longer enough. Cities should also promote justice and the health of its residents. In *L'An 2440, rêve s'il en fût jamais* (1770/1786) eighteenth-century Louis-Sébastien Mercier awakes from a sleep of centuries and finds himself in a dream image. He describes the city of the future: 'I was lost in vast and beautiful streets, all properly aligned. I entered spacious intersections so well ordered that I saw not a hint of obstruction. I heard none of those confusedly bizarre cries that once rent my ears. I encountered no vehicles ready to crush me. A blind man would have been able to walk easily. The city had an animated air, but without trouble or confusion.' Apparently, this was how an enlightened city looked: civilized, and promoting health and happiness. Filled with optimistic ideals of the Enlightenment, and an unshakeable confidence in the infinite power of human reason, designers began to make themselves heard and started to increasingly shape the city as they preferred it to be. Whereas before, cities would more or less be

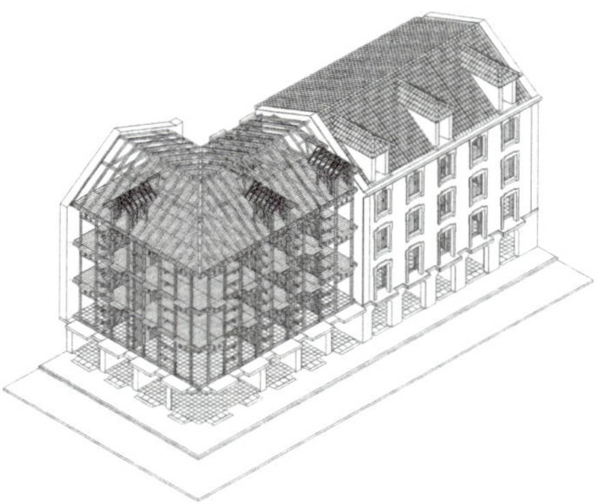

Pombaline cage construction with timber bracing system, used to earthquake-proof buildings in areas prone to seismic activity

formed organically in most regards, now reason, science, and technique opened up vistas of a better functioning city. This new organization came with a new aesthetics, one that was very much inspired by classical antiquity.

In cities such as Bordeaux, Nancy, and Lisbon, urban plans were realized that are somewhat reminiscent of Mercier's descriptions. Take, for example, the Baixa neighbourhood in Lisbon, rebuilt after the devastating earthquake of 1755. Planning and construction are an admirable, ingenious exercise in both organizational and scientific terms. Here arose an earthquake-proof district based on science, with fireresistant walls and buildings that are equipped with so-called Pombaline cages, wooden constructions that could distribute the forces unleashed by earthquakes. The walls not only contained flames but also dampened sound, improving health and sleep. And they brought privacy, now that residents could retreat behind these walls. Aesthetically speaking, the neighbourhood is characterized by a rational, methodical layout with grand public spaces and straight, orderly streets in a fashionable, classicist style. The result was a new, efficient, and safe district with a respectable image, heralding a new age for Lisbon.

Baixa de Lisboa, Lisbon, Portugal

A truly healthy city requires a different starting point, takes into account the whole system of flows, and is designed from thorough knowledge of all the six pillars of a healthy urban metabolism: the cycles of materials, a vital economy, healthy living, sustainable energy, flexible infrastructure, and sociocultural solidarity.

There were also other functions driving the urban transformation of the eighteenth and nineteenth centuries. The need to promote the distribution of knowledge among the population resulted in various new types of buildings: public theatres, libraries, and museums. Existing building types, such as hospitals, prisons, and courthouses were revised on the basis of new scientific insights. Another century later, modernism would give a new and decisive impulse to a reorganization of the city. This restructuring was indeed necessary, as industrialization and the progress made in healthcare resulted in an unprecedented population growth. Production methods were changing radically and a huge increase in scale took place. The working class grew and new political movements such as socialism and communism were on the rise. In 1901 the Housing Act was passed in the Netherlands, in response to the effects of a fast-growing urbanization and the concomitant rise of a growing group of poor urban dwellers in abominable living conditions. The Act outlined the importance of democratically established regulations and requirements with regard to public housing. For example, promoting the health of residents became an important requirement in the building and layout of homes. This transformed the look of the city. As more daylight had to enter apartments, the use of glass in Dutch cities increased exponentially. Also, industry and commerce grew and infrastructure also became a central task for designers as mobility drastically changed with the advent of the automobile.

In 1922, Le Corbusier presented his design for a Ville Contemporaine at the Salon d'Automne in Paris. His own description of entering this 'contemporary city' gives an impression of the spatial experience: 'Suppose we are entering the city by way of the Great Park. Our fast car takes the special elevated motor track between the majestic skyscrapers: as we approach nearer there is seen the repetition against the sky of the twenty-four skyscrapers; to our left and right on the outskirts of each particular area are the municipal and administrative buildings; and enclosing the space are the museums and university buildings

…. Then suddenly we find ourselves at the feet of the first skyscrapers. But here we have, not the meager shaft of sunlight which so faintly illumines the dismal streets of New York, but an immensity of space. The whole city is a Park.'[1] If Mercier envisioned a city in the far future, for the modernists this future was quite near. There was a huge social urgency, and all the progress made in science and industry also made it feasible that the city of the future would soon be pulled into the present.

Peter Behrens' Turbinenfabrik for the General Electric Company, Berlin, 1883

The longing for that new present was passionate and it came with a different form language. A new, rational aesthetics was in the making. In it, initially known architectural forms could still be recognized in a more abstract shape, such as the Turbinenfabrik by the architect Behrens, which featured pillars and a tympanum. Gradually, however, designs became more radical. New materials such as steel and concrete and the new machine-based production methods formed the basis of the modernistic aesthetics that made a clean break with the past. The founding manifesto of the Congrès Internationaux d'Architecture Moderne (CIAM) from 1929 stated: 'They [the CIAM architects] therefore refuse categorically to apply in their working methods means that may have been able to illustrate past societies; they affirm today the need for a new conception of architecture that satisfies the spiritual, intellectual, and material demands of present-day life.'

Not only in Europe did performance define the look of cities. And it wasn't always and everywhere that aesthetic innovations were driven by high-flown ideals. Besides, those ideals have taken quite a severe beating over the past century. The optimistic sense of the limitless progress that reason would bring has been tempered by an equally passionate criticism of that same rationality. Besides Western prosperity, industrialization turned out to have a serious drawback in the form of international economic inequality. The trumpeting of rational man was more and more emphatically muted and subjected to criticism of an anthropocentrically organized world in which the planet itself gets the worst of it and is meanwhile starting to rebel forcefully in the form of global warming, the rise of sea levels, desertification, and exhausted resources. The answer to these problems as well will give rise to new forms and different cities in which the sustainable use of natural resources and conditions will be crucial.

In terms of aesthetics, this development may also bring benefits. In a completely different context and area than described above,

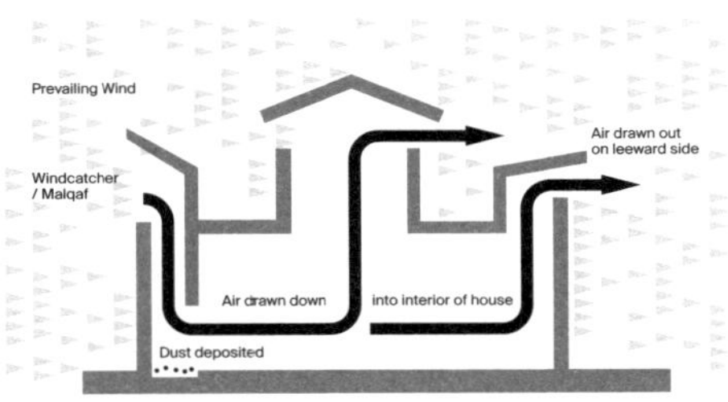

The principle of a wind catcher

Wind catchers in Yazd, Iran

the wind catchers of cities such as Hyderabad in Pakistan and Yazd in Iran — known in Sindhi and Urdu, respectively, as 'City of Wind Catchers' — are interesting realizations of a functional requirement leading to a specific aesthetic expression. In the street scenes of Hyderabad these wind catchers are prominently present as diamond-shaped pipes that catch the south-western evening breeze above the city during hot summers and bring them to street level to create a natural air-conditioning effect. Because they catch the winds as high as possible there is minimal influx of unwanted dust. In the winter time, when the winds have turned, the wind catchers function as heating by making use of the afternoon air that has been warmed by the sun. The architectural identity created by this technique is both unique and a decisive factor in the look of the city. In Yazd, where the winds do not always come from the same direction, the towers have a round structure, catching winds from different sides. In the extremely hot summers these wind flows are sometimes also led to cool underground water basins — sometimes filled with ice from nearby glaziers — where they vaporize the water and fill the living spaces with cooled air.

Producing Energy Is Not Discrete

The wind catchers form an interesting inspiration for the smart use of local natural conditions to create a healthy urban environment. They also prove that setting such a goal can result in an exciting aesthetic identity for cities. Therefore, designing with an eye to the functional requirements of the system is not necessarily at odds with appealing urban environments. On the contrary: the look of a city is always also already an effect of functional requirements. That does not change the fact that, for example, the sheer size of the current energy task also challenges designers aesthetically. The infrastructure of the energy network has always led to prominently present elements in the landscape with typical forms such as those of gas and pumping stations, and the gas and electricity networks. Whether green or brown, producing energy never happens discreetly. Power pylons are prominently present in the landscape and the smoking chimney stacks of incinerators can hardly be called subtle. But these parameters are currently changing considerably and the list of requirements is expanding. The aesthetic consequences of this therefore present themselves in various ways. This often leads to heated political debates, as in the case of wind turbines claiming a place in the landscape, frequently vehemently criticized by local residents. On the other hand, there are currently new buildings being designed — also as part of the new energy mix — that enrich the urban landscape both functionally and aesthetically.

One nice example of this is CopenHill, the waste-to-energy plant in Copenhagen, designed by BIG in 2017. This striking building doesn't look at all like you would expect from such a plant and it also has functions one does not usually associate with an incinerator. One eyecatcher is the oblique twisted and sloping roof of the plant, which has lodged itself in the city like a mountain. It also provides the leisure functions of a natural mountain: you can climb it, hike or walk across it, and ski down off it. Inside the plant of more than 40,000 m² the machinery has been organized in such a fashion that it fits perfectly inside a building with a sloping roof providing 10,000 m² of outdoor sports space and leisure activities. And so the industrial Amagar harbour suddenly has a sizeable hill in the otherwise flat Danish landscape; a hill that not only contributes clean energy and leisure facilities to the city, but also, thanks to the trees high up, provides it with cleaner air, better ecological circumstances, and heat mitigation. Thanks to this building there is suddenly room for forestation and greening in the midst of an industrial zone. The slope also has catering facilities and a centre for environmental education. Those who take the glass elevator up the mountain are treated to an educational look into a modern, climate-friendly energy plant. Because of this transformation, instead of a necessary building hidden at the edge of the city, a healthy relaxing and educational destination was created for families and athletes, making a cultural contribution to the city in a completely new way. Mixing functions goes hand-in-hand here with aesthetic and cultural enrichment, inspired by a circular and carbon-neutral agenda. The new infrastructure that is the result of realization of a progressive climate agenda, functions here as the catalyst for improving the urban conditions with regard to physical and social health, ecology, and circularity in a truly new form.

Local Aesthetics

The educational Food Forum pavilion designed by DoepelStrijkers for the Floriade Expo 2022 in Almere, Flevoland (NL) may be less spectacular and may not have the same spatial impact as CopenHill, but it too is a building that experiments with design based on performances in several areas. The result is a rather striking shape. The Pavilion stands four metres below sea level. That fact was visually processed by lifting a floor with a clay façade — a reference to the soil that used to be the sea bottom in this young province — up to sea level and placing it on top of the glass-enclosed ground floor. The building is both an educational and meeting space, while at the same time it is a test case for using recycled and bio-based building materials. Its aim is to be a knowledge centre about and visual translation and concrete realization of making various flows circular: water, energy, building material, waste, and food. An interesting aspect in this is that part of the furnishings and various elements of the building are leased, meaning that they are basically replaceable and are not assigned a permanent place in the building per se. For the use of materials that are not leased, not only the limitation of material application has been taken into account but also the possibility of reuse and dismantlement. All this makes for a building that provides a uniquely different expression both from within and from outside. The ample application of wood, the clay façade, and the use of recycled and fully recyclable concrete enriched with elephant grass for the floors on the first floor result in a clear identity.

This building concept is inspired by the principles of Nature-Based Building and incorporates principles of 'circular building' by closing water, energy, material, waste and food cycles as far as possible in a didactic manner

Biobased building materials in Living Monument, by Darina Bleumink

Many aesthetic developments are driven by applying less traditional materials. Circular use of materials is also leading in the design of the Living Monument project by the young Arnhem designer Sarina Bleumink. Living Monument is the new destination of the old potato flour plant De Centrale in Coevorden, which is reused as a building with living/working studios. The former factory was heavily damaged in a bombardment in the Second World War, was rebuilt, but fell into disuse later. Bleumink uses the potato flour that used to be made here as the basis for the concrete with which she restructures and reconstructs the old foundation and remnants of the building. The potato starch is added as a bio-based binding agent to the crushed bricks of the former factory, preserving the history of the building in a material sense as well. The starch concrete blocks are cast in traditionally hydrated wooden formwork made from trees in the surroundings. These leave a specific and unique imprint in the concrete blocks. After having served their purpose, the work forms are used in the façade. As the crushed bricks are not perfectly even in composition and colour, the starch concrete has different hues, as a permanent reminder of the historical background of the building. Older debris and grit contain more brick, younger remnants have more concrete. By using the debris in exactly its original location, the colour of the concrete changes as one walks through the building from the older to the newer part. The starch therefore functions not just materially but also symbolically as a binding agent between present and past. In Bleumink's design the circular application of building materials, augmented with a within the context meaningful bio-based binding agent, defines the aesthetic value of the old building. The design thus functions as the custodian of the local cultural value of the old factory. Also, the people who know this culture and have made it their own will be the ones living in this building.

They are the offspring of the former employees and some of them are still living in the adjacent labourer's cottages. Once they have moved into the building, they will be able to pass on this cultural heritage to new residents.

Just like a large biodiversity is an indication of a healthy green structure, aesthetic diversity reflects a healthy urban culture. It is precisely the insight into the local system of the spatial problem — whether we are talking about architecture, urban planning, or landscape architecture — that provides interesting access to metabolic solutions that also contribute to an enhanced identity of a place.

The very much local cultural and historical value of the building defines Bleumink's design. This demonstrates an attitude that was also expressed a number of times in the interviews with designers included in this publication. In a number of conversations the word 'vernacular' is mentioned, referring to an aesthetics that is strongly inspired by local traditions and techniques. It's an attitude that opposes technical solutions that rely on materials with a large carbon footprint, materials that are mined and transported across the globe. Instead, they prefer local knowledge and materials to address local problems. David Gianotten calls this 'contextual'; design that springs from a local logic. Lola Sheppard and Mason White also mentioned this and in addition point to the fact that it is exactly the spontaneous nature of local customs that forms an innovative force and an aesthetically appealing challenge. In his interview, Daniel Ibañez advocates a simply much more frugal use of materials and optimizing them locally. In reaction to the trend of adding more and more layers to buildings in the search for a higher resilience against all possible external threats, he states that one locally mined material often suffices to make a building function. Provocatively, he posits that all the really necessary layers can also be obtained from a single thick piece of material. And, he adds: 'Maybe you would object by saying that the energy efficiency of that building might not be less than when there are these 25 layers. That might be right. But what I'm telling you is that the overall metabolic power of my building versus another one made with thousands of layers that are contaminating, emitting emissions and were built with non-renewable materials, is going to be hundreds of times worse.'

Arguing in favour of an expressly local aesthetics with very local use of materials also helps to combat another shortcoming of a more generic approach, which is that the entire world is starting to look the same. It compels us to embrace the very diversity that makes the world so appealing and — to draw yet another parallel with biology — also forms a measure of systemic success. Just like a large biodiversity is an indication of a healthy green structure, aesthetic diversity reflects a healthy urban culture. It is precisely the insight into the local system of the spatial problem — whether we are talking about architecture, urban planning, or landscape architecture — that provides interesting access to metabolic solutions that also contribute to an enhanced identity of a place.

Sustainability and Proximity

For most of human history an aesthetics that was largely defined by the use of local materials was evident. Materials were primarily selected on the basis of their proximity. That is why the built environment, of necessity, is largely made of materials that are acquired at a short distance from the building site. When materials came from afar it was usually for the ostentatious display of power and wealth. The use of practical, local materials also ensured that buildings fitted into their surroundings in a natural, matter-of-fact way. In spite of the application of an imported, 'generic' classical ordering of columns, the stonecarving in Petra, Jordan, is unmistakably location-specific and unique in its material strategy.

Ad Deir, also spelled ad-Dayr and el-Dir, is a monastery carved out of rock in the ancient Jordanian city of Petra

Locally produced architecture was simply a practical necessity for most of our history and therefore it is not primarily a representative strategy. Guilds were organically organized around craftsmanship with regard to locally available materials, which resulted in social-cultural networks that then created a specific signature for certain regions. Probably people only became aware of these regional signatures and styles with the growth of international trade, when they became visible and could be compared. Local materials were like water to fish: their omnipresence made them invisible. Initially, the use of materials from far away was the method of choice to emphasize something special. Regionalism, the representative and functional strategy to use location-specific conditions to inform a design, therefore only became a 'strategy' when this simply no longer

Lina Bo Bardi's SESC Pompéia

Balkrishna Doshi's Sangath

was an unavoidable limitation.

The universal ambitions of the modernists and their dislike of local political, cultural, and geographical differences also inspired opposition to standardization. This led to the so-called 'critical regionalism', a movement that, in a remarkable way, expressed a strategy to mix the technology-inspired progress of modernism with local sensitivities. Famous examples of this are works by Geoffrey Bawa, Lina Bo Bardi, and Balkrishna Doshi.

By now, the relation with proximity is much less evident and materials from the other side of the world may even be cheaper than those from local quarries. Globalization has exchanged the limitations imposed by proximity for limitations imposed by labour and logistics. In rich countries local materials now have the nostalgic shine of authenticity, craftsmanship, and lost solidarity, but are not cost-efficient. Recent projects from countries such as Chile, India, and China — celebrated for their craftsmanship — are often only made possible by the availability of cheap labour and by dubious mining practices. The Venice Architecture Biennale 2016, 'Reporting from the Front', included a lot of examples that presented interesting riddles: is it not so that the authentic design practices we long for are simply unaffordable in many places, or otherwise inherently linked to the exploitation of nature and people?

Buying materials locally is often presented as a sustainable building strategy. The main arguments for this are savings in cost and less pollution because of shorter transport routes; the increased capacity to control buying and production, thereby preventing exploitation of the environment and people; the greater advantages for communities when supply chains are more integrated and coincide with personal relations, trust, and reciprocity. But the distance metrics can be elusive. Is it more sustainable in Europe to use concrete from a local concrete factory or to use premium labelled sustainable wood (Accoya) from New

Geoffrey Bawa's Steel Corporation Offices and Housing

Zealand? According to the BREEAM certificate the wood from the other side of the world scores best. Buying locally often competes with the economic scale brought on by globalization. It does not come as a surprise that affordable CLT wood comes from regions with large pine forests and related wood industries, such as Canada and Scandinavia. In the Netherlands it would be difficult to start up an industry that can compete on such a scale, unless the costs of transport would rise drastically or protectionist tariffs would be imposed. Such a policy would of course, have far-reaching consequences that go way beyond the building sector.

Reuse

In countries with few or no natural resources, reuse of materials can be a solution. Reuse is gaining momentum, but the reality is that when an investor speaks with a contractor, the latter will always say that demolition and building something new is cheaper than transforming an existing building. Preserving buildings and reusing materials is even more expensive because careful disassembling is infinitely more time-consuming than demolition. In addition, reassembling is often much more cumbersome. As the reuse industry grows, these processes will become more cost-efficient but for now the argument to be presented here is not a financial one.

In other regards reuse comes out quite favourably. Reuse projects often lead to remarkable architecture with multiple layers of meaning and unique aesthetic qualities. Truth be told, most examples of this are modest boutique projects in which the building costs are manageable. Bigger reuse projects are less common. One recent example proving the opposite is the transformation of the World Trade Centre in Brussels into the multifunctional ZIN building. This structure of 110,000 m² (1.2 million sq ft) is comprised of apartments, offices, a hotel, and various shared functions. The Belgian government took the lead here by enforcing reuse in the rental agreement with the project developer. The project has not yet been completed and its scale and ambition are new to all parties involved. Whether it will be a success can only be determined when it's finished. Still, realizing a project of this scale with all the risks of innovation involved, will undoubtedly be expensive. The idea is that as recycling companies will grow in scale, costs will go down. This is a hopeful development, but one that is hard to assess until more work is being done. Remarkably, a look at the architecture of the ZIN building is, despite its laudable performance, aesthetically disappointing. In the end, the new building hardly distinguishes itself from the generic company apartments in Brussels North. Perhaps this is where the bigger problem lies at the moment: that the challenge is more of an aesthetic nature than anything else. Why go to all this trouble if the result doesn't look different? The transition towards a cleaner building practice is more in need of aesthetic than of economic courage.

The transition towards a cleaner building practice is more in need of aesthetic than of economic courage.

After all, doesn't the prospect of reuse — as *spolia* in ancient Rome has taught us — have the potential to create a much richer aesthetics for the reuse of architecture? Shouldn't reuse and transformation be the natural architectural effects of the need for locality and authenticity? However, over the past few decades, globalization has driven the building sector into the opposite direction. It's the waterbed effect: factories were closed in places where labour and environmental regulations made production too expensive and cumbersome, to be reopened in places where companies could easily circumvent such legislation.

Two firms, both based in Brussels, do interesting work that tries to oppose this trend. One of them is BC Architects, a company that started in 2012 with modest, clever rammed-earth projects and has meanwhile scaled up to a materials-producing company that uses earth from building site excavations throughout Belgium. They have realized buildings of 10,000 m² (108,000 sq ft) and more using their own materials, which they produce in the city centre. Another example, also from Brussels, is Rotor DC. This firm focuses more on materials salvaged from demolished buildings and boasts an impressive online store with a large variety of second-hand products, varying from partition walls to façade panels. What share companies such as BC Materials and Rotor DC will have in the overall building volume is not known yet, but their approach does point in a hopeful direction that may make a relevant and contemporary contribution to the long tradition of building with locally available materials.

Spolia (spoils): re-used stones in ancient Rome

Construction workshop by BC architects & studies

An Aesthetics of Proximity

What role do designers have in these transition processes in the building sector? Are we relegated to the status of designers who critically browse materials catalogues and make responsible decisions based on

Rotor DC reclaiming the marble wall cladding of the Brussels North Station

what's on offer? Should we start our own materials companies, like our examples from Brussels? Is there still room for experimentation within projects, despite the limitations imposed by standardized labels and sustainability criteria?

It is evident that the focus on sustainability in design has resulted in a new agenda that puts the entire production chain from mining to refuse heap into question, creating a sometimes frustrating and complex context for designers to work in. Exploring the ensuing possibilities has the potential to fundamentally change how we work with materials, but may also bring the risk of creating a rigid straitjacket of strict criteria.

Meanwhile, we observe a trend among designers to take a firmer stand in these transition processes in the building world and to seek design freedom in a solid understanding of local culture and circumstances. Over time, the work of architects has become fragmented into specialisms that today have mostly become the province of other parties in the building process. Designing details and engineering façades is done much more efficiently, in an economic sense, by the suppliers of materials and products than when a designer would do this. This is partly the result of the willingness with which architects have conceded to limit their role to that of making a supply-driven design based on simplistic sustainability criteria. However, just because the results are often not very creative doesn't mean that the current context no longer leaves us room for aesthetic innovation. On the contrary. It is exactly the limitation inherent in a less varied supply of materials and in the desire to support and do justice to local customs and cultures that can be an inspiration for aesthetic creativity and innovation. By taking the underlying system as the starting point of design, we force ourselves to arrive at fundamental innovations for buildings, cities, and landscapes that are not only aesthetically appealing but also make a bigger contribution to healthy urban ecosystems. Because they are more sustainable, result in less CO_2 emissions, and create a safe place for the effects of climate change. By designing from the system opportunities arise to design the space for urban programmes in a different manner by creating new mixed forms of living, working, and learning in neighbourhoods. And that facilitates healthy living, by expanding the possibilities for sports and exercise, providing healthy food, and banning substances that are bad for our health. Using sustainable sources and materials and gathering local knowledge in the design process leads to location-specific solutions with an intrinsic aesthetic value.

Does this mean that the traditional role of the architect as an artist
will be lost in favour of that of the architect as a sustainability agent?
We emphatically think not. For the design of the contemporary city
it is precisely values such as beauty and cultural expression, in addition to sustainability and optimized performance of designs, that are
crucial to its success. Working from a notion such as 'the vernacular',
designers are looking for the sublimation of beauty in a very innovative
manner. It's just that what drives beauty is not so much to be found in
traditional, historically grown aesthetic principles that are interpreted
anew. Nor does it come from translating economic rules into specific
building details, as in architects' drawings of a hundred years ago.
Designing a systemic change necessarily leads to a new form language.
A language, or rather an infinite number of languages, that cannot be
laid down in universal aesthetic principles but lead to always new artistic and spatial experiences. Just as 'Graham' is an absolutely new figure
in reaction to an absolutely different question. A question, moreover,
that is site-specific and may differ from one place to the next and therefore must have a different spatial expression in every place. This new
spatial experience can take the form of a ski slope on top of a waste-to-
energy plant, but also that of the skyscraper made of salvaged wood by
the US firm RISD Ultramoderne, whose only function is to store CO_2.
The aesthetic experience of such a building is beyond beauty. Beauty
problematizes our conception of architecture and of the function of the
building, of our spatial imagination and of our understanding of beauty
as such. A building such as this, therefore, touches upon the sublime.

1   Le Corbusier, 'A Contemporary City', in *The
    City of To-morrow and its Planning* (1929),
    New York 1987, pp. 163-178.

With an Eye to Diversity

'Franny is listening to a program on wolves.
I say to her, Would you like to be a wolf? She
answers haughtily, How stupid, you can't be
one wolf, you're always eight or nine, six or
seven. Not six or seven wolves all by yourself
all at once, but one wolf among others, with
five or six others. In becoming-wolf, the
important thing is the position of the mass,
and above all the position of the subject itself
in relation to the pack or wolf-multiplicity:
how the subject joins or does not join the
pack, how far away it stays, how it does or
does not hold to the multiplicity.'

— Gilles Deleuze & Félix Guattari, 'One or
Several Wolves?', in *A Thousand Plateaus*,
1980

Designers play a crucial role in making our cities healthy. Research by
design is the pre-eminent method for feeding this transition with the
required knowledge, thereby helping to realize it. The publication at
hand lists and explores a number of new methods and developments
that contribute to the crucial transformation of the city — and of its
designers. Because it is no longer a question of whether designers and
their methods should change in order to improve the performance of
our cities. The agenda laid out in this book is anything but noncom-
mittal. It sets a task for designers who have no choice but to address it,
a challenge that must be met if we are not to be overtaken by events.
The social, circular, and climate-adaptive tasks of the city require integral, multi-layered solutions that address a diversity of problems. This
requires research that takes on these various layers simultaneously and
always includes them in potential design. The traditional methods and
tools of the designer simply no longer suffice.

This is why designers first have to reinvent themselves and become
as versatile and layered as the designs the contemporary city demands.
This takes innovation, going beyond the borders of our own discipline,
and collaboration. In 'One or Several Wolves', the French philosophers'
duo Deleuze and Guattari conjure up the image of the Wolf-man, a key
patient of Sigmund Freud, the father of psychoanalysis. To Freud, this
patient was a neurotic whose blockages were the result of set patterns
that were obscured by an obsession with the father figure and latent
homosexuality. Deleuze and Guattari completely reverse this image:
it is precisely the Wolf-man who has a perfectly healthy relation with
reality and sets an example to others — he is someone who understands
himself from his multiplicity, his pack, his community, which help
define his identity and behaviour. 'You can't be one wolf, you're always

eight or nine, six or seven. Not six or seven wolves all by yourself all at once, but one wolf among others, with five or six others', they note. In doing so, they point out the importance of adopting a much more flexible identity that is determined to a high degree by the individual's attitude to the group and the situation. With these philosophers, identity is never fixed but always becoming, and therefore constantly changing and changeable. In that sense the Wolf-man, or rather Wolf-human, as the model is not confined to this male historical patient, may also be a model for the contemporary designers who must let go of their old fixed identity and can no longer hide behind their lofty, unique genius. Designers too must actively commit to a community and engage in all kinds of collaborations in order to be successful in making the city healthy. A lone wolf is a dangerous lunatic, whereas a healthy wolf thrives thanks to active collaboration and exhibits due modesty where it is needed and decisiveness where it is appropriate and opportune.

Designers too must actively commit to a community and engage in all kinds of collaborations in order to be successful in making the city healthy.

Designers who are willing to engage in the required new collaborations and know how to resign themselves to their role in processes of research and design, open up all sorts of new possibilities for thoroughly deepening and expanding their own design practice. This produces different, layered, and versatile designs that make cities more resilient, healthier, and more inhabitable. A different attitude or a different question coming from other interests and perspectives results in different cities with different buildings and different functionalities. In our exploration of future solutions for cities, of which this publication is a reflection, we advocate layered solutions that, in optima forma, try to do justice to the six pillars of a healthy city at once (circularity, climate adaptation, economy, health, social-cultural cohesion, and a versatile infrastructure). A new neighbourhood, such as Porte de la Chapelle in Paris, connects social improvements, new jobs, and educational functions with forms of production close by the urban client, thus minimizing transportation and promoting circularity. This helps the city with adapting to climate change, with reducing material flows, improving existing transport networks with a too large ecological footprint and making them more efficient, which also benefits the health of the local residents. And neighbourhoods such as these also help with problems outside the city. For example, by bringing production capacity into the city the landscape becomes less 'messy' and it can free itself from anonymous boxes, enhancing the aesthetic quality of the landscape and the city fringes.

By mixing functions at different scales a whole range of urban innovations can be implemented, touching upon the various pillars of a healthy urban metabolism. The latter is no side issue. The complexity of the contemporary city no longer affords the luxury of creating buildings and neighbourhoods that perform in one aspect only. Our cities must become climate-neutral and circular in the short term if we are to counter global warming and the exhaustion of natural resources, but not at the expense of inclusivity in the city. A perfectly circular design solution that increases the economic exclusion of certain groups of urbanites, is a bad solution. An improvement of the urban infrastructure at the expense of urban nature in a neighbourhood is a bad solution. The same goes, by the way, for areas outside the cities as well, where mixing functions is just as necessary. Layered agriculture can combine energy generation with growing crops. At sea too, such hybrid forms of using the space are possible, and probably necessary. Wind turbines at sea can be the basis for new forms of agriculture that serve to improve water quality and biodiversity, which eventually will also benefit a responsible form of fishery. Such layered, complex interventions do however ask a lot of the research by design that forms the basis of it and of the designers who must keep an eye on all these agendas and watch over their interconnectedness.

A healthy urban metabolism is a diverse urban metabolism.

These interventions also require us to redefine the design tasks, together with clients and commissioners. One important task of the designer of the future is to combine various agendas and involve new players in defining the future design tasks. In that process too, which already takes place long before the actual designing starts, designers must play an active role.

In formulating the design tasks for a healthy, layered city and for the places directly connected to that space, diversity should be a core value. A healthy urban metabolism is a diverse urban metabolism. Just as a healthy forest safeguards and promotes biodiversity, likewise a healthy city should safeguard and promote metabolic diversity. This implies that the ambition is always to optimally promote performance on all six pillars of a healthy metabolism at the same time. Design interventions must serve to improve both climate conditions and social liveability and greenery in neighbourhoods, also when these goals appear to be difficult to reconcile. The various pillars of a healthy urban metabolism are after all not hierarchically ordered. And they are interrelated, often forming communicating vessels, and therefore cannot be approached separately. Like the various vital organs in a body, they should function well individually, but most of all work together well in order to function as a healthy whole. A healthy urban metabolism therefore *is* a metabolism that safeguards the diversity of the city. It is up to the present-day designers to watch over that diversity, develop new spatial typologies for it, and, where necessary, intervene in the urban fabric in order to promote and improve the opportunities for a healthy urban ecosystem. This is not an easy task that can be accomplished without extensive study. But no matter how complicated it is, there is no alternative.

It is in the inevitability and complexity of the task that we find the aesthetic and intellectual challenge to designers. The present-day designers are forced to be innovative in their approach of the city. Forms and functions of the future city are not yet established and are often not even defined as such. Designing the healthy city of the future therefore requires a designing avant-garde that should produce these definitions and translate them into spatial designs. To then adapt these designs again where necessary, because the city of the future will always be in the making, as will be its designers. The healthy city will not have a definite form but will have to adapt itself time and again to changing demands, just like its makers will have to keep transforming themselves if they are to meet these demands. The challenge of urban transition is a permanent one and it starts with the metamorphosis of the designer. May this book be an encouragement in this.

Biographies

DAVID DOOGHE works as a Senior Scientist Integrator at TNO, Strategic Analysis & Policy Unit. He works on the spatial and policy integration of new technologies linked to healthy urbanization, energy, or mobility transition. Before this, David worked as a project leader for metropolitan strategies at the Deltametropool Association. There, within the theme of metropolitan strategies, various urban transitions came together and approaches by (inter)national urban regions were compared. This was done by comparing their administrative models and responsibilities, policies, and concrete projects. David's interest in the role of actors in spatial projects linked to transitions is also reflected in his appointment as researcher at the Future Urban Regions research group. Here, he looks at the role of actors (new or existing ones with a changing role) in new urban challenges such as energy transition, climate adaptation, new economy, and social issues.

ERIC FRIJTERS, founding partner at FABRICations, has over fifteen years of experience in designing, implementing, and consulting about projects in architecture, urbanism, and regional strategies in both the Netherlands and abroad. He has a background in architecture at the Karlsruhe Institute of Technology, studied Philosophy at the University of Amsterdam, and graduated with distinction at the Eindhoven University of Technology. His research has been published in several books and appears in various journals. Eric received recognition for his work with several prizes as a designer and researcher with a hands-on approach who experiments with innovative architecture and urban design. For over a decade now, he has been initiating and leading research into healthy urban ecosystems and design thinking methodology and is involved in testing productive strategies on urban metabolism.

CATJA EDENS is an independent architectural historian and writer. She teaches architectural history at Delft Technical University and the Academies for Architecture in Arnhem and Rotterdam. With her PhD research at Eindhoven University of Technology she explores the archiving of women architects and how it has affected architecture culture in the twentieth century. Edens works from a historical awareness perceiving architecture as a cultural expression defined by its place and time, and the specific values, circumstances, and challenges involved. In the Future Urban Research group, she focused on the cultural expression of new forms of spatial design and how these can fit into and add onto layered urban contexts. With her work as a teacher, writer, moderator, and podcast maker she builds bridges between the worlds of architectural design, academic research, government, education, and the general public.

MATTHIJS PONTE is a writer, editor, and journalist with a background in literature and philosophy. He was the director of Perdu, Amsterdam's renowned poetry space, and co-founded the international literature festival Read My World as well as a publishing house for literature in translation. His writing, teaching, and research concentrates on—the intersection of—politics, cultural and postcolonial theory, philosophy, the arts and current affairs. He is drawn to experiment and interdisciplinarity in all his activities. Being the philosopher among spatial designers, he was the odd one out in the Future Urban Regions research group and operated as critical interlocutor and editor. After finishing this book, his primary focus has been on writing fiction.

THIJS VAN SPAANDONK is co-founder of
BRIGHT, a research, design, and development cooperative for urban development.
BRIGHT produces observations and
prototypes to investigate and intervene
in the impact of the systems of energy,
food, mobility, and economy on our surroundings. Project outcomes range from
GIS-based serious games to large public
exhibitions, from housing for bats to public
buildings and from speculative scenarios to
policy advice for the national government.
Currently, BRIGHT works on the design
of the built infrastructure of the electricity grid, prototypes of decentralized data
centres and the development of communi-
ty-owned real estate.
Thijs was curator Energy Transition as
Leverage for the 2020 International Architecture Biennale Rotterdam. The focus of
his curatorial work was to see the necessary
energy transition as a cultural act and as
impossible without a transition of ownership, representation, and values, a necessity
of new value and ownership models. Thijs
is currently the programme director for the
Urban Design Master programme at the
Rotterdam Academy of Architecture and
Urban Design.

ROOSJE VERSCHOOR is a visual artist with a
deep fascination for cultural history. Verschoor was trained as a photographer at
the Gerrit Rietveld Academy in Amsterdam. She works in several media, such as
photography, video, performance, and
experimental print techniques. Her work
is research-based and she often travels to
explore (oral) histories and cultural practices. Recently she spent extensive research
periods in Surinam, resulting in exhibitions
in Moengo, Paramaribo, and Amsterdam.
Her work has been on show in group exhibitions in many countries, including Spain,
Canada, and the United Kingdom, and in
Puerto Rico. In 2020 Verschoor was granted
the Young Talent Stipend by the Mondrian
Fund.

CHRISTOPHER DE VRIES is co-founder of
Rademacher de Vries Architects. The office
works on concrete architectural projects
through a broad research-driven conception of design that particularly focuses on
questions of scale. In this view, architecture, the city, and the landscape form an
integral design assignment that inextricably links spatial, ecological, social,
cultural, and political questions. Christopher received his Bachelor's degree in
Delft, after which he obtained a Master's
degree in architecture and urban planning
at the Massachusetts Institute of Technology (MIT). In the US, he was affiliated with
the New Geographies Lab at Harvard GSD
and worked at OPSYS Landscape infrastructures. Christopher's academic work
has examined post-disaster urban redevelopment and infrastructural design as a tool
for territorial and urban planning. This
research is continued through research and
teaching at several universities and publications in various journals.

JET VAN ZWIETEN is a community-oriented
designer, graduated with distinction from
the Design Academy Eindhoven. She
co-founded social design collective Foundation Projects, initiating interventions in
public space, using locally sourced building materials. She is also the co-founder
and former creative director of Vechtclub
XL, a business centre and meeting place
for creative entrepreneurs in Utrecht. In
her management, she tried to increase
mutual contact in order to achieve maximum cross-pollination between tenants
and applied a strict admissions policy
to achieve a diverse and durable ecosystem. She aimed at organic and innovative
redevelopment of the former OPG site [a
pharmaceutical wholesale business] with
a permanent position for Vechtclub XL.
When she moved to Arnhem in 2018, she
co-initiated a community centre where preventing social isolation is combined with
energy transition on a neighbourhood level.
This is where she met the business partner
with whom she now runs the interior design
agency Poelmann & van Zwieten.

About the visual contribution of Roosje Verschoor

AMSTERDECKS (P.162) When visiting the Amsterdecks I noticed how everyone changed into and out of their swimming clothes without rush or shame. Sometimes the swimmers would take a moment to dry, standing fully naked in the sun. This struck me, since in the greater area of Amsterdam I have seen less and less nudity. Somehow, the idea of swimming in natural water gives an opening to wearing your natural nude suit. The jetty Amsterdecks lies about a five-minute walk into the Amsterdamse Bos in the waters called the Nieuwe Meer (The New Lake). The jetty is equipped with sensors that inform swimmers about the quality of the water, and even pumps oxygen into the water if necessary. But it also serves as an easy passage for swimmers to access the Nieuwe Meer.

MOUNTAIN AIR, (COPENHILL) (P.168) During a tour of the waste disposal factory inside Copenhill, I learned that the smoke that is produced is cleaned to the extent that it is of the same quality as the air that we breathe in the inner city. Reflecting on the concept of clean air for people, the images of tuberculosis patients in their pyjamas recovering in the mountains of Switzerland soon came to mind.

FEDRIK, (KIRUNA) (P.172) Fredrik is a local jeweller in Kiruna who is forced to close his store due to the relocation of the town. He explained to me that he refused the reimbursement that the mining company offered him, since it was too low. He is yet to hear back from them. This photo is taken on the spot of the former city hall, which has been demolished. The inside of the new city hall is entirely golden. Even though Fredrik is a jeweller, he thinks it looks ridiculous. The original clocktower from the old city hall has been placed next to the new city hall in New Kiruna. Fredrik regrets that he can no longer see the clock at the edge of town. Instead, it is now hidden in the valley between the new apartment buildings of New Kiruna. It makes it impossible to tell the time.

WASHING, (SCHOONSCHIP) (P.180) 'In Amsterdam, a community of floating homes shows the world how to live alongside nature' is what the Washington Post wrote about the neighbourhood Schoonschip. Schoonschip is beautiful and almost fully self-supporting and independent from public utilities. The residents are very happy to live there. Most of them are friends with the initiator.

MATTER OUT OF PLACE, (ROTOR DC BRUSSELS) (P.184) The store of Rotor DC, where they sell recycled construction materials, feels like a giant art installation. While reading about Rotor DC I found out they researched when waste is produced and what role waste plays in our society. This led me to the theory of Mary Douglas who wrote that 'dirt is matter out of place'. It is strange to imagine the objects inside Rotor DC's store as dirt, as they are so aesthetically pleasing and 'in place'.

JARDIN ROSA-LUXEMBURG (P.190) From an old railway emplacement Jardin Rosa Luxemburg emerged, a beautiful park with a neighbourhood garden, apartments, a café, a library, and more. The cultivated areas are irrigated by rain collected on the roofs, which are also covered with solar panels. In short, this place sounds like paradise. And when I entered it, from the busy streets of Paris, it immediately felt that way too. I noticed, however, that besides residents sitting in front of their houses drinking wine, there were also groups of young men drinking beer on the public benches. Although this surprised me in such an elite space, I perceived it as a successful design for a free and open park for everyone. After a while though, I noticed that there were also people sleeping in the bushes and heating a substance in aluminium foil behind a shed. Alina, the young woman in the photo, explained to me that there are so many addicts in Paris that all the parks are filled; when they are searching for a place to rest, they don't care if it is shabby or fancy, open or hidden.

SMALL CITY (P.192) This photo was taken in
Parc de la Villette, which has been tailored
to every sort of human desire. It is filled
with many playgrounds, an amusement
park, a museum, a concert hall, architectural follies and different outdoor gyms
with a variety of devices. Only the heavy
lifting has to be done with found urban
objects.

TEA TIME (P.198) In Eerbeek I met Carmen,
whose husband had worked in one of the
paper factories surrounding the small town.
She told me that many people in Eerbeek
complain about the pollution of the factories, the noise of the trucks, and so on.
She, however was very grateful that her
husband had been employed by the factory
right behind her house for so many years,
providing their family with an income.
This factory makes paper for tea packaging.
Carmen showed me the house next door,
which was abandoned. The factory director
had lived there, but after he died, the house
was occupied by squatters until the beginning of 2022. It now stands empty, but as
it was damaged by the squatters, its future
is uncertain. This gave way for a lot of
rumours in the community about how habi-
tats are valued by the surrounding industry.

Colophon

THE CITY AS A SYSTEM
METABOLIC DESIGN FOR NEW
URBAN FORMS AND FUNCTIONS

The publication is a cooperation between
trancity×valiz and the Future Urban Regions
lectorate, which is connected to the Dutch
Academies of Architecture in Amsterdam,
Arnhem, Groningen, Maastricht, Rotterdam
and Tilburg.

Editors
Eric Frijters, Matthijs Ponte

Text and Research
David Dooghe, Eric Frijters, Catja Edens,
Matthijs Ponte, Thijs van Spaandonk,
Christopher de Vries, Jet van Zwieten

Copy Editing
Leo Reijnen

Translation
Leo Reijnen

Proofreading
Els Brinkman, Vivi van Leersum

Image editing
Jet van Zwieten, Pia Pol

Photography
Roosje Verschoor

Design and Typesetting
Catalogtree, www.catalogtree.net

Paper Inside
115 grams Munken Print White
90 grams houtvrij gesatineerd mc

Paper Cover
250 grams Nordland offset

Printing and Binding
Wilco Art Books, Amersfoort

Publisher
Simon Franke — Trancity,
Pia Pol / Astrid Vorstermans — Valiz
trancity×valiz, Amsterdam, 2023
www.valiz.nl

Future Urban Regions
The Future Urban Region lectorate explores
urban (eco) systems and innovative design
tools for the existing city. From a changing
understanding of the use of space, it works to
improve urban environmental performance,
the economicsituation, and/or socio-cultural
participation. This agenda guides the assign-
ments of (specific forms of) design research,
which are commissioned by local and regional
authorities, to be embedded in the education
curriculum of the six Dutch Academies of
Architecture.

trancity×valiz
trancity×valiz is a collaboration between two
independent publishers that share a common
understanding regarding the function of publications. Their books provide critical reflection
and interdisciplinary inspiration, and establish
a connection between cultural disciplines and
socio-economic issues. Publications on the city,
urban change and the public domain are at the
core of the collaboration between Trancity and
Valiz.

This publication was made possible through
the generous support of the Creative Industries
Fund NL and the Van Eesteren-Fluck en Van
Lohuizen Foundation

International Distribution
• NL/LU: Centraal Boekhuis,
www.centraal.boekhuis.nl
• BE: EPO, www.epo.be
• GB/IE: Central Books,
www.centralbooks.com
• Europe (excl. NL/BE/LU/GB/IE)/
Asia: Idea Books,
www.ideabooks.nl
• Australia: Perimeter,
www.perimeterdistribution.com
• USA, Canada, Latin-America:
D.A.P., www.artbook.com
• Individual orders: www.valiz.nl;
info@valiz.n

ISBN 978-94-93246-14-0

Printed and bound in the Netherlands